KERSHAW COUNTY, SOUTH CAROLINA MINUTES OF THE COUNTY COURT 1791-1799

∂C

BY
BRENT HOWARD HOLCOMB
CERTIFIED GENEALOGIST

HERITAGE BOOKS
2008

HERITAGE BOOKS

AN IMPRINT OF HERITAGE BOOKS, INC.

Books, CDs, and more—Worldwide

For our listing of thousands of titles see our website
at
www.HeritageBooks.com

Published 2008 by
HERITAGE BOOKS, INC.
Publishing Division
100 Railroad Ave. #104
Westminster, Maryland 21157

International Standard Book Numbers
Paperbound: 978-0-7884-3509-6
Clothbound: 978-0-7884-7281-7

INTRODUCTION

Kershaw County was formed in 1791 from the counties of Fairfield, Lancaster and Richland. Therefore, prior to 1791, the county records of those counties should be researched for persons who appear in the county court minutes herein. The seat of Kershaw County was and is the town of Camden, which was formerly in Lancaster County. The original volume from which these abstracts were made is preserved at the South Carolina Archives. The original pagination is given. Actually, court minutes themselves are abstracts, and very little can be omitted in publishing these records. The court minutes begin in 1791 with the formation of the county and continue through 1799, when the county court system in South Carolina was abolished. In the year 1800, counties (including Kershaw) became known as districts. The term county was not resumed until 1868.

The records themselves are fairly typical of county court minutes in South Carolina. Of great interest to genealogists are the entries from the court acting as a court of ordinary or probate court. Many entries having to do with orphans, wills, estates, and the like provide vital clues and establish relationships which might prove difficult to find otherwise.

This volume is the last of the county court minutes of South Carolina to be published. The other counties with extant court minutes are Newberry, Fairfield, Edgefield, York, Chester, Spartan or Spartanburgh, Union, Pendleton, Winton (Barnwell), and Marlborough. All of these have been published as separate volumes, with the exception of the Pendleton County Court Minutes, which were published serially in *The South Carolina Magazine of Ancestral Research.* Separately and collectively, these records are some of the most valuable genealogical tools for the period 1785-1799 in South Carolina.

[16 May 1791]

[Pages 1-5 torn out]

[Page 6]

Ordered that the Recognizance of FREDERICK ROBINSON & ALEXANDER GOODALL be Laid Over Untill the 28th July Next.

Ordered that the Recognizance of JOHN McCAW and JAMES PEIRSON be Laid Over Untill the 28th July Next. Adjourned till to Morrow 10 O'clock. ADAM F. BRISBANE, SAMUEL BOYKIN, JOHN KERSHAW.

Agreeable to Adjournment the Hon'ble ADAM FOWLER BRISBANE, SAMUEL BOYKIN & JOHN KERSHAW Esquires met according to Law and Open Court.

Ordered that Licence be Granted JOSEPH THOMSON for Retailing Spirituous Liquors the Securities are MOSES FERGUSON & NATHANIEL PACE.

Ordered that the Will of HUMPHREY BARNET be Recorded and letters Testamentary be Issued.

Ordered that Licence be Granted JOHN RUSSEL for Retailing Spiritous Liquors the Securities are ADAM THOMSON & DAVID RUSSEL.

Ordered that the Clerk of the County be allowed five Pounds 2/6 for three large Books purchased for the purpose of recording Deeds Mortgages Wills & Ca to be paid out of any Monies that may come into his Hands for the use of the County.

[Page 7]

ROBERT BROWN son of JOHN BROWN Dec'd an Orphan Boy of about 17 Years of age came into Court chose DARLING JONES his Guardian who was approved. Ordered that he give Bond in the sum of L 600 for the faith Discharge of his [duties]. JOHN MICKLE & MICHAEL BARNETT were approved of as Securities.

Ordered that a Bench Warrant issue against ROGER GIBSON on the Oath of FREDRICK LAMB charged with assaulting & beating him.

Ordered that Licence be Granted ZACHARIAH CANTEY for Selling Spiritious Liquors the Securities are JOHN CHESNUT & BENJAMIN CARTER.

Ordered that Licence be Granted to JAMES PIERSON; DAVID BUSH, ISAIH BUSH, Securities.

DAVID BUSH; JAMES PIERSON, ISAIH BUSH, Securities.

ISAIAH BUSH; JAMES PEIRSON, DAVID BUSH, Securities.

[Page 8]

Ordered the the Letters of Administration be Granted PATTY [stricken] MARTHA SUTTON upon the Estate of RICHARD SUTTON [stricken: Upon her Producing a Certificate from under the hand of the Clerk of Lancaster County] the Securities are GEORGE ROSS and JASPER SUTTON.

Ordered that a Notice be Served on the following Persons to give an Account of the Estrays in their Possession to the Clerk within Thirty Days: WILLIAM NETTLES, JACOB SHANDY, JOHN BRADLEY SENR.

Ordered that the Following Persons be Appointed Overseers Over the Different Roads herein Mentioned.

- 1 -

From Pintree Bridge to Town Creek, Town Creek to Claremont Line, Pinetree Creek to Sandres Creek, Little pinetree Creek to Camden ferry) ZACHARIAH CANTEY.

Sanders Creek to Flat Rock ... JO'S THOMSON
Flat Rock to Lancaster Line ... JA'S INGRAM
Little Pinetree to Canteys Bridge including the Bridge   JA'S KERSHAW
from the end of the new Road to the long Bluff next to Cam'd to Little Lynches Creek   JA'S WILLIAMS
Little Lynches Creek to great Lynches Cr.   R'D MIDDLETON
Canteys Bridge on Pinetree to Great Lynches Cr.   J'O BREVARD
From ferry to Richland Co. Line on the Road to Columbia   W. WHITAKER
JOHN MARTINs to Richland line on McCORDS Ferry.   D. OQUIN
Camden to Granys Quarter on the Rocky Mount Road. AB KELLY
Grany Qt's to Lancaster Line.   SAM BELTON
Road towards Rocky mount on west side of the River untill it meets Chesnuts ferry Road.   A. LESTER

[Page 9]

From Chesnuts ferry by the Plantation of JOHN ARMSTRONG at Coll'o Creek to fairfield County line... ALEX STEWART.

from Rocky Mount Road to JOHN MICKLEs Ferry...   SAML BELTON.

Ordered that SAMUEL BOYKIN Esqr. be empowered to contract in behalf of the County with a Physician for the Care of _____ Spencer a poor Woman the expence not to exceed Seven Pounds.

Ordered that SAMUEL WHITAKER is appointed as Deputy Clerk and duly Qualify's as Such.

Ordered that M'r ZECHERIAH CANTEY is appointed to Advertise Immediately for the building of Pintree Creek Bridge with hand Rails not to exceed Twenty Five Pounds.

Ordered that Licence be Granted to JAMES BROWN the Securities are SAM'L LEVY & CUTHBERT COLEMAN.

Ordered that a Sorrel Mare an Estray be sold to day.

The Court then adjourned to the 28th July next at 10 O'Clock.   ADAM F. BRISBANE, SAMUEL BOYKIN, JOHN KERSHAW.

[Page 10]

28th July Court.   The Honorable A. FOWLER BRISBANE & JOHN KERSHAW 'Esq'rs met & opened Court agreeable to Adjournment & Proceeded to draw Jurors.

Grand Jurors: 1 DOUGLASS STARK, 2 ALEXANDER CREIG CORUTH, 3 JOHN RUTLEDGE, 4 ISAAC KNOX, 5 GEORGE RICHARDSON, 6 SAMUEL TYNES, 7 GEORGE GATON, 8 JAMES CANTEY, 9 ARON FERGUSON, 10 WILL'M DUNLAP, 11 ARTHUR CUNNINGHAM, 12 JOHN MARSHALL, 13 JOHN INGRAM, 14 WILLIAM WELCH, 15 GEORGE ROSS, 16 JOHN WEBB, 17 WILLIAM SAUNDERS Raftin Creek, 18 WILLIAM SAUNDERS SEN'R, 19 JOHN HORTON, 20 THOMAS CRAYTON, 21 BUR'L BOYKIN, 22 WILLIAM KIRKLAND, 23 SILAS CAMMEL, 24 JOHN GRAHAM, 25 JAMES CORUTH, 26 THOMAS LENOAR, 27 JACOB GREY, 28 JOHN BOYKIN, 29 WILL'M BOND, 30 ____ VAUGHAN Sawneys Creek.

Petit Jurors: 1 WILL'M HICKMAN, 2 CORENLIUS MALONE. 3 GEORGE HAYS, 4 GEORGE PYLAND, 5 JESSE FLY, 6 JOHN TRANTHAM, 7 ARCHIBALD

[28 July 1791]

WATSON, 8 WILLIAM YOUNG, 9 HENRY HUNTER, 10 BENJAMIN FERGUSON, 11 JOSIAH SAUNDERS, 12 W'M MOORE SEN'R, 13 MATHEW BOWEN, 14 ROBT. MARSHALL, 15 CHARLES GREY, 16 JAMES JOHNSON, 17 ROBERT THOMPSON, 18 JAMES ROBINSON JUN'R, 19 WILLIAM GRIFFIN, 20 SAM'l McKAY.

[Page 11]

21 Petit Jurors, 22 WILLIAM BREWER, 23 JAMES WILLIAMS, 24 NATH'L ROGERS, 25 JOHN JONES, 26 JESSE MINTER, 27 JOSHUA LEE, 28 WILLIAM SHIVER, 29 WILLIAM PEACH, 30 BERRY KING.

Common Pleas Juror: 1 JAMES CAIN, 2 JOSIAH SCOTT, 3 JOHN GATON Bever Creek, 4 PATRICK LATON, 5 JONATHAN ENGLISH, 6 JOHN LOVE, S Creek, 7 JOSEPH McADAM, 8 WILLIAM SUTTON, 9 JOHN KERLEE, 10 ANDREW GRAHAM, 11 PHILIP PAYNE, 12 GEORGE SAUNDERS JUN'R, 13 EDW'D NARRIMORE, 14 CHARLES CASSITY, 15 GEORGE KING L Creek, 16 THOMAS SHROPSHIRE, 17 HUGH THOMPSON, 18 ISAAC FORTENBERRY, 19 WILLIAM ELKINS Sawney C, 20 JOSEPH WELLS, 21 SOLOMON OWEN, 22 DANIEL HARKINS, 23 THOMAS SMITH, 24 BENJ'N WATTS, 25 JAMES LOVE, 26 JAMES BELVIN, 27 _____ VAUGHAN S, 28 LEWIS GRANT, 29 DAVID TODD, 30 W'M WILLIAMS.

On a Motion being Made by the County Attorney, that the Recognizence of _____ DRAKEFORD be laid over untill the next court.

[Page 12]

WARE vs DeBUSSY. Case in Attachm't. JOHN CLAUDE BAPTISTE Le DRAT DeBUSSY appeared in person & put in a please to the Jurisdiction of the Court and offered the following affidavid which he made in open Court.

JOHN CLAUDE BAPTISTE Le DERAT de BUSSY of Camden in the County of Kershaw Store Keeper maketh Oath and saith that the Cause of his putting in a plea to the Jurisdiction of the Judges of the County Court of Kershaw in the aforesaid Case on attachment arises from his having had a Writ served upon him issued out of the Superior District Court and returnable to the DIstrict Court at Camden aforesaid for the Damages to be dued from the Deponant to the said Plaintiff in attachment; and to which said Writ the Deponant hath appeared by his Attorney and is ready to answer to the same. And that the Deponant Knoweth other Complaint which the Plaintifff in this Case hath against him than what is Contained in the said Writ served to which the Debt hath appeared in the Superior Court as aforesaid and therefore that the putting in the said Plea is not meant by the Deponant to be in any wise delatory but that he cannot appear in the said County Court to the said attachment, having already by his attorney made his apperance to the Writ in the Superior Court as aforesaid. JN'O LeDRAT deBUSSY. Sworn in open Court this 28 day of July 1791. F BOYKIN, CC.

Ordered that the said plea be overruled & the Parties Proceed to Tryal.

[Page 13]

Ordered that CHARLES ELLIS be sworn as Administrator of ... JOHN THOMPSON Deceased and that letters do Issue; the securities are JOSIAH SCOTT & HENRY HUNTER.

Ordered that MARGARET LUCKY be sworn as Administratrix of ... SAMUEL LUCKY Deceased and that letters do Issue; the securities are DAVID MARTIN & S. MARTIN.

Ordered that WILLIAM NETTLES be sworn as Administrator of ... DAVID CHERY Deceased and that letters do issue; the Securties are NICHOLAS SWILLA

[28 July 1791]

& JOHN SWILLA.

Ordered that NICHOLAS ROBINSON & SAM'L DOBY be taken as Securities for JOHN BARRON, SAM'L DOTY instead of ISABELLA REID for Retailing Spirituous Liquors.

Ordered that Licence be Granted HUGH YOUNG to Retail Spirituous Liquors; the Securities are JOHN ADAMSON & DAVID BUSH.

Adjourned Untill to Morrow 10 OClock. ADAM F. BRISBANE, JOHN KERSHAW.

The Hon'ble ADAM FOWLER BRISBANE & JOHN KERSHAW met and Opened Court agreeable to adjournment.

[Page 14] 29th July Court 1791.

EDWARD MORTIMER & Co vs SAMUEL TYNES. Sum Pro L 4-11-10. Decree for Plaintiff Four Pounds eleven Shillings & ten pence with Interest from the 25 Feb 1791 & Costs of Suit.

PETER OLDGOOD vs HEZ'H LOVE. Sum Pro L 3-16-4. Decree for plaintiff as pr. Specialty with Interest from the first of November 1790. Stay the Executions three months.

THOMAS HOOPER vs BRYANT SPRADLEY. PERKINS Pltfs atty. Sum Pro. MATHIS Dfd'ts atty. Decree for Plaintiff as pr Specialty with interest from the first of March 1790. Stay the Execution three months.

JOHN EGLESTON vs CHARLES IRBY. BROWN Pltfs Atty. Att. Ordered that the Property of CHARLES IRBY now in the hands of JOHN REID be sold & the Balance of his account with JOHN REID be first Paid Which is L 3 s 12 d 11 and a note of hand for L 12 sterling, he being Garnishe.

[Page 15]

JAMES PIERSON V't N. JOHNSON. Att. L 7. moved by Mr. MATHIS that the Writ be Quashed. The Court was divided therefore the Cause remain in Statu Quo.

DAN'L Brown v't N. JOHNSON. Att. Writt. Moved by Mr. MATHIS that this writ be Quashed the Court was divided therefore the Cause remains in Statu Quo.

JOHN MARSHALL v't DAVID ROBINSON. Writt Att. L 8 13 9. Sci facias. Judgement by Default and that Fieri Facias be Issued to Summons ROBERT McCAIN, the Garneshee to Shew Cause why Judgement should not go against him.

THOMAS GATHER v't MOSES BROWN. Writt Att. a Motion being Made to Set a Side the Attachment on the Ground that it was Serv'd by an Improper Officer but the Court Were Divided in Opinion. Ordered that WM. CLAUDIAS INGRAM be Declared Plaintiff. Ordered that the Negroe be Sold and the Money Returnd to Court.

[Page 16]

Ordered that letters of administration of ... John Brown deceased be Issued to DARLING JONES his Securities are MICHAEL BARNETT, BENJAMIN McKINNEY.

BRYANT SPRADLEY vs JOHN WILSON. Ordered that Judgement be given by Default.

[29 July 1791]

Ordered that MATHEW JONES be held to Special Bail on the Case of WILLIAM TWADDLE.

JAMES PERRY v't W'M CLAUDIUS INGRAM. BROWN Pltffs atty. T. P. Decree for Plaintiff with Cost of Suit. Stay the Execution three months.

JOSHUA McHENRY v't JOSEPH PAYNE. PERKINS Pltfs atty. S. P. Settled at Plaintiffs Cost.

-Adjourned Untill to Morrow Ten OClock. ADAM F. BRISBANE, JOHN KERSHAW.

[Page 17] July 30th Term 1791.

The Hon'bl ADAM FOWLER BRISBANE & JOHN KERSHAW Esqrs. met and Opened Court agreeable to Adjournment.

Ordered that the Sheriff do contract upon Reasonable terms with some workman to erect a pari of Stocks before the Goal on one side of Broad Street.

Ordered that the County Attorney do enter an appearance at the next Superior Court in this Destrict to answer to a Writ of Sci. fa. Served upon the Justices of this Court.

Ordered that ROBERT COOK Linches Creek & JOS PAYNE Swift Creek be appointed to act as Constables for the District Court for One Year agreeable to an order thereof and that a Copy of this order be given to the Clerk of said Court.

Ordered that the Estate of HUMPHREY BARNET be Sold and a Credit Given Untill first of Jan'y 1793 after giving legal Notice of said Sale.

[Page 18]

Ordered that WILLIAM NETTLES & JOHN BRADLEY Who have Estrays in their possession & have neglected to make Due return thereof to this Court be proceeded against by the County Atty according to Law.

The Minutes being Read the Court Adjourn'd Untill the third Monday in October Next 10 OClock. ADAM F. BRISBANE, JOHN KERSHAW.

16 October Court 1791

Agreeable to adjournment the Honorable ADAM FOWLER BRISBANE & SAMUEL BOYKIN Esqr's met and opened Court and then Proceeded to business ---

Ordered that the Estate of SAMUEL LUCKY be Sold on a Credit to the first of January 1793 Taking Bonds With Approved Security With Interest from the Day of Sale.

Ordered that FRANCIS ADAMS be appointed Over seer of that part Cain Creek Road from the fork of Rocky Mount Road to Beaver Creek and PHILEMON HILLIARD to the County Line of the above Mentioned Road.

SAMUEL KIRKLAND v't JOHNATHAN BARNS. Ordered that the Plaintiff in this Action Within the age of 21 Years to Prosecute his Suit by DAN'L KIRKLAND his Next Friend.

[another page numbered 18]

Ordered that the Estate of JOHN THOMSON be Sold and Credit of Three Months.

[16 October 1791]

Ordered that THOMAS WHITAKER be Appointed Administrator of ... the Unadministered Part of JOHN WILLIAMS Estate Who was Duly Qualify'd.

The Minutes being first Read the Court Adjourned Untill to Morrow Ten OClock. ADAM F. BRISBANE, SAMUEL BOYKIN.

The Honorable ADAM F. BRISBANE Esq'r met at the Court House according to Adjournment and Proceded to Business.

Ordered that there be a Road Opened from JOSEPH McCOYs to Little Lynches Creek at PATRICK McCAINs Bridge from thence to JOSEPH BREVARDs ferry on great Lynches Creek and that GEORGE EVANS be Appointed Overseer of the said Road.

Ordered that Fifty five Shillings and five Pence be Paid the Sheriff for Erecting the Stocks agreeable to an Order of Court.

Ordered that the Estate of DAVID CHERRY be sold & a Credit of three months be Given.

[Page 19]

Ordered that WILLIAM BOND be Appointed Overseer of the Road Leading from Camden to CHESNUTs Ferry and to Open a New Road from Camp Creek to S'd Ferry.

An application from M'r JOHN REED praying that the Tavern Rates as heretofore established by the Court be altered so far as it respects the articles, Punch, Cider Toddy Grog Sangaree & Lodging it is therefore ordered that the articles Punch Toddy Grog & Sangaree be struck out of the Rates. That Country Cider be rated at 15 d p'r bottle & that the charges for Lodgeing be 6 d p'r night.

Ordered that LAMUEL PERRYs Will be Proven and Recorded and that Letters of Testamentory do Issue.

Ordered that Estray taken up by WILLIAM HANDY[stricken] MORROW be Sold To Morrow and a Horse taken up by WILLIAM NETTLES and a Horse taken by WILLIAM NETTLES Which horses Were Advertised before the County was Divided.

The Minutes being first Read the Hon'ble Court Adjourned Untill to Morrow Ten O Clock. ADAM F. BRISBANE, SAMUEL BOYKIN, JOHN KERSHAW.

[Page 20]

The Hon'ble JOHN KERSHAW Esq'rs Met according to adjournment and Proceeded to business.

Ordered that the Petition for Opening a Road from McCULLUMs Ferry on Great Lynches Creek to PEOPLES Mill and From thence to Camden be Laid Over Untill the 28 Feby Next.

Ordered that Licence be Granted BRYANT SPRADLEY the Securities are HUGH McDOWL & NICHOLAS ROBINSON.

Ordered that the Estate of JOHN WILLIAMS Deceased be Sold on the 22 November Next and a Credit Given to the first of May following with Int. from Day of Sale.

Adjourned untill the 28th Feby. next. JOHN KERSHAW.

28th February Court 1792

The Honorable ADAM FOWLER BRISBANE and JOHN KERSHAW Esq'rs Met agreeable to Adjournment & Proceeded to Draw the Jurors from Box No 1 to No 2.

GRAND JURORS: 1 JOHN HORTON [stricken], 1 ROBERT LEE, 2 HENRY HORTON, 3 JOHN MIDDLETON, 4 WM BOND, 5 ANDREW LESTER, 6 JAMES INGRUM, 7 THOMAS BALLARD, 8 RICH'D MIDDLETON, 9 JAMES MARSHALL, 10 WM. KIRKLAND, 11 REUBIN PATTERSON, 12 GEORGE MILLER, 13 LOVICK ROCHELL, 14 GEORGE EVANS, 15 JAMES CORROTH.

[Page 21]

16 WILLIAM WHITAKER, 17 JOHN GUEERY, 18 THO'S WATS, 19 DAN'L KIRKLAND, 20 THO'S LENORE [jurors 21 through 30 are stricken] 21 HENRY HUDSON, 22 DAVID JONES, MOSES REEVES, 23 DAN'L OQUIN SEN'R, 24 WM TWADDLE, 25 LEWIS COLLINS, 26 JACOB GREY, 27 THOS ENGLISH, 28 _____ VAUGHN, Sawney c, 29 JONATHAN GREYHAM, 30 GEORGE DURING.

DRAWN FROM BOX N. 3 to N 4. PETIT JURORS: 1 BRYANT SPRADLEY, 2 DAN'L McMILLIAN, 3 JOHN DENNIS, 4 DAVIS COATS, 5 GEORGE SAUNDERS, 6 GEORGE PAYNE SEN'R, 7 DAVID CLANTON, 8 NICHOLAS THOMSON, 9 WM. COOK, 10 JOHN BRADLEY SEN'R, 11 JOHN FAULKINGBERRY, 12 THOMAS BIRD, 13 JOSEPH COATS, 14 WM BRASWELL, 15 JACOB CHERRY, 16 THO'S CANTY, 17 SAM'L JONES, 18 LUKE GIBSON, 19 EDWARD ROGERS, 20, JOHN HICKSON, 21 SAM'L MARTIN, 22 THO'S MILLS, 23 SAM'L PAYNE, 24 WM. MAXWELL, 25 DAN'L GARDNER, 26 ROB'T MACKAY, 27 SAM'L BRADLEY, 28 REUBIN BRADFIELD, 29 ROB'T FAULKINBERRY, 30 SAM'L SMITH, 31 THO'S SHURLEY, 32 JOHN CLANTON, 33 JOHN OWEN, 34 WM. EGLINSTON, 35 JOHN LENORE, 36 RICH'D DRAKEFORD, 37 CHA'S SPEARS JUN'R, 38 REUBIN COOK, 39 JOSEPH McCOY, 40 JOSEPH PERDY, 41 JOSEPH FLY, 42 ROB'T WHITE, 43 JAMES SEWEL.

[Page 22]

From Box No 3 to N. 4

Common Pleas Jurors: 1 JAMES TOLAND, 2 WM LAYTON, 3 JAMES BATES, 4 ABRAHAM WIMBERLY, 5 JOHN KILI, 6 ALEX'R McKEE, 7 CHA'S McLELAND, 8 GEORGE PERRY, 9 MARTIN TRANTHAM, 10 WALTER SROPSHIRE, 11 JAMES WREN, 12 JAMES SMITH, 13 JESSE CURLEE, 14 RICH'D CURLEE, 14 RICH'D GARNER, 15 ROB'T DUMBLE, 16 JOHN McCLURE, 17 CH. RAYLEY, 18 JOHN McKEE, 19 JOHN RIDDLE, 20 JOHN COOK, 21 CHARLES ROBINSON, 22 WM. WIMBERLY, 23 ABRAHAM SHIVER, 24 JOHN SAUNDERS, 25 WM GREYHAM, 26 RICH'D CLANTON, 27 JOHN TRUSDALL, 28 MATHEW PAYNE, 29 BENJ. ALEXANDER, 30 ALEX'R STEWART.

The following persons Were Impanneld on the Grand Jury & Sworn.

DOUGLAS STARKE, foreman; a ALEX'R C. CORRUTH, JOHN RUTLEDGE, GEORGE RICHARDSON, SAM'L TYNES, GEORGE GAYTON, JAMES CANTEY, a AARON FERGUSON, a WM DUNLAP, ARTHUR CUNNINGHAM, GEORGE ROSS, JOHN WEBB, JOHN HORTON, JOHN MARSHALL.

[Page 23]

The following Persons were Impanneled on the Petit Jury & Sworn[stricken].

WILLIAM BREWER, foreman; JOHN TRANTHAM, ARCH'D WATSON, WM YOUNG, JOSIAH SAUNDERS, MATHEW BOWEN, a ROB'T MARSHALL, ROB'T THOMSON, JAMES WILLIAMS, JESSE MINTON, WM PEACH, BERRY KING.

[28 February 1792]

The Court admits of the Excuse Made by NATH'L ROGERS & THOS. SHROPSHIRE as Jurors.

Ordered that letters of Administration do Issue to ELINOR ELKINS on ... JOHN ELKINS Deceased the Securities are JN'O ABBOT & GIDEON LOWRY.

Ordered that letters of Administration do Issue to WM SCOTT on ... JOHN SCOTT Deceased the Securities are BURWELL BOYKIN & WILLIS WHITAKER.

the following Persons Were Impaneld on the Common Pleas Jurors: JAMES CAIN, PATRICK LATUN, JOHN KERLEE, ANDREW GREYHAM, GEORGE KING, JAMES LOVE, WILLIAM WILLIAMS, JOHN GAYTON.

[Page 24]

Ordered that Letters of Administration do Issue to ROBERT COOK of ... GEORGE UNDERWOOD the Securities are REUBIN COOK & FEDRICK JONES [stricken] WM CHANCELER.

The Court Adjourn'd to Morrow ten Oclock. ADAM F. BRISBANE, JOHN KERSHAW.

The Hon'ble ADAM FOWLER BRISBANE and JOHN KERSHAW Esquires Met & Opened Court agreeable to Adjournment.

GEORGE ROSS Appeared in Open Court and Acknowledged a Deed of Conveyance to JAMES COWSART.

Ordered that Letters Testamentary Do Issue to REUBIN COLLINS & JOHN GAYDEN Executors of the last Will & Testament of ... WM COLLINS Deceased.

Ordered that the Sale of Property belonging to the Estate of LEMUEL PERRY made by WM KIRKLAND & LEWIS COLLINS the Executors be Approved of by the court.

[Page 25]

Ordered that SAMUEL TYNES be taken off the Grand Jury as a Prosecuter & Witness.

The State vs ROGER GIBSON. Retur'd by the Grand Jury. a True Bill. Traversed.

The State vs W'M SIMMS. Retur'd by the Grand Jury a true Bill. Traversed.

The State vs FREDRICK ROBINSON. Retur'd by the Grand Jury a True Bill. Traversed.

The State vs CHARLES BARBER. No bill.

The State vs JOHN BOLDING. Retur'd by the Grand Jury a true Bill.

The State vs FREDERICK ROBINSON. Assault. Verdict Guilty. W'M BREWER foreman.

The Petit Jury being Impanneld and Sworn Which are as follows: W'M BREWER, foreman, JOHN TRANTHAM, ARCH'D WATSON, WILLIAM YOUNG, JOSIAH SAUDNERS, MATHEW BOWEN, (affirms) ROBERT MARSHALL, ROBERT THOMSON, JAMES WILLIAMS, JESSE MINTON, WM. PEACH, BERRY KING.

[Page 26] [29 February 1792]

Ordered that letters Testamentary DO Issue to BURWELL BOYKIN Executor of the Estate of DURRET LONG Deceased....

Ordered that letters Testamentary Do Issue to BURWELL BOYKINS Executor on ... SAMUEL BOYKIN Deceased.

ROBERT CARTER vs SAM'L BOYKIN. MATHIS Pltffs atty. PERKINS Def't atty. The Executors of the Parties agree to leave this Cause to Arbitration and the Award be a Rule of Court.

Cap't ISAAC DUBOISE & Capt JOHN CHESNUT appointed Arbitrators With Power to appoint an Umpire & that they Make their award on or before the 15th May Next.

SAM'L BOYKIN Adm'r T. RICHARDSON vs ALEX'R IRWIN. PERKINS Pltffs atty. Trover. MATHIS Deft's atty.

The Petit Jurors Cal'd & Sworn Viz. WILLIAM BREWER foreman, JOHN TRANTHAM, ARCH'D WATSON, WILLIAM YOUNG, JOSIAH SAUNDERS, MATHEW BOWEN, ROBERT MARSHALL, ROBERT THOMSON, JAMES WILLIAMS, JESSE MINTON, WM PEACH, BERRY KING. We find for the Plaintiff Fifty Pounds Sterling.

[Page 27]

Ordered that JAMES HOLLY Renew his Recognizance to appear at Lancaster Court.

The Court Adjour'd till Morrow 10 OClock. ADAM F. BRISBANE, JOHN KERSHAW.

1st March 1792. The Hon'ble ADAM FOWLER BRISBANE & JOHN KERSHAW Esq'rs Met and Opened Court agreeable to Adjournment.

Ordered that FREDERICK HEATH be appointed as Guardian to STEPHEN TERRY.

Ordered that the Estate of JOHN SCOTT SEN'R be sold & Made payable the first of Jan'y Next With Interest thereon and that it be Advertized three Weeks in Camden and agreeable to Law.

The State vs JOHN BOLDING. Verdict Not Guilty for Stealing Tobacco.

The Petit Jurors Cal'd & Sworn viz. WILLIAM BREWER foreman, JOHN TRANTHAM, ARCH'D WATSON, WM YOUNG, JOSIAH SAUNDERS, MATHEW BOWEN, ROBERT MARSHALL affirm, ROBERT THOMSON, JAMES WILLIAMS, JESSE MINTON, WM PEACH, BERRY KING.

Witnesses SAM. TINES, DAVID MEYER, W'M CAMP, ____ JONES, A. BASKINS.

[Page 28]

Ordered that letters Testamentary Do Issue to JAMES KERSHAW on ... JOSEPH KERSHAW Deceased.

Ordered that letters Testamentary Do Issue to JAMES KERSHAW on ... STERLING PETTIWAY Deceased.

REUBEIN STARKE vs NATHANIEL CLANTON & RICHARD CLANTON. PERKINS Pltffs. Debt Judgement by Default.

[1 March 1792]

Ordered that the Estate of JOHN ELKINS be Sold and a Credit Given Untill the first of October Next.

WREN vs COLLINS. Att. Ordered that W'M KIRKLAND do enter as Special Bail.

JAMES PEARSONS vs N. JOHNSON. PERKINS Pltfs Atty. Att. Dismissed at the Plaintiffs Cost. MATHIS Def't Atty.

State vs JOHN DRAKFORD. Basterdy.

State vs PATCHET. Basterdy.

Ordered that the Defendents Enter into Security in the Sum of Fifty Poiunds to Indemnify the County DAVID HUNTER & RICH'D DRAKFORD Securitys & to pay Costs.

[Page 29]

JONES & OSGOOD vs WYAT COLLINS. MATHIS Plfts Atty. S. P. L 2. 11 & In't. Decree for the Plaintiff as P Specialty With In't from 3rd Jan'y 1790.

HENRY HUDSON vs JAMES TOLAN. Att. PERKINS Plfts Atty. NOTT Def't Att'y. Judgement Confessed. Stay Execution three Months.

FREDERICK ROBINSON who was yesterday found Guilty on an Indictment for an Assault & Battery on JNO McCAW Was sentenced to suffer One Months close Confinement in the Common Goal of Camen to pay a fine of Five pounds Sterling & Give Security to keep thePeace & For his good behaviour for twelve Months himself in L 100 & 2 Securities to be approved by one of the Judges of the Court in L 50 each & pay Costs and stand committed till the Judgment of the Court be performed.

Ordered that ROBERT FORD, ISHAM POWELL, JOHN MORGAN, JAMES HUNTER, & FREDERICK ROBINSON each of them Enter into Recognizance in the sum of L 100 each and two securities each in the sum of L 50 each for the Persons above Mentioned to hold them to their good behavour.

[Page 30]

and for their Appearance at this Court and not to Depart Without leave and to do and Receive What Shall be Enjoined by them the Said Court.

Adjourned Untill to Morrow ten OClock. ADAM F. BRISBANE, JOHN KERSHAW.

2 March 1792

The Hon'ble ADAM FOWLER BRISBANE & JOHN KERSHAW Esq'r Met agreeable to Adjournment and Opend Court.

Ordered that the Estate of GEORGE UNDERWOOD be sold and a Credit Given to the first of January next.

Ordered that Letters Testamentary do Issue to DOUGLAS STARKE on ... JOHN PLATT Deceased.

J. WELSH vs JUDITH ROBERTS. NOTT Pltf Atty. By Consent of the Pltfs & Defts Atty a Commission to issue to take the Depo. of ROBERT LOVE in Georgia the Pltf receiving the right of Exception to his Compentence as a Witness.

[2 March 1792]

[Page 31]

Ordered that the Estate of W'M COLLINS Deceased be sold and Made payable the first of Jan'y 1793.

EDWARD MORTIMER & Co vs Exor of JOHN BELTON. S. MATHIS Pltf. PERKINS Def't. We find for the Plaintiff Forty pounds 4/7 With the Interest due thereon agreeable to Note. W'M BREWER foreman.

The Jury Call'd & Sworn: W'M BREWER, foreman; JOHN TRANTHAM, JAMES WILLIAMS, JESSE MINTON, ARCH'D WATSON, JOSIAH SAUNDERS, ROBERT MARSHALL affirm, ROBERT THOMSON, W'M PEACH, BERRY KING, WILLIAM WARE, W'M HICKMAN.

Ordered that the Recognizance of ISHAM POWELL & Others, JAMES HUNTER & Others, JOHN MORGAN & Others, ROBERT FORD & Others, and the Witness be laid Over to Appear at Our Court on the Twenty fifth Day of July Next.

WM TRADDLE vs MATHEW JONES. CASE. MATHIS Pltf Atty; NOTT Dft atty; We find for the Plaintiff L 20 with twelve Months Interest and Costs. W'M BREWER foreman.The Jury Call'd Sworn [same jury as previous case].

ROBERT FORD vs RICH'D YANCEY. PERKINS Pltfs Atty. T. P. Dismissed at Pltfs Costs.

[Page 32] MICHAEL BULGER vs TH'S BALLARD, WILLIAM & JOHN CRAIG & ALEX'R FLEMING. Case. PERKINS Pltfs Atty. BROWN Defd't Atty. Dismissed at Defendants Costs.

HUGH McGEE vs JAMES NICKLE. BROWN PLtfs. S. P. Dis missed at Dfdts Costs.

SAM'L LOWRIE vs DAVID WILLIAMS. PERKINS Pltfs Atty. S. P. Judgement by Default.

ZACHARIAH MARTIN vs JOSHUA McHENRY. Case. Abated by the death of Defend't. BROWN Pltfs Atty. PERKINS Defdts Atty.

JOSEPH KERSHAW vs WILLIS WHITAKER. CASE Abated by Death of Pltf. MATHIS Plfts atty.

JAMES OGILVIE vs GEORGE ROSS. NOTT Pltfs Atty. S. P. Judgement Confessed.

WREN vs MOSELEY COLLINS. The Defendant having appeared & attended the Court & no attch't retained ordered that the same be dismissed at the Plaintiffs Costs.

[Page 33]

DAN'L BROWN vs JOHN VERRILL. Att. PERKINS Pltf. Find for the Defendent. W'M BREWER, foreman. The Jury Call'd & Sworn: W'M BREWER foreman, JAMES WILLIAMS, JOHN TRANTHAM, ARCH'D WATSON, JOSIAH SAUNDERS, ROBERT MARSHALL, ROBERT THOMPSON, JAMES PIERSON, WM PEACH, WM HICKMAN, WM WERE, BERRY KING.

Court Adjourned Untill to Morrow ten OClock. ADAM F. BRISBANE, JOHN KERSHAW.

3 March 1792. The Hon'ble ADAM FOWLER BRISBANE & JOHN KERSHAW Esq'rs met agreeable to Adjournment and Open'd Court.

[3 March 1792]

Ordered that letters of Administration do Issue to JULIA CHAMPION on ... RICH'D CHAMPION Deceased.

ANDREW LESTER vs FIELDING WOODRUF. Debt. PERKINS. Plea WithDrawn and Judgement Confessed on Note.

Ordered that the following Persons be appointed Constables & that they be summoned to Appear at Court the 16th May Next to be qualified & all those Who have Not qualified on the former appointment in May 1791 WM NETTLES JUN'R, JOHN SWILLEY, JOHN McNEAL & JOSEPH PAYNE.

[Page 34]

Ordered that the following have permission to take out Licence to Sell Spirituous Liquors: RICHARD BLANKS, JOHN ADAMSON, THOS. DINKINS, GERSHAM CHAPMAN, BROCKWAY & PAYNE, JOHN McNEAL, JOHN KERSHAW, JOSEPH McCOY, JAMES COUSART, JESSE MINTON, JOHN REID, SAMUEL LEVY, DAVID KING.

WALTER ROWE vs JAMES ROBINSON. PERKINS. Att. Judgement by Default on an account proved by JN'O ADAMSON in Lanc'st County and a Small Note of Hand.

FRANCIS ADAMS vs SAM'L LEVY. Case. BROWN Pltf. Atty. We find for the Plaintiff L 16 s 6 d 3. WILLIAM BREWER, foreman. The Jury Cal'd & Sworn: WM BREWER, foreman, JOHN TRANTHAM, ARCH'D WATSON, JOSIAH SAUNDERS, BENJAMIN CARTER [stricken], ROBERT MARSHALL, ROBERT THOMSON, JAMES WILLIAMS, WM PEACH, WM HICKMAN, ROB'T HOOD, WM WERE [stricken], WM YOUNG, WM NETTLES.

JOHN EGLESTON vs WM. CAMMOCK. NOTT Pltfs. Atty. S. P. Judgement for Pltf Stay Execution Three Months.

DAN'L BROWN vs N. JOHNSON. Att. Discontinued.

[Page 35] WM WARE vs J. L. DeBUSE. Att. LEft to JOHN REID, DOCTOR ISAAC ALEXANDER, & Cap't ISAAC DUBOISE, be arbitraters.

ALEXANDER CARROOTH vs WILLIAM COLLINS. Sum: Pro: MATHIS Att'y for Pl'f. Decree for Plaintiff as P Note of Hand.

JOHN WALLACE vs JOHN CALLENDER. BROWN Pltf Atty. S. P. Judgement Confessed.

JN'O CHESNUT & DUNCAN McRA vs WM SCOTT Ex'r of JOHN SCOTT. Writ. We find for the Plaintiff L 14 s 2 d 3 with Lawful Interest. WM BREWER, foreman. JOHN TRANTHAM, ARCH'D WATSON, JOSIAH SAUNDERS, ROBERT MARSHALL, ROBERT THOMSON, JAMES WILLIAMS, WM. PEACH, WM HICKMAN, ROB'T HOOD, WM YOUNG, WM NETTLES.

Ordered that JOHN TAYLOR & ABRAHAM CHILDERS be Sworn Depitty Sheriffs appear'd and Sworn accordingly.

[Page 36]

HUGH McDOWL vs ROBERT DOW. Appeal from Justice of Peace. Judgement affirmed L 3 6 5 Each party paying his Own Costs.

Ordered that a Bond With Security be taken agreeable to Law for the Amount of the Appraisement of Eleven Stray hog taken up by BRYANT SPRADLEY & that they Continued advertized the two Next Courts.

[3 March 1792]

SAM'L DUNLAP vs LEWIS HUDSON & RUSH HUDSON. BROWN Pltf att'y. S. P. Order for Judgment Stay Execution three Months.

Ordered that JOHN McNEAL be Appointed Deputy Sherif and be Sworn Accordingly. Met and Sworn.

REUBIN COOK vs JAMES McMANUS. Att. Laid Over.

THOMAS GATHER vs MOSE BROWN. Att Dismissed.

JOSEPH BREVARD vs ROGER GIBSON & WM. SUTTON. Debt. On motion of the Plfs Attorney, Ordered that the bail taken by the Sheriff in this Case, be Entered as Special Bail to the Action.

[Page 37]

JOHN P. WAGNON vs ABRAHAM FLEMING. Att.

On a Motion of the Plaintiffs Attorney to have the Garnishee called the Court Were of Opinion that he Was not Obliged to appear the Attachment having been Levyed by EDWARD RUTLEDGE Who had only been Nominated & approved by the Court but never had been Sworn in Whereupon the court Dismissed the above attachment as Well as One brought against Said FLEMING by FRANCIS BOYKIN upon the Same Grounds.

ROBERT HENRY vs JOHN KERSHAW. JO BREVARD Pltfs Att'y. Debt. Confessed Judgement.

DUNCAN McRA & ZACHARIAH CANTEY vs JOHN KERSHAW. JO BREVARD Pltfs Att'y. Debt. Confessed Judgement.

Ordered that Process Do Issue against the Several Persons Presented by the Grand Jurors for Offences and Also for the Overseers for the Several Road that are Out of Repair.

JOHN RUSSEL vs HEZEKIAH LOVE. MATHIS Pltf Atty. Debt. Judgement by Default.

BRYANT SPRADLEY vs JOHN WILLSON. MATHIS. Att. Judgement by Default L 9 6 3. Ordered that the land Attached in this Case be sold being first advertized in the State Gazett.

Adjourn'd Untill Monday ten OClock. ADAM F. BRISBANE, JOHN KERSHAW.

[Page 38]

5th March 1792 Feby Term.

The Court Met & Open'd Agreeable to Adjournment When ADAM F. BRISBANE & JOHN KERSHAW Esq'r Were Present.

Agreeable to an Order of Court JOHN DRAKEFORD and MARY PATCHET has Given Bond with Security [stricken: Agreeable to the above Order]

Agreeable to an Order of Court JAMES HOLLY Gave Recognizance to Appear at Lancaster Court.

The State vs JAMES GUN. Recognizance. Nole Prosequi.

Ordered that Letters Testamentary Do Issue to JOHN BOYKINS & ZACHARIAH CANTEY on ... SAM'L BOYKIN Deceased.

[5 March 1792]

Ordered that Twenty Pounds Sterling be Paid to M'r ZACHARIAH CANTEY by the Clerk fo Building a Bridge Over Pine tree Creek.

Ordered that Seven Pounds Sterling be paid to DOCTOR THOMAS WRIGHT for a Cure Performed on a MR'S SPENCER.

[Page 39]

Ordered that the County Attorney do take the Most Effectual Method to Prosecute the following Persons for not Producing the Estrays return'd by them Viz The Representatives of ARCH'D McNEIL, JAMES SAUNDERS, ALEXANDER STEWARD & DAN'L Brown.

Ordered that the Several Estrays that are produced & Legally Advertised Be Sold.

Ordered that EDWARD RUTLEDGE be Appointed as Deputy Sheriff. Accordingly Appeared and Sworn.

Ordered that the County Attorney Do Take the Most effectual Method of having the Recognizance of ISHAM POWEL returnable to the Superior Cort Estreated in Case it should prove on his trial to be forfeited & that the Recognizance of FREDERICK ROBINSON be sued for if it should on his trial for the Riot appear to be forfeited.

The Hon'ble Court Adjourned Untill the third Monday in May Next. ADAM F. BRISBANE, JOHN KERSHAW.

[Page 40]

The Hon'ble JOHN KERSHAW Esq'r Met agreeable to Adjournment and Opened Court.

Ordered that the Different Persons be Appointed Overseers of the Different Roads herein Mentioned.

From Camden to Town Creek Inclusive, DAN'L PEAK; Town Creek to Claremont Line, JOHN BOYKIN; Pinetree Creek to Saunders Creek, NICHOLAS ROBINSON; Saunders Creek to Granys Quarter Creek, WM. NETTLES; Granys Quarter Creek to Flat Rock Including Granys Q. Creek, SAM'L SMITH; Flat Rock to Lancaster Line, GEORGE MILLER; Cowsar to Gunswamp New Road, E'D ROGERS; Camden Ferry to Canteys Bridge, MICHAEL GAUNTER; Fork of Road to Little Lynches Creek at Fords, JAS. WILLIAMS; Little Lynches Creek to Great Lynches Creek, Great Lynches Creek, JESSE MINTON; Canteys Bridge to Tillers Ferry, JO'S McCoy; JO MCCOYs to Brevards Crossing place, GEORGE EVANS; Rocky Mount Road to Grayns Quarter Inclusive, FRANCIS BELVIN; Granys Quarter Bridge to White Oak both Roads, W'M DANIEL; White Oak to Lancaster County Line, MICHAEL BARNET; From White Oak the Beaver Creek Road, REUBIN COLLINS; Saunders Creek to Hanging Rock Creek at NETTLES, SAM'L JONES; Hanging Rock to Buffalo Cr., THO'S WELSH; Buffalo to Kinningtons ford at Lick Creek, RICHMOND TERRIL; Lockarts to Buffalo by TINES, W'M JONES SEN'R;

[Page 42]

Buffalo to Chesterfield County Line, JOHN CATO; Camden to Chesnuts Ferry, W'M BONDS; Chesnuts ferry to Colo Cr., PETER CRIM; From Camden Ferry to the Rocky Mount Road Untill it meets Chesnuts Ferry Road, ROGER GIBSON; Camden Ferry to Richland County Columbia Road, ISAAC ROSS; JOHN MARTINs to County Line on McCords Road, JAS. ENGLISH; Pinetree Creek to the Line near Carters Crossing Place on Scape Whore, GEO PAYNE SEN'R.

[21 May 1792]

Ordered that the following Persons Obtain Licence for Retailing Spirituous Liquors: DAVID BUSH, ISAIH BUSH, McRA & CANTEY, JAMES BROWN JUN'R, WILLIAM YOUNG[stricken].

Ordered that JOHN SWILLA be appointed as a Deputy Sheriff appeared and Sworn Accordingly.

Ordered that MR. DINKINS be permitted to erect a Gate on the Publick Road between Camden & the ferry for the term of Seven Months provided it shall be at least Ninety feet Wide & Made to Open on Either Side With Iron Hinges & An Iron Latch & Catch. Ordered That JAMES KERSHAW be permitted to Build One of the Same Demensions & Descriptoin as the fore going on or near Canteys Bridge.

Ordered that the Overseer of the Charraw Road on this side of Little Lynches Bridges Do Open a New One from the house of JAS WILLIAMS in as direct a line as Possible to the Sd Bridge.

[Page 42]

Ordered that JAMES KERSHAWs Accot presented this Day be paid Amounting to 59/1.

Ordered that the Purchasers of Estrays Sold by Order of this Court be proceeded Against According to Law in all cases Where the Money is become Due.

The Honble Court Adjourned Untill to Morrow ten OClock. JOHN KERSHAW.

The Hon'ble JOHN KERSHAW Esq'r Met and Opened Court Agreeable to adjournment.

Ordered that Letters of Administration Do Issue to MARY & JAMES AYRES on ... DAN'L AYRES Deceased, the Securities are JOHN RUTLEDGE[stricken] TAYLOR & GEORGE ROSS.

Ordered that the Credit given to the Purchasers of the Estate of WM COLLINS as Ordered for Sale the 2nd MArch 1792 be extended to the first Day of January 1794.

Ordered that a Seal for the Use of this Court be Procured as early as Possible Which Will Make a suitable Impression.

[Page 43] (22'nd May)

Ordered that the property belonging to the Estate of JOHN SCOTT JUN'R Deceased be Sold on a Credit till the first of January next.

Ordered that LYDIA & FERRABY HOWARD the Orphan Children of WILLIAM & MARTHA HOWARD Do remain in the Care of JOHN ABBOT Untill a Proper and approved person can be procured to take Charge of them.

Ordered that the Estrays be sold this day Which have been advertised the legal time & For Which no Owner have appeared.

Ordered that the County Attorney be & is required to take the legal Steps for causing all Persons returned as defaulters Working on the Roads to be fined & that those Overseers of Districts of Road Who have neglected to Make a Return to this Court be required to Make excuse on the first Day of Next Court for such Neglect on Pain of being Proceeded against agreeable to Law.

Ordered that JOHN MILLHOUSE & WILLIAM LANG Who were appointed Executors (as it is said) of the last Will and Testament of JOHN GALBRAITH

[22 May 1792]

Esquire late of Camden Deceased Do shew Cause to this Court at the next Meeting thereof Why they or either of them Do not Prove the said Will and take the burthen of the Administration thereof upon them. And in case of their Declining to Act as Executors thereof

[Page 44]

or Either of them then to shew cause Why the said Will should Not be Delivered up to this Court to be proved & Letters of Administration With the Will Annexed granted to some proper person or Persons.

The Court Adjourned Untill the Twenty Eighth Day of July Next. JOHN KERSHAW.

28th July Term 1792. Agreeable to adjournment the Court Was Opened and Adjourned Untill Monday 10 OClock.

30th July. Agreeable to Adjournment the Court was Opened Present ADAM FOWLER BRISBANE, JOHN KERSHAW Esqr's.

1 Grand Jurors, 2 WILLIAM TWADDLE, 3 HENRY HUDSON B. Creek, 4 JACOB GREY, 5 LEWIS COLLINS B. C., 6 DAN'L OQUIN SEN'R, 7 THOS ENGLISH, 8 JOHN GREHAM B. C.[stricken] MICAIAH VAUGHN, 9 GEORGE DURAN, 10 BURWELL BOYKIN, 11 SAM'L BELTON, 12 JOHN BOYKIN, 13 A. B. ROSS, 14 ROB'T DUNLAP, 15 SILAS CAMBLE,

[Page 45]

16 ANDREW BASKINS, 17 JOHN NICKSON, 18 THO'S GARDNER, 19 CHARLES McGINNEY, 20 JAMES COWSAR.

PETIT JURORS: 1 RICHMOND TERRIL, 2 RICH'D WILSON, 3 WM. TERRILL, 4 ARCH'D McAFFEE, 5 HUGH McLESTER, 6 DENNIS QUINLEY, 7 ROGER GIBSON, 8 STARKE HUNTER, 9 ANDREW NUTT JUN'R, 10 BIRD OWEN, 11 WILLIAM SCOTT G. Quarter, 12 ISRAEL MOORE, G. Q., 13 JOHN COOK JUN'R, 14 JAMES TATE, 15 JONATHAN BUNCKLEY, 16 JAMES ENGLISH, 17 JOHN HOOD B. C., 18 WILLIAM WELL T. C., 19 PATRICK McCAIN, 20 WILLIAM DANIEL, 21 THO'S WATTS, 22 JOHN TAYLOR, 23 JOHN DRAKEFORD, 24 DAN'L OQUIN JUN'R, 25 JOHN OQUIN, 26 MOSES SAUNDERS, 27 PAUL SMITH, 28 WILLIAM CURLEE, 29 ROB'T DICKSON, 30 PETER CRIM.

GRAND JURORS: 1 ANDREW LESTER, foreman, 2 HENRY HORTEN, 3 WILLIAM BOND affirm, 4 ANDREW LESTER [stricken], 4 JAMES INGRAM, 5 THO'S BALLARD, 6 RICHARD MIDDLETON, 7 JAMES MARSHALL, 8 JAMES MARSHALL [stricken], WM KIRKLAND, 9 GEORGE MILLER, 10 JAMES CORRUTH aff, 11 DAN'L KIRKLAND, 12 THO'S LENORE, 13 ROB'T LEE, 14 GEORGE EVANS.

[Page 46]

1 JAMES MILLER foreman, 2 BRYANT SPRADLEY, 3 DAVID COATS, 4 THOMAS BIRD, 5 JACOB CHERRY, 6 SAMUEL JONES, 7 LUKE GIBSON, 8 JOHN HICKSON, 9 SAMUEL MARTIN, 10 GEORGE PAYNE, 11 JEFRY HUTSON, 12 WILLIAM McGILL.

Ordered that JOHN CAULKINS be Appointed in the Place of BENJAMIN PERKINS in the suit of

JOHN McCAMBRIDGE vs JAMES BEVANS. Judgement Confessed.

JEREMIAH BROWN vs JOSEPH McCOY. Judgement Confessed With Costs.

[30 July 1792]

RICHARD SPRINGS vs ROBERT FORD & JOHN MARSHALL. Judgement Confessed With Costs.

Ordered that the Last Will and Testament of William Tate be Proved and Letters Testamentary Do Issue to JOHN CHESNUT & ZACHARIAH CANTEY Executors of the Above Will.

[Page 47]

Ordered that the following Persons have Licence for Retailing Spirituous Liquors: JOHN BARREN, JAMES LOVE, GEORGE MILLER.

Ordered that Letters Testamentary Do Issue to SAMUEL SLONE & JEFRY HUDSON on ... WILLIAM SLOAN Deceased, the Will being Duly Proved and SAML SLONE & JEFRY HUDSON Qualified as Executors thereof.

REUBIN COOK vs JAMES McMANUS. Att. Judgement for L 24 s 13 With Int. from 13'th May 1776. Old Currency.

Robert McCAIN Sworn as Garnashee is Indebted to the Defd't but Cannot Ascertain What amount Which he is to Render in to Clerk in future.

Ordered that the Presentments of the Grand Jury be Received and A Copy made Out for to be Printed in the State Gazett.

The Court then Adjourned Untill Tomorrow Morning at Nine O'Clock. ADAM F. BRISBANE, JOHN KERSHAW.

[Page 48]

Agreeable to Adjournment the Court was Opened: Present ADAM F. BRISBANE, JOHN KERSHAW, Esq'rs.

WM NELSON vs JOSEPH McCOY. PERKINS. Plaintiff Nonsuited.

JOHN L. DeBUSEY vs MICAJAH VAUGHAN. Judgement for Pltff. Confessed for Debt. Int. & Costs.

EDWARD CHRISTIE vs HENRY MOORE. MATHIS. NOTT. [stricken: Nonsuit Appeal]

Jury Sworn: JAMES MILLER foreman; BRYANT SPRADLEY, DAVID COATS, THOMAS BIRD, JACOB CHERRY, SAM'L JONES, LUKE GIBSON, JOHN HICKSON, SAMUEL MARTIN, GEORGE PAYNE, JEFRY HUTSON, WILLIAM McGILL.

Ordered that the Return of the Appraisement of the Estate of M'r SAM'L BOYKIN be Defer'd untill Next Court the Executors not being Perfectly prepared to Make a Return.

[Page 49]

EDWARD CHRISTIE vs HENRY MOORE. Writ Case. The Pltf produced a Copy of his A/C compared with his Books before a Justice of the Peace at Charleston which he offered as Evidence of his Debt and The Defendant objected That the original Books of Entry ought to be produced in Court Whereupon the Court were of the Opinion that such Copy ought not to be rec'd as Evidence. the Plaintiff is Non suited.

JOSEPH BREVARD vs ROGER GIBSON & WM. SUTTON. NOTT. Judgement Confessed. BROWN.

[31 July 1792]

MOSELEY COLLINS vs WM WALKER. BROWN. Judgement by Default according to Specialty for the Monies Goods & Chattles in the hands of JOSEPH COTES JUN'R Garnishee.

PETER OSGOOD vs NICHOLAS ROBINSON & FREDERICK ROBINSON. MATHIS. We find for the Pltf. the note with In't (deducting L 3 10 With Interest). Debt Note. NOTT.

[same jury as previous case]

[Page 50]

Ordered that JOSEPH TILLER JUN'R Be Sworn as Constable appeared and Sworn in Accordingly.

WILLIAM YOUNG vs GEORGE PERRY. BROWN. Debt on Note. The Defts Att'y withdraws his Plea. Judg't by default according to Specialty with Interest & Costs.

THO'S WELSH vs ROB'T LOVE & JUDITH ROBERTS. Ordered to be Continued upon the Defendent Giving Security to Appear and abide the Decision of Next Court HENRY EDEY Sec'y for the Def't.

DAN'L PAYNE vs ARCH'D WATSON. MATHIS. Decree for Plaintiff Ten Pounds.

Ex parte JOSEPH NETTLES an Infant of the Age of fourteen years & upwards, a Motion was made, Suggesting that the said Infant being intitled to an Estate & property in his own right, Desirous of choosing a Guardian to take the Custody of his person & Estate, to protect & manage for his benefit; and the said Infant being produced in Court in his proper person & examined touching the freedom of his choice; and WILLIAM NETTLES the Infant's father being also examined in open Court & consenting thereto, & agreeing to relinquish his right of Guardianship; And the said Infant having chosen

[Page 51]

JOSEPH BREVARD for his Guardian; and the said JOSEPH BREVARD having consented take upon him the Burthen of the same Guardianship. Ordered, That the said JOSEPH BREVARD do give Bond with Security in the sum of L 500 for the due execution of the said Trust; and that thereupon Letters of Guardianship do issue consistituting and authorising the said Joseph Brevard to act accordingly.

JOHN R. HUTCHINS vs JN'O ARMSTRONG TRUL, JAMES CAMBLE, & SAMUEL SLONE. Judgement by Default.

DAN'L BROWN vs JOHN RUSSELL & DAVID HUNTER. NOTT. Judgement Confessed by DAVID HUNTER and by Default against JN'O RUSSEL With Costs.

SAM'L DUNLAP vs HENRY HUDSON & JN'O BALLARD. BROWN. Judgement by Default according to Specialty with In't and Costs. MATHIS.

ABRAHAM CHILDERS vs JAMES TOLAND & JN'O NARRIMORE. MATHIS. Att. We find for the Plaintiff L 8 5/ With In't from the 6th August 1791. JAMES MILLER foreman.

JAMES MILLER, BRYANT SPRADLEY, DAVID COATS, THOMAS BIRD, JACOB CHERRY, SAM'L JONES, LUKE GIBSON, JOHN HICKSON, SAM'L MARTIN, GEORGE PAYNE, JEFRY HUTSON, WM. McGILL.

[31 July 1792]

[Page 52]

JOSHUA LUCAS vs THO'S LANGFORD. Judgement for the Costs the Debt being Satisfy'd.

JAMES WILLIAMS vs JOHN NORRIS. PERKINS. Att. Plaintiff Nonsuited. BROWN. [same jury as preceding case]

Ordered that the Name of JOHN BARREN be left Out in the Copy of the Presentments that is to be Published he Giving the Court a Sufficient Excuse.

SAM'L MATHIS SNR. of Kershaw vs Adm'r of WM LECONTs Estate. MATHIS. We find for the Pltf. L 26 13/1 Sterling with IN't from 1 Jan'y 1786. Plea of Plene Administravit being put in & allowed this Judgment is for Future assets. JAMES MILLER, foreman. [same jury as preceding case]

SUSANNAH BROWN vs FREEMAN LEWIS. NOTT. Att. Judgement by Default for L 10 with Costs.

[Page 53]

HENRY FOSTER vs WM LANG. S. P. Judgement by Default according to Specialty With Costs.

Ordered that the Estate of DAN'L AYRES Deceased be Sold on a Credit Untill the first of January next.

JONATHAN BELTON vs ARCH'D WATSON. MATHIS. S. P. Decree for Plaintiff as pr Specialty With Costs of Suit.

ALEXANDER MOORE vs JOSHUA DINKINS. BROWN. S. P. Judgement by Default as Pr Specialty.

JAMES COWSAR vs JOHN KERSHAW JUN'R. BROWN. S. P. Set a Side for Singular and I'll Legal [sic] Proceedings at [stricken: Pltfs. costs] and that the Defd't be allowed the Costs of this Application.

EDWARD MORTIMER & Co vs JAMES WILLIAMS. S. P. Judgement Confess'd for L 5 16/6 Stelg. and Costs of Suit Stay Execution 2 Months.

FRANCIS BOYKIN vs LEWIS DINKINS & JO. CANTEY. BROWN. S. P. Judgement Confess'd as P Specialty Stay Execution 3 Months. MATHIS.

W'M TWADDLE vs JAMES GUNN. MATHIS. Judgement Confessed as Pr. Specialty Debt Stay Exeuctino Untill 25 Dec'r next.

[Page 54]

JOSEPH BREVARD vs JAMES TOLAND. BROWN. Judgement by Default a Writ of Enquiry to be Executed.

JOHN EGLESTON vs ROB'T FULWOOD. Judgement agreeable to Specialty With Costs.

DAN'L BROWN vs JOHN JONES. Judgement agreeable as Pr Specialty With Costs.

ROBERT HENRY vs WM. BRUMMET. DEBT on Note. Judgement Confessed as Pr Specialty With In't & Costs Stay Execution 4 Months.

EDWARD MORTIMER & Co. vs Rob't Bowen. S. P. Decree for Pltf. at 10/ Pr Hundred amounting to 70/ & In't Pr Specialty With Cost of Suit.

[31 July 1792]

Ordered that the Estrays that has been Legally Advertized be Sold to Morrow.

ROBERT CARTER vs SAM'L BOYKIN. Case. This Case been Left to Arbitration last time the Arbitrators Award for the Plaintff L 6 s 11 d 3 With In't from the first of Jan'y 1791.

Ordered that the said Award be Made Absolute.

The Court Adjourned Untill to Morrow 9 OClock. JOHN KERSHAW, ADAM F. BRISBANE.

[Page 55]

Agreeable to Adjournment the Court Opened. PRESENT ADAM F. BRISBANE, JOHN KERSHAW, Esq'r.

Ordered that the Following Persons have Licence for Retailing Spirituous Liquors: JAMES PIERSON, HUGH YOUNG.

[stricken: JOHN McCAMBRIDGE vs JAMES BEVENS. Judgement Confessed With Costs]

WILLIAM WERE vs JOHN DEBUSEY. Settled by Award of Arbitrators for the Plaintiff the Arbitration Confirm'd.

ROBERT HOOD vs ROBERT CARNS. Dismiss at Plfts Costs.

JOSEPH LOCKHART vs JOSIAH PARKER. Dismiss'd at Plfts Costs.

[stricken: DAN'L PAYNE vs ARCH'D WATSON. Decree for Pltf. With Costs of Suit.]

DAVID DANIEL Vs JOHN TRANTHAM & RACHAEL TRANTHAM. Judgement by Default With Costs.

Executors of COL'O KERSHAW vs PAUL SMITH. Judgement by Default with Costs.

[stricken: LION & LEVY vs NEEDAM CATO. Settled]

[Page 56]

ALEXANDER FLEMING vs JOSIAH PERRY. Judgement by Default.

Ordered that a Tax Amounting to One Sixteenth part of the General tax of this State for the Year 1791 be imposed on all property Within this County Made taxable by the act of Assembly for Raising Supplies for that year and the same be Collected and Paid to the Clerk of this Court on or before the first Day of the Court of Police to be held in May Next.

Ordered that JOHN PLUNKETT be Allowed the sum of three Dolars Pr Month for the Maintenance and Supporting two Idiots his Sons this Allowance to Continue Untill the May Court Next if they both live.

Ordered that the Sheriff be Directed after Advertising to sell the Estray Cows Return'd by A. B. ROSS Esq'r on Saturday 11'th Ins't at Westerham it not being Possible Without great Difficulty to Produce them at the Court House.

Ordered that all Other Estrays Which have been Advertised the legal time be Sold this Day & that the Justices of Peace Within the County be Desired to give Notice to all Persons tolling Estrays before them to have them Produced at Court on the first day of the third Court after taking them up.

[1 August 1792] [Page 57]

Ordered that the Foregoing Order be Advertised in Different Parts of the County.

HUGH McGEE vs JAMES NICKLE. MATHIS. Judgement Confessed stay Ex. 1 Nov. 1792.

Ordered that a Dedimus Do Issue Directed to JOHN KERSHAW & JOSEPH BREVARD Esq'rs Appointing them Commissioners to Receive the Ackowledgement of MRS. BRISBANE relative to her Renunciation of Dower in the following undermentioned Real Estates and of her execution of the Deeds of conveyance passing the Fee Simple of the same viz't Five Lots or parcells of Land in the Town of Camden known by the Numbers 239, 240, 241, 242 & 243 also a Lot or parcell of Land on broad Street in said Town convey'd by A. F. BRISBANE to MARGARET SMITH on the 15 Aug't 1788 And also Four other Lots in the said Town, No. 262, 263, 276 & 277.

In consequence of a Petition from Sundry Inhabitants of this County, residing on & near to Great Lynch's Creek, to the Judges of this County, stating the public advantages and convenience of having a Bridge erected over the said Creek, at the crossing place on JOSEPH BREVARD's plantation, praying that such order and proceeding may be made, as shall be considered necessary & proper for the same purpose.

[Page 58]

It is therefore Ordered, That GEORGE EVANS, JOSIAH CANTEY, and ROBERT COOK be appointed Commissionesr with power to Contract for such Bridge, provided the expence thereof to this County exceeds not Seven Pounds ten shillings.

Ordered that Lettes of Administration do Issue to MARGARET ENGLISH on ... THO'S ENGLISH Deceased.

Or'd that the Clerk be Empowered to Grant a Licence for Retailing Spirituous Liquors at any time When Apply'd to at his Office.

Ordered that the Sheriffs Clerks Account be paid Amounting to Twenty Seven Pounds ten Shillings.

[stricken: Ordered that letters of Administration Do issue to JOHN LENORE the Securities are]

ISAAC ALEXANDER this Day was Qualify'd as a Judge of this Court in the Room of SAM'L BOYKIN Deceased and took his Seat.

The Hon'bl Court Adjourned Untill the third Monday in October Next. ADAM F. BRISBANE, I. ALEXANDER.

[Page 59]

OCTOBER COURT. The Court met Agreeable to Adjournment. Present JOHN KERSHAW Esq'r. The Court Adjourn'd Untill Tomorrow Nine O'Clock. JOHN KERSHAW.

16th October. The Court met according to adjournment. PRESENT JOHN KERSHAW, ISAAC ALEXANDER, Esq'rs.

Appeared this day in Open Court MR'S SARAH MARTIN and Proved the Last Will & Testament of JOHN WALTERS Deceased.

JEREMIAH PARISH also appeared & proved the Last Will & Testament of JACOB EVANS Deceased.

[16 October 1792]

Ordered that the Estrays be sold this day which have been advertised the legal time & for which no owners have appeared.

That letters testamentary do issue to WILLIAM EVANS on ...   JACOB EVANS deceaesd. WILLIAM EVANS appeared & qualified as Executor.

[Page 60]

Ordered that Letters of Administration do Issue to SARAH TINSLEY With the Will Annexed on ...   JOHN WALTERS Deceased and that the Securities are DUGLAS STARKE & JAMES CANTEY.

Ordered that the Account of Mr JAMES KERSHAW be Paid, amounting to Thirty five Shillings & Seven Pence for the Repairs of the Bridges Near Camden.

Ordered that Letters Testamentary Do Issue to JOHN CHESNUT, GEORGE ROSS & JONATHAN SUTTON Executors of the last WIll & Testament of JASPER SUTTON Deceased....

Ordered that a Dedimus be Issued to Qualify JONATHAN SUTTON as an Executor of the Last Will & Testament of JASPER SUTTON.

Ordered that JAMES ENGLISH be appointed to Open & Oversee a Road Leading from JOSHUA ENGLISH Ferry to the Main Charleston Road on the West Side of the River and those Persons Do Work thereon Who may live Within four Miles above & below the said Rode that are liable to Work on Rodes that have not Worked the time prescribed by Law & that he doe Make his return at the Next May Court.

Ordered that ARON FERGUSON be Appointed to Open & Oversee Rode leading from ENGLISH Ferry to the Main Charleston Rode on the East Side of the River and all those persons do work thereon Who may be lieable to Work on Rodes within four miles above and below....

[Page 61]

Ordered that ARCHIBALD McDONALD be Appointed administrator of the Estate of JAMES CONDYN and that letters of Administration do issue on ...   the said JAMES CONDYN Deceased the Securities are DUNCAN McRA & JOHN CRAVEN.

The Executor of Wm SLOAN Deceased Rendered into Court an Inventory & Appraisement of the Estate of the said SLOAN. Ordered that the Same or so much thereof as the Executors may Judge Necessary be sold to Wit the Negroes to be Sold to Camden on the 28th of Next Month on three Months Credit the Executors to take Bonds or Notes (& Mortgages in such Cases as they may think Proper) and the Other Property to be Sold at the Plantation of the said Deceased on the first Tuesday in Next Month on the like Credit and on the Same Terms.

[portion of page cut out] [Lett]ers Testamentary Do Issue CLANTON Executrix [ ] Executor To the last Will and [ ] CLANTON Deceased on all Rights & Credits, Lands & [ ] RICHARD CLANTON [ ] Deceased

JOHN CALVET having appeared & proven the Will of the aforesaid RICHARD CLANTON.

Ordered that letters of Administration be issued to THOMAS BROWN on ... JOHN GALBRAITH deceased the Securities being approved are JOHN ADAMSON & JAMES BROWN JUNIOR.

[16 Oct 1792]

[Page 62]

Ordered that Letters of Administration do Issue on ... JOHN CANTEY Deceased to JAMES CANTEY & ZACHARIAH CANTEY the Securitys are DUNCAN McRA & JOHN CHESNUT.

Ordered that all persons Residing Within four miles of the New Rode of Which JAMES WILLIAMS is Overseer and Who have not Worked the Legal Number of Days be liable to work on Said New Rode.

Ordered that ARTHUR BROWN ROSS & REUBEN STARKE Esquires be & they are hereby appointed Commissioners to join the Commissioners from Fairfield County for ascertaining the line between Kershaw & Fairfield Counties.

The Court then adjourned untill the twenty Eighth day of February next. [Signatures cut out]

[Page 63]

February the 20'th 1793. The Court met and Proceeded to Draw the Jury. Present JOHN KERSHAW, BURWELL BOYKIN, Esqr's.

From Box No. 1 to No. 2.

GRAND JURY: 1 THOMAS WHITAKER, 2 ISAAC ROSS, 3 JOSEPH THOMSON, 4 WM NETTLES L. Creek, 5 NICHOLAS ROBINSON, 6 DAVID BUSH, 7 DAVID MARTIN, 8 WM SANDERS SEN'R, 9 JOSHUA ENGLISH, 10 SAM'L BRADFORD B. Creek, 11 JOHN MIDDLETON L. Creek, 12 ISAAC ALEXANDER, 13 JOHN REID, 14 JAMES BROWN JUN'R, 15 ABRAM CHILDERS, 16 SAM'L LEVY, 17 ISAAC DUBOSE, 18 WILLIAM WARE, 19 WILLIAM LANG, 20 HUGH McDOWL.

From Box No. 3 to No. 4.

PETIT JURY: 1 WYLY COLLINS, 2 ZACHARIAH NETTLES, 3 WM SLOAN, 4 JORDEN ASHLEY, 5 DAVID PEEBLES, 6 WILLIAM ARCHER, 7 ROBERT BARCKLEY, 8 AARON ATKINS, 9 STEPHEN GLANDEN, 10 GEORGE PAYNE JUN'R, 11 JOHN PAYNE SEN'R, 12 W'M WALDEN, 13 ROBERT COOK, 14 BERRY ROBINSON, 15 JAMES SHARPLEN, 16 WILLIAM PAYNE G. S. 17, FRANCIS ADAMS, 18 REUBIN COLLINS, 19 JAMES NIPPER, 20 ISAAC BLANCHARD, 21 HEZEKIAH LOVE, 22 JOSHUA WATSON, 23 WILLIAM RUSSEL, 24 JAMES SCOTT, 25 JOHN ROBINSON, 26 JACOB SHIVER, 27 JACOB BRASWELL, 28 ALEX'R ARCHER, 29 WM. NETTLES G. W., 30 WM. RANDOLPH.

The Court was Opened and Proceded to Business.

[Page 64]

Grand Jurors Call'd and Appear'd: 1 LEWIS COLLINS, 2 ROBERT DUNLAP, 3 HENRY HUDSON.

PETIT JURORS: 1 ROGER GIBSON, 2 JAMES TATE, 3 JOHN TAYLOR.

Ordered that Letters of Administration do Issue to HESTER COOK on ... JOHN COOK Deceased the Securities are RICHARD DRAKEFORD & ISRAEL MOORE (Sworn in).

On Application from JOHN CHERRY a Minor of the age of Nineteen to have ARTHUR B. ROSS appointed a Guardian for him. Ordered that the said ARTHUR B. ROSS be and is hereby appointed.

[20 Feb 1793]

Ordered that JOSEPH McCOY be appointed a Constable he appeared & Sworn in.

Ordered that Licence be Given to the following persons for Retailing Spirituous Liquors:

THOMAS SMERRILL; Securities, ROB'T & JAMES GUNN.

JO McCOY: Securities, WM NETTLES & SAM'L TYNES.

[Page 65]

JOHN COATS appeared in Open Court and Proved the Will of WILLIAM SCOTT Deceased.

Ordered that the Distribution of the Estate of JACOB EVANS be Complied With agreeable to the Will.

Ordered that HENRY KENT be allowed seven shillings Pr Month for the Subsistance of his family Untill Next July Court.

Ordered that HUGH BROWN be Sworn in as a Constable.

The Court Adjourned Untill to Morrow Ten OClock the Minutes being first Read. BUR'L BOYKIN, JOHN KERSHAW.

Agreeable to Adjournment the Hon'ble Court Met. Present JOHN KERSHAW & BURWELL BOYKIN, Esq'rs.

Grand Jury Called: 1 WILLIAM TWADWELL, 2 ROBERT DUNLAP, 3 LEWIS COLLINS, 4 GEORGE DURIN, 5 HENRY HORTON, 6 THOMAS ENGLISH, 7 DAVID BUSH, 8 JOHN BOYKIN, 9 ABRAHAM BELTON, 10 SAM'L DOTY, 11 WM COOK, 12 JO McCOY, 13 WM PARKER.

Petit Jurors: 14 JN'O ADAMS excused, 15 JO. LLEMANG, 16 BENJ. CARTER.

[Page 66]

March 1st 1793. ISRAEL MOORE Appeared in Open Court and Proved the last Will and Testament of DRURY CAMPBELL.

Jury Drawn from Box No. 5 to No. 6 to Serve as Grand Jury men:

1 JOHN R. HUTCHINS, 2 JOSEPH LLEMANG, 3 JOHN ADAMSON, 4 BENJ. CARTER, 5 ABRAHAM BELTON, 6 WILLIAM COOK, 7 ROBERT HOOD, 8 JAMES BROWN SEN'R, 9 JOHN CRAVEN, 10 W'M PARKER, 11 SAM'L DOTY, 12 DAVID BUSH, 13 MICHAEL GAUNTER.

Ordered that ARTHUR MASSY be Sworn in as Constable appeared and Sworn accordingly.

State vs ISHAM POWELL for Assault & Battery on DAVID SAUNDERS. Dismiss at Defendts Costs.

On a Motion of the County Attorney.

Ordered that JOHN R. HUTCHENS, JOSEPH LLEMANG, JOHN ADAMS, DAVID BUSH, BENJAMIN CARTER appeared before the Court Immediately to Shew Cause Why an Attachment should not Issue Immediately for Contempt against them.

[1 March 1793]

[Page 67]

State vs RICHARD EVANS. Ordered that RICHARD EVANS Enter into a Recognizance to appear at the Next Chesterfield County Court & the Witnesses and Prosecutors be bound to appear at the same time.

SAMUEL MATHIS appeared in Court and Acknowledged a Deed Given to PERRY PARISH.

The Grand Jury Impannel'd and Sworn: 1 DAVID BUSH foreman, 2 WILLIAM TWADWELL, 3 ROBERT DUNLAP, 4 LEWIS COOK, 5 GEORGE DURIN, 6 HENRY HUDSON, 7 THOMAS ENGLISH, 8 JOHN BOYKIN, 9 ABRAM BELTON, 10 SAM'L DOTY, 11 W'M COOK, 12 JO. McCOY, 13 WILLIAM PARKER, 14 JO LLIMANG, 15 BEN'J CARTER. The Court Adjourn'd.

Ordered that Letters of Administration do Issue to MARY LEE on ... ROBERT LEE the Securities are HENRY LOWREY & EDWARD COLLINS.

State vs THO'S WILLIAMS. Felony. The Prosecutor Not appearing Ordered that the Defendant Recognizance be Continued Untill July Court WILLIAM HINSON Prosecutor & HENRY REAVES Securities being Solemnly Call'd to appear and Prosecute and failing Ordered that a Ciria Facias do Issue to Appear at July Court to Shew Cause Why their Recognizance Should not be forfeited & Execution Issue Accordingly.

[Page 68]

State vs WILLIAM NORRIS. Indited Petit Larceny. The Grand Jury Returned a True Bill. DAVID BUSH, Foreman.

Ordered that it be hereafter Considered a Rule of this Court that the Sheriff Shall always When in Court Wear a Sword & In Case of his absence the Under or Deputy Sheriff.

ROBERT BROWN an Infant 16 Years of Age applied to have WILLIAM KIRKLAND Esq'r appointed his Guardian Which Was ordered Accordingly.

State vs ROGER GIBSON. The Defendent Withdrew his Plea and Confesd Guilty, the Court Deferr'd Judgement untill further Consideration.

State vs WILLIAM SIMS. Not Guilty. SAMUEL TYNES, Foreman. Petit Jury Sworn: 1 SAMUEL TYNES foreman, 2 ARCH'D McAFFE, 3 HUGH McCLESTER, 4 ANDREW NUTT 5, ISRAEL MOORE, 6 JAMES TATE, 7 JAMES ENGLISH, 8 JOHN TAYLOR, 9 PAUL SMITH, 10 MALACHI MURPHY, 11 LEWIS DINKINS, 12 GERSHON CHAPMAN.

[Page 69]

BRYANT SPRADLEY vs JOHN WILSON. Attachment. Advertisements in the Gazettes having been produced & read in open Court requiring the Defendant to plead to this Action accordingly to Law & the time having expired on this Day in which the said Defendant was allowed to plead, and no plea having been put in for him; It is therefore ordered that the said Plaintiff have final and absolute Judgment against the said Defendant for his Debt in this case and that the Land in this case Attached be sold to discharge the same.

WILLIAM HOUSTON coming into Court Drunk being summoned as a +Witness in behalf of the State and behaving insolently the Court ordered him to be committed to Close prison till further Orderd.

The Court adjourned Until to Morrow Ten OClock. BUR'L BOYKIN, JOHN KERSHAW.

- 25 -

The Hon'ble Court met Agreeable to Adjournment. Present JOHN KERSHAW & BURWELL BOYKIN, Esq'rs.

[Page 70] 2 March 1793

Ordered that WILLIAM HOUSTON be Released from Confinement after paying the Fees.

Ordered that the Exors. of WILLIAM SLOAN be allowed to sell the personal Est. of Said Deceased on three Months Credits at the Plantation of the Said Deceased on the first Saturday in Next Month or the first Saturday in May or the first Saturday in June.

Ordered that letters of Administration do Issue to EDWARD HULAND on ... CULLIN HULAND the Securities are ISRAEL MOORE & JOHN JACKSON.

DAN'L PAYNE Appeared in Open Court and Proved the Last Will & Testament of SAMUEL BELTON.

Ordered that letters Testamentary do Issue to MR'S RACHEL BELTON Executrix of the last Will and Testament of SAMUEL BELTON Deceased.

THO'S WELSH In'dsee of WILLIAM YOUNG vs ROBERT LOVE and JUDITH ROBERTS. Debt. The Plaintiff appeared in Court and agreed to Suffer a Non Suit and pay the Costs.

Ordered that the Exortrix of SAML BELTON be allowed to Sell that part of the personall Estate that May be Required for a Devision or payment of Debts or to present the loss of Perishable Articles belonging to the Estate of the Deceased

[Page 71]

on the first Saturday in Next Month or on the first Saturday in May or the first Saturday in June at the plantation Where on She lives on a Credit of three Months.

JON'N BELTON vs DAVID CLANTON. Debt. Judgement Confes'd for L 13 s 19 d 7 and Costs of Suit.

SAMUEL MATHIS vs SAMUEL TYNES. S. P. Judgement agreeable to Note With Interest Confess'd and Costs of Suit.

State vs ROGER GIBSON. AJB. Guilty and the Defendant is Fined s 40 with Costs of Suit and not to Depart the Court Untill Paid.

Ordered that Letters of Administration Do Issue to JOHN HORTON on ... ROBERT BLACK the Securities ISRAEL MOORE, THOMAS WELSH.

State vs WILLIAM NORRIS. Petit Larceny. GUILTY. SAMUEL TYNES, foreman. the Jury Call'd and Sworn: 1 SAMUEL TYNES foreman, 2 JAMES ENGLISH, 3 GERSHAM CHAPMAN, 4 JAMES TATE, 5 JOHN TAYLOR, 6 ARCH'D MCFEE, 7 HUGH McLESTER, 8 ANDREW NUTT JUN'R, 9 ISRAEL MOORE, 10 PAUL SMITH, 11 ROGER GIBSON, 12 JOHN COOK.

[Page 72]

DAVID COATS vs JOHN HARVELL. Attach't. Ordered & Agreed that THOMAS KELLEY the Garnashee in this case do make oath before Mr. FRANCIS BOYKIN or some other Magistrate of the monies &c that he has in his hands of the absent debtors, that the same be filed in the Clerk's Office & be considered as if done in open Court. [entire entry stricken]

State vs JAMES PIERSON. Indictment. It appearing to the Court That the Defendant had been duly Served With a Process to appear and answer to the

[2 March 1793]

Indictment having failed to appear tho Solemnly Call'd Ordered the same Jury be Sworn Accordingly Returned a Verdict Guilty. SAMUEL TYNES, foreman. [entire entry stricken]

Ordered that SAMUEL SLOAN be put in Close Confinement Untill the Court Adjourns till Next Court and pay the fees and a fine of Twenty Shillings before Liberated.

SIMON WILLIAMS vs MARTIN TRANTHAM. S. P. Settled.

JAMES BROWN vs JAMES TOLAND. S. P. Decree for Plaintiff as pr Specialty With Costs of Suits.

DAVID BUSH & C'o vs WILLIAM STUBS & JOHN GREYHAM. S. P. Decree for Plaintiff as Pr Specialty against JOHN GREYHAM With Costs of Suit.

[Page 73]

JAMES MARKS vs WILLIAM SUTTON. S. P. Decree for Plaintiff as PR Specialty With Costs of Suit.

WILLIAM TWADDLE vs GEORGE PERRY. Scire facias. Ordered that the same be made absolute and that Execution do Issue against him.

JOHN TWADDLE vs JAMES HUNTER. S. P. Decree for Plaintiff as pr Specialty With Costs of Suit.

The State vs JAMES PIERSON. Jud't on a Pres't of grand Jury for retailing spirituous Liquors without Licence. Mr. MATHIS excepted in behalf of M'R PIERSON as Amicus Curio to the service of the Process that there was an Error in the Date. The Court overruled the Exception on the Process & ordered the Jury to be sworn. The Jury sworn as last Verdict "We find the Defendant Guilty." SAM TYNES, foreman.

The Court Adjourn'd Untill Monday Ten OClock. BUR'L BOYKIN, JOHN KERSHAW.

[Page 74]

March 4th 1793. The Hon'ble Court Met Agreeable to Adjournment. Present JOHN KERSHAW, BURWELL BOYKIN. Esq'rs.

State vs FREDERICK ROBINSON. Discharged of the Recognizance for Conterfeit Money.

State vs JOEL NORRIS. Larceny. Discharge of the Recognizance.

State vs PHILIMON HILLIARD. Present Dismiss'd at Def't Costs.

State vs JAMES GUNN. A. & Battery. Compromised at Defendants Costs.

State vs ROBERT McCAIN. A. & Battery. Dismiss at Defen'dts Costs.

Ordered that the Sheriff do make Out a Compleat Jury list against the Next July Court.

State vs FEDRICK ROBINSON. Assault & Battery. Dismiss'd at Def'dts Costs.

SAMUEL TYNES Foreman of the Jury having Given Sufficient Reasons to the Court Obtained leave of Absence Whereupon GERSHON CHAPMAN was appointed in his Room.

[4 March 1793]

D: BROWN vs CUTHBERT COLEMAN & JNO PEMBERTON. Qui tam action.
Discontinued against CUTHBERT COLEMAN who agrees to pay Clerks & Sheriffs
fees. also against JOHN PEMBERTON on the same terms.

[Page 75]

State vs JESSE MINTON. Present for Retailing Liquors. Guilty. G. CHAPMAN,
foreman.

The Jury Being Call'd and Sworn: 1 GERSHAM CHAPMAN foreman, 2 JAMES
TATE, 3 JOHN TAYLOR, 4 ARCH'D MCAFFEE, 5 WILLIAM JONES, 6 HUGH
McCLESTER, 7 ANDREW NUTT JUN'R, 8 ISRAEL MOORE, 9 PAUL SMITH, 10
JOHN COOK, 11 ALEX'R GOODALL, 12 W'M SCOTT.

WILLIAM SCOTT Administrator of JOHN SCOTT SEN'R presented in Court an
account against the Estate of JOHN SCOTT JUN'R for L 224 s 2 sterling & the
same account was Ordered by the Court to be filed with the Accounts & papers
of the Estate of JOHN SCOTT SEN'R.

The Court also ordered that WILLIAM SCOTT Executor of JOHN SCOTT JUN'R
do produce an Inventory of the Estate of his Testator & lodge the same with the
Clerk of this Court.

WILLIAM CASTON vs ARNOLD BERRY. A. B. Decree for Pltff. L 4 with
Interest & Costs of Suit.

JOSEPH BREVARD vs WILLIAM SUTTON. S. P. Decree for Plaintiff L 7 With
Costs of Suit.

[Page 76]

DAVID WILLIAMS vs ROBERT McCAIN. Trover. Decree. The Plaintiff is
Nonsuited.

CHARLES MCGINNEY vs SAM'L REYNOLDS. Att. Writ of Enquirey. Jury
Sworn: 1 GERSHAM CHAPMAN, 2 JAMES TATE, 3 JOHN TAYLOR, 4 ARCH'D
McAFFEE, 5 ROGER GIBSON, 6 HUGH McLESTER, 7 ANDREW NUTT JUN'R, 8
ISRAEL MOORE, 9 PAUL SMITH, 10 JOHN COOK, 11 ALEX'R GOODALL, 12
WILLIAM SCOTT.

We find for the Plaintiff L 25 s 6 d 8 sterling & interest thereon from the 9'th
December 1789 with Costs of Suit. G. CHAPMAN, foreman.

MINOR WINN vs ROBERT McCAIN. S. P. Decree for Plaintiff L 7 s 15 With
Costs of Suit.

MINOR WINN vs ROBERT McCAIN. S. P. Decree for Plaintiff as Pr. Specialty
With Costs of Suit.

Ordered that Letters of Administration do Issue to THOMAS BROWN on ...
COLLIN BROWN & WILLIAM BROWN the Securities JOHN ADAMS & JAMES
BROWN JUN'R.

[Page 77]

JOHN KERSHAW Esq. versus JEAN LeDROICT DeBUSSY. On Attachment. M'R
BURWELL EVANS who was summoned to answer in this Corut, as Garnishee of
the Defendant, appeared personally in Court and being duly Sworn declareth that
to the best of his recollection and belief he owes a Ballance of L 9 sterling or
thereabouts to the Defendant on Account for Goods Wares and Merchandizes; and
that he hath no property of the said Defendant in his hands power or possession,
nor doth owe him any further or other Sum than as above mentioned.

The Court then Adjourned untill tomorrow ten o'clock. BUR'L BOYKIN. JOHN KERSHAW.

Agreeable to adjournment the Hon'ble Court Met. Present: JOHN KERSHAW, BURWELL BOYKIN, Esq'rs.

State vs JAMES COWSAR. Presentment, Continued.

State vs ZACHARIAH CANTEY. Presentment fined 5/ & Costs.

[Page 78] 5 March 1793.

Ordered that the Administratrix of the Estate of RICHARD CHAMPION Esq'r deceased be allowed to sell the negroes and other personal Estate of the said dec'd; the negroes to be sold in Camden on Monday the 15 day of April next for Cash & the household furniture &c on Tuesday the 16 at the plantation of the said Deceased, on Rockbranch on a Credit of 3 Months giving due notice thereof.

Ordered that JOHN LISSENBY and NICHOLAS COOK be appointed Commissioners in the Room of ROBERT COOK and JOSIAH CANTEY appointed Commissioners by an Order of this Court in August last for Contracting for the building of a Bridge over Lynches Creek.

State vs JOSEPH MILLER. Presentment. Not Guilty. G. CHAPMAN, foreman.

The Jury Call'd and Sworn: 1 GERSHAN CHAPMAN foreman, 2 JAMES TATE, 3 JOHN TAYLOR, 4 HUGH McLESTER, 5 ANDREW NUTT JUN'R, 6 ISRAEL MOORE, 7 PAUL SMITH, 8 JOHN COOK, 9 ROBERT HOOD, 10 ROGER GIBSON, 11 MICHAEL GAUNTER, 12 WILLIAM SCOTT.

Executors L. PERRY Estate vs JOSEPH COTES. Attch't. Judgement by Default according to Specialty With Costs of Suit.

WILLIAM PARKER vs ALEX'R GOODALL & SAM'L BREED. Debt. Discontinued at the Def'dts costs.

[Page 79]

ARCH'D JAMISON & C'o vs GEOR BARNES. Debt. Plea With Drawn. Judgement Agreeable to Specialty With Costs.

HENRY HUGHES vs HUGH YOUNG. Case. The Defendent Non suited with the Costs of Suit.

JESSE HAYS vs W'M WARD, Executors JNO WILLIAMS, vs JOHN LOCKHART & WILLIAM WILLIAMS. Debt. We find for the Plaintiff according to Note With Interest And Costs. [same jury as preceding case]

JESSE REAVES vs HUGH MCGEE & JAMES LOVE. We find for the Plaintiff according to Note With Interest With Costs of Suit.

RICHARD SPRINGS vs ROBERT FORD & JOHN MARSHALL. Case. Judgement by Default With Costs of Suit.

THOMAS BRADFORD vs THOMAS BALLARD. Debt. Judgement Confess'd as Pr Specialty Stay Execution three Months.

DAVID HUNTER vs ARCHIBALD McAFEE. Debt. Judgement Confess'd after allowing the proper Discounts.

[Page 80] 5 March 1793

DAVID BUSH & C'o vs HUGH McGEE. S. P. Judgement Confess'd for L 5 s 16 & In't from the 30th May 1793 with Cost of Suit.

JOHN SWILLA Came into Open Court and Resign'd his Office as Under Sheriff.

DANIEL BROWN vs DANIEL BROWN, GIDEON BROCKWAY, BEMAN BROCKWAY & BURBON BROCKWAY. Att. Ordered that the Defdt. Do Plead to this Action at or before the Next Court.

JOHN CHESNUT Survivor of KERSHAW BOYKIN & C'o vs Admin'r of DAN'L BRITON. S. P. Decree for Plaintiff for the amount of Account With Interest Defd't having Pleaded Plene Administravit & filed his Affidavit. Plaintiff Suggested that there Were Lands Which Were liable for the payment of said Debt agreeable to an Act entitled "An Act for the More easy Recovery of Debts..." Ratified by the Legislature 7th Day of April 1759. The Defendant Demurr'd thereto....

[Page 81]

BLAIR & PATTERSON vs JOHN JONES. S. P. Decree for Plaintiff as Pr. Specialty With Interest and Costs of Suit.

JOSEPH COATS vs HENRY HUDSON. S. P. 2 Notes. Judgement Confess'd. Stay Exo'n four Months With Costs of Suit.

Exors of ROBERT CARTER, Exor of CHA'S McKAY vs JOHN McKERKEY and JOSEPH McCOY. Stands over; the writ having been served on JOSEPH McCOY only, the other Deft non est inventus. Alias to issue ag't JOHN MACKEY.

SAMUEL THOMSON vs THOMAS KELLY & DAVIS COATS. Debt. Judgement Confess'd as Pr Specialty With Interest Stay Execution three Months with Costs of suit.

JOHN TAYLOR is No Longer to Act as Deputy Sheriff of this County.

MARY BELTON vs GEORGE PETERSON & CHARLESS McGINNEY. S. P. Decree for Plaintiff stay Execution three Months With Costs of Suit agreeable P Specialty.

HEZEKIAH LOVE vs JOHN RUSSEL. Appeal. Judgement Confirm'd.

JASPER SUTTON vs DAVID WILLIAMS. Debt. Judgement Confest. for L 9 14/6 With Interest from the 25th July 1790 & Costs of Suit.

[Page 82] March 5'th 1793.

SAMUEL TOMLINSON vs JOSHUA ENGLISH Exor ROBERT ENGLISH. Debt. Verdict for Plaintiff L 27 s 12 on Note. Defd't having pleaded Plina Administravit & filed his Affidavit. Plaintiff suggested that there were Lands Which Were liable for the payment of the s'd Debt. Agreeable to an Act entitled an Act for the More easy Recovery of Debts in his Majestys Plantations & Colonies in America Which said Act was Recognized & ratified by the Legislature of this State on the 7th Day of April 1759. The defendant demurred thereto... We find for the Plaintiff 27:12 with Int. G. CHAPMAN, foreman.

JOSEPH BREVARD vs JAMES TOLAND. Case. The Same Jury. We find for the Plaintiff L 11 d 9 with Interest from July 1790 to this Date. G. CHAPMAN, foreman.

ROGER GIBSON vs LEWIS DINKINS. Ordered that this cause be refered to the Arbitrament of JOHN REID and JOHN RUTLEDGE and that their award be made a rule of this Court & that the same be of equal force and validity as a Verdict

[5 March 1793]

of the Jury on the said [case]. Arbitrators are to make their award & return the same into the Court immediately.

[Page 83]

Exors of JOSEPH KERSHAW vers. JOSHUA DINKINS. On a Bond. Judgment per Default, according to Bond.

JESSE REAVES vs THOMAS JONES. S. P. Judgement by Default agreeable to Specialty With Costs.

THOMAS HAWFIELD appeared and Acknowledged himself the father of the Child of which MARY BRADLEY is Ensient Whereupon it was Ordered that he do Give Security before F. BOYKIN Esq'r at the next July Court to Answer to the Same & abide the Order of the Court.

DAVID BUSH & C'o vs PETER CRIM. Debt. Judgement by Default agreeable to Specialty. Stay of Exeuction three Months With Costs of suit.

PETER OSGOOD vs JAMES LEWIS. S. P. 2 Notes. Judgement by Default as Pr Specialties With Costs of Suit.

NAZEROUS WHITEHEAD vs ANDREW LESTER. S. P. Judgement by Default as Pr Specialty With Costs.

JERRY PETMAN vs JESSE MINTON. S. P. Dismissed at the Def'dts Costs.

JAMES TOLLAR vs ROBERT HOOD. S. P. Judgement by Default as Pr Specialty With Costs of Suit.

[Page 84]

BRYANT SPRADLEY vs CHARLES TAYLOR. Discontinued.

Ordered that SAMUEL SLOAN be Released on Paying the Customary fees.

EDWARD MORTIMER & C'o vs ABRAM CHILDERS. S. P. Judgement Confess'd as per Stay Execution Untill July Court Next. Note With Costs of Suit.

Ordered that the Estate of JOHN SCOTT JUN'R be sold for Cash on the Nineteenth Day of April next.

JOHN KERSHAW vs JOHN LeDUBESEY. Att. Decree for the Plaintiff for the Ballance of Account With Interest Three Pounds fifteen shillings with Costs of Suit. And ordered that the Garnishees Summoned in this case who have Answered thereto do pay the Same and Costs of Suit, Otherwise Execution to issue against them for the same, as far forth as they are respectively indebted unto the Defendant.

Ordered that the Property of ROBERT LEE Deceased be Sold on a Credit Until the first of January next and the Sail be on the fifteenth of April in Camden for the Negroes and on the Sixteenth for the Remainder of the Property at the Plantation of ROBERT LEEs Deceased.

[Page 85]

ROGER GIBSON vs LEWIS DINKINS. The Arbitrators Appointed by a Rule of this Court in this Case Award as follows. We the Subscribers ... have convened & the parties heard their Several Obligations as Well as the Testimony of Witness do award unto ROGER GIBSON L 11 s 12 d 8 to be paid by said LEWIS DINKINS in full of all Demands. Camden 5th March 1793. JOHN REID, JOHN RUTLEDGE.

[5 March 1793]

GEORGE KERSHAW being Appointed as Under Sheriff and Was Sworn Accordingly.

Ordered that Letters of Administration Do Issue to HENRY HUDSON on ...WILLIAM HOLMES Deceased the Securities are JOHN RUSSEL & JOHN TAYLOR.

The Court Adjourned Untill to Morrow Ten OClock. BUR'L BOYKIN, JOHN KERSHAW.

[Page 86] 6'th March 1793

Agreeable to Adjournment the Hon'ble Court Met. Present JOHN KERSHAW & BURWELL BOYKIN, Esq'rs.

Exors of JOSEPH KERSHAW vs GEORGE BROWN. Judgement Confess'd as Pr Specialty With Interest & Costs.

DAVID COATS Vs JOHN HARWELL. ATT. THO'S KELLY Garnishee.

THOMAS SMIRRELL vs JOHN MILLHOUSE. Appeal. Settled.

ROBERT FULWOOD vs ROBERT DUNLAP. Settled.

HENRY KENT vs LAZERUS KELLY, JAMES KELLY & ANN KELLY. Continued at Pltfs Costs.

NICHOLAS COOSENBERRY Vs THO'S BALLARD & JOHN TAYLOR. Dismiss'd at Def'dts Costs.

JOHN JONES & Wife vs FINELY HOLMES & Wife. With Drawn on Payment of Costs.

REUBIN STARKE & Wife vs CHARLES MCGINNEY. Settled.

[Page 87]

WILLIAM TUCKER vs JOHN COOK. The Defendent to pay the Costs of Sheriff & Clerks fees.

Ordered that the Sheriff be Paid L 12 s 10 as pr Account Rendered in and likewise the sum of L 10 to the Clerk as Pr Account.

Ordered that ABRAM CHILDERS be authorised to Draw upon the Clerk of this Court for the sum of ten shillings pr month for the Support of the Orphan Child of JAMES CONDYN deceased untill next July Court and that LYDIA HOWARD an Orphan Child in the Charge of this Court be indented an Apprentice to JOHN ABBOT untill the day of her Marriage or her arrival to the age of Eighteen years that he be required to give her the usual time of Education viz't One Year.

Ordered that the Estrays which have been advertised the usual time be sold this Day.

Ordered that a new Road be opened to the County Line from PAYNES Old Field below Camden by ENGLISH Mills a Course to MOORES Mill before the first day of March Next & that JAMES CANTEY & THOMAS ENGLISH be appointed to Carry the same into Effect the Hands liable to Work are those Who Work on the Publick Road to Charleston.

On Motion of the County Attorney on Affidavit of GEO ROSS and others ordered that a Warrant issue against W'M PARKER to appear at next Court to answer to an Information for trading with Negroes.

[Page 88] 6 March 1793

Ordered that the Administrators of the Estate of JOHN CANTEY Deceased be authorized to sell the same for Cash at JAMES CANTEY's Plantation on Monday the twenty fifth instant.

Ordered that the Exo'r of RICHARD CLANTON deceased be authorized to sell his Estate at the Plantation of the said Deceased on Monday the 15 Day of April Next on a Credit to the first Day of January next after giving due notice.

Ordered that the Executors of JASPER SUTTON's Estate be authorized to sell the same at the Plantation of the Deceased on Monday the 29th Day of April the Personal Estate on a Credit of One & two years.

Ordered that the Exor's of the Estate of WILLIAM TATE be authorized to sell the Perishable property of the same on the first Monday in Next Month on a Credit of One Year.

State vs JAMES PIERSON. fixed Twenty Pounds. The day SAMUEL MATHIS present to the Court a Proteste Which he had Drawn up against the Proceedings in this Case on the 2nd Instant alledging in the same that the Minutes of that Day did not properly and sufficiently set for the Circumstances of the said Trial & the Proceedings therein and Alledged that his Said Protest did set forth the same more full & Clear and prayed that his said protest Might be entered on the Minutes of this Court but the Court refused the same.

State vs JESSE MINTON. Presentment. Ordered that a New trial be Granted on the Def'dts paying the fees.

Ordered that HENRY HUDSON be Cited to appear at May Court to Shew Cause Why his letters of administration on the Estate of WILLIAM HOLMES Deceased Shall not be Withdrawn.

[Page 89]

State vs WILLIAM NORRIS et alias. Sci fa. On Recognizance.

Ordered that the remainder of the business in which the State is a party be continued untill next Court Which has not been decided.

The Court then adjourned untill the third Monday in May next. BUR'L BOYKIN, JOHN KERSHAW.

20th May 1793. Agreeable to Adjournment the Hon'ble Court Mett. Present JOHN KERSHAW, BURWELL BOYKIN and ISAAC DUBOSE Esquire he being Qualified Out of Court took his Seat.

Ordered that JOHN KERSHAW be authorized to contract With a Workman for Repairing Pinetree Creek bridge and Affixing substantial hand rails thereto at the Expence of the County.

Ordered that letters of Administration Do Issue to JAMES SCOTT on the last Will and Testament of WILLIAM SCOTT Deceased the Securities are RICHARD DRAKEFORD & WILLIAM SCOTT.

On the Petition of WILLIAM & THOMAS WHITAKER respecting a Road to their Plantation, Ordered that ISAAC ROSS Do give a Passage of 16 feet from the Corner of his Corn field nearest to the ferry to the Corner of I. DUBOSE's Corn field fence and that

[Page 100]

[20 May 1793]

ANDREW LESTER, WILLIS WHITAKER and JOHN DYE be and are hereby appointed to Carry the same into Effect.

HENRY HUDSON having been Cited on the Application of SUSANNAH BROWN a Creditor of WILLIAM HOLMES Deceased to Shew Cause Why the letters of Administration granted him on the Estate of said HOLMES should not be revoked, it appearing to the Court that the letters of Administration aforesaid Were improperly & illegally Obtained the said HUDSON being Neither a Relation or Creditor of the Deceased but on the Contrary a Debtor.

It is Ordered that the same be revoked and annulled and Administration thereof be Granted to the said SUSANNAH BROWN by her Giving Good Security for L 150.

The Minutes being first read the Court adjourned Until to Morrow 10 OClock. IS. DUBOSE, BUR'L BOYKIN, JOHN KERSHAW.

Agreeable to Adjournment the Court Met. Present JOHN KERSHAW, ISAAC DUBOSE, BURWELL BOYKIN.

Ordered that the District of Road of which THO'S WELSH Was Overseer the last Year to Continue to the County Line.

[Page 101] 21 May 1793

The Court then proceeded to the appointment of Overseers of the Roads When the following Persons were appointed. THOMAS ENGLISH in the Room of DANIEL PEAK.

THOMAS LENORE	JOHN BOYKIN
THO'S DINKINS	NICH'S ROBINSON
JAMES LOVE	W'M NETTLES
DAVID HUNTER	SAM'L SMITH
JAMES COWSAR	GEO MILLER
GEORGE ROSS	E'D ROGERS
M. GANTER	M. GANTER
JAMES WILLIAMS	JAMES WILLIAMS
ROBERT FORD	JESSE MINTON
JOHN COOK JUNIOR	JO. McCOY
PATRICK McCAIN	GEO. EVANS
FRANCIS BELL	FRANCIS BELL
including the Bridge	
LEWIS COOK	W'M DANIEL
W'M TWADDLE	MICH: BARNET
LEWIS COLLINS DAN'L KIRKLAND	REUBIN COLLINS
JOHN LOCKERT	SAM'L JONES
to the County Line	
ED NARRIMORE	THO'S WELSH
WILLIAM CATO	JOHN CATO
REUBIN PATTERSON	W'M BOND
THO'S VAUGHN	PETER CRIM
ANDREW LESTER	ROGER GIBSON
WILLIS WHITAKER	ISAAC ROSS
DAN'L O'QUIN JUN'R	JAMES ENGLISH
JACOB SHIVER	GEORGE PAYNE

Ordered that the Clerk be required to give a List to the County Attorney of those Overseers of Rodas, Who have been Deficient in keeping their Several Districts in Repair & Who have not Performed the Duty required of them by Law.

[Page 102] 21'st May 1793

Ordered that three Dollars P Month be Paid JOHN PLUNKET for the Maintenane of his two Sons untill Next May Court.

Ordered that One Dollar Pr Week be paid M'rs TOLLOUCT[?] for the time She Supported N. COOSENBERRY While Under the Care of DOCTOR ALEXANDER.

Ordered that the Sheriff of the County Collect One Twelfth of the Gen'l Tax for the Use of the County and make his Return Next May Court.

Ordered that STEPHEN WHITE be appointed as a Deputy Clerk in the Room of LEMUEL WHITAKER, appear and Sworn Accordingly.

Ordered that JOSEPH McCOY be added to JOHN LISSENBY & NICHOLAS COOK for Contracting of the Building a Bridge Over Lynches Creek.

Ordered that JAMES BOWLES be Committed to Goal for Insolent and Contemptious behaviour in presence of the Court and thereto to Remain Twenty four Hours.

Ordered that those Estrays that have been legally Advertised be Sold Immediately after the Adjournment of the Court.

Ordered that the Clerk of the Court be required to give a list ot the County Attorney of those Who have taken up Estrays and not Complyed With the Tenor of the Law in Such Cases.

After the Minutes being Read the Court adjourned Untill the Twenty Eighth of July Next. BUR'L BOYKIN, JOHN KERSHAW.

[Page 103] Monday 29th July 1793 Camden.

Grand Jury Drawn from Box No. 1 to No. 2:

1 JAMES SMITH, 2 E'D COLLINS B. Creek, 3 WILLIAM LAYTON G Quarter, 4 DENNIS QUINLEY, B. Creek, 5 RUSH HUDSON, 6 MATHEW NUTT, 7 JOHN O. QUIN, 8 THOMAS DICKSON, 9 W'M TWADDLE, 10 ROBERT DUNLAP G. Q., 11 BENJAMIN ALEXANDER, 12 SHAW BROWN, 13 VINCENT JONES, 14 JOSIAH PARKER, 15 GEO. SAUNDERS JUN'R, 16 THO'S BROWN, 17 W'M HORTEN, 18 THOMAS BALLARD, 19 W'M DANIEL JUN'R, 20 ISRAEL MOORE.

Petit Jury Drawn from Box N'o 3 to N'o 4:

1 SAM'L CLANTON, 2 DAVID RUSSEL, 3 W'M MOORE SEN'R, 4 MEX'R C'R HEAD CORRUTH, 5 DAN'L O. QUIN JUN'R, 6 JOHN COTES, 7 ANDREW PRESTLEY, 8 THOMAS WAGGONER, 9 JOSEPH HYE, 10 JACOB CHAMBERS, 11 JOHN SINGLETON, 12 HENRY STRANGE, 13 JOHN PLUNKET, 14 DAVID SAUNDERS, 15 GEORGE PERRY, 16 ROWLEY HAMMOND, 17 JOHN NICKSON, 18 JESSE FLY Buffelow Creek, 19 W'M KEMP, 20 STEPHEN GLANDALL 25 M. C., 21 JAMES SHARPLIN, 22 JOSEPH McADAM, 23 ANDREW SPRADLEY, 24 EDMUND DEASON, 25 FRANCIS BELL, 26 LAURENCE BURNS, 27 PETER CRIM Saw C., 28 ANTHONY PRESTLEY, 29 NATH'L ROGERS G. Q., 30 NIGHT NIGHT.

The Hon'ble Court Met Agreeable to Adjournment. Present: JOHN KERSHAW, ISAAC DUBOSE, Esq'rs.

Ordered that Letters of Administration do Issue to REBECCA LEE on the Estate of JOHN LEE ... Securities are RICHARD GAYDEN and EDWARD COLLINS.

[Page 104] [29 July 1793]

Exors of ROBERT CARTER Exor of C. McKAY vs JOHN McKAY & JOSEPH McCOY. Capias in Debt. In Motion of Mr. BREVARD Attorney for the Plf. Ordered that a pluries Writ in this case do issue against JOHN McKAY, returnable to next February term. N. B. The other Defend't JOSEPH McCOY having been served before last Term.

The Grand Jury being Cal'd & Impanneld:

1 JOSEPH THOMSON, 2 W'M NETTLES, 3 NICHOLAS ROBINSON, 4 DAVID MARTIN, 5 JOSHUA ENGLISH, 6 SAM'L BRADFORD, 7 W'M WARE, 8 HUGH McDOWEL, 9 ISAAC ROSS, 10 DAVID BUSH, 11 JAMES BROWN JUN'R, 12 WILLIAM SANDERS, 13 SAMUEL LEVY.

Petit Jury Call'd:

1 JORDIN ASHELY, 2 DAVID PEEBLES, 3 W'M ARCHER, 4 ROBERT BARCKLEY, 5 ARON ATKINS, 6 GEORGE PAYNE JUN'R, 7 BERRY ROBINSON, 8 JAMES SHARPLIN, 9 W'M PAYNE, 10 HEZEKIAH LOVE, 11 JAMES SCOTT, 12 JACOB SHIVER, 13 ALEX'R ARCHER, 14 FRANCIS ADAMS.

THOMAS GARDNER Esquire appeared in Court & Took the Oaths of Qualification as a Justice of Peace for this County.

Ordered that the Estate of JOHN COOK Deceased be Sold on a Credit untill Next January and January following One fourth of the Purchase Money Made Payable Next January and the Remaining part in January following.

[Page 105]

Ordered that LEWIS COLLINS be appointed Overseer of the District of Road for which DANIEL KIRKLAND was appointed the 21'st May last he living out of that District and that he do Continue Untill the third Monday in May Next.

State vs THOMAS WILLIAMS. On motion of the Defendant's Council Ordered that in consequence of the prosecutors failing to appear against the Defendant, that a Scire facias do issue to the Sheriff of Richland County against them, to shew cause, at the next Trial Court of this County in Feb. next, why their Recognizances should not be forfeited, and Execution go to Levy the same. And that the Defendant & his securities be discharged from their Recognizance.

WILLIAM NELON vs J'O McCoy and JAMES COOK. Debt. Judgement Confess'd as Pr Specialty With Interest & Costs of Suit Stay of Execution two Months.

EDWARD MORTIMER & C'o vs JOSEPH McCOY. Debt. Judgement Confessed according to Specialty Stay Execution five Months.

JONATHAN BELTON vs JEREMIAH McDONALD & W'M BRYAN. Debt.

Judgement Confessed for L 28 s 10 With Interest thereon from the 23rd April 1792 and Costs of Suit the Execution to be lodged to bind the property.

JAMES BROWN & Co vs JAMES MATTOCKS. S. P. Judgement Confess'd for L 9 13/8 and Costs of Suit Execution to Issue but not to be Levyed Until the first December.

The C. C. Society vs THOMAS BROWN. S. P. Judgement Confess'd as Pr Specialty With Costs of Suit Stay Execution Six Months.

[Page 106] July 29'th 1793

PHILLIP G. CHION & JOSEPH DULLIS vs JAMES GUN. Debt. Judgement as Pr Specialty Stay of Execution Untill the first day of October next with Costs of

Suit.

W'M CRAIG vs JAMES AYRES. S. P. Judgement Confest for L 6 s 16 d 4 With Interest as Pr Specialty and Costs of Suit. Execution to Issue but not Levyed Untill the first of October Next.

MICAJAH VAUGHS vs SAMUEL SELLS. Case. Judgement Confess'd for L 10 With Costs of Suit. Stay of Execution to the first Day of November.

ROBERT HENRY vs JAMES BROWN JUN'R. Debt. Judgement Confess'd for L 244 s 16 the Execution to Issue and Not Levyed Untill further Orders.

State vs WILLIAM NORRIS & Others. Ordered that Scire Facias DO Issue to Shew Cause Tomorrow Why Exeucution Should Not Issue on their forfeited Recognizance.

EDWARDS MORTIMER & C'o vs WILLIS WHITAKER. Debt. Judgement Confess'd for L 10 s 5 d 2 with Costs the Execution to Issue and not be Levyed Untill further Orders.

ZACHARIAH NETTLES Appeared in Open Court and Sworn as a Constable.

Ordered that the Clerk of the Court pay to DAVID MARTIN Two Shillings & four pence Pr. Week for a Bushell of Corn for the Use of RITTENBURY's family Untill New Corn Comes in and then two Shillings Pr Week untill July Court Next.

[Page 107] July 29'th 1793

JOHN JACKSON vs SAMUEL CLARKE. Debt. Judgement Confess'd as Pr Specialty With Costs of Suit & Stay Execution Untill the first February Next.

ALEX'R STEWART vs JAMES GUNN. Case. Judgement Confess'd for the Value of 3200 W't of Tobacco at Ten Shillings P Hundred and Interest Thereon from the Twenty first Decem'r last with costs of suit.

JAMES WILLIAMS vs JOHN NORRIS, CADER HAROLD. Att. Dismis'd. [entire entry stricken]

The Court then adjourned untill Tomorrow Ten O'Clock. IS. DUBOSE, JOHN KERSHAW.

30th July 1793. The Court Met Agreeable to Adjournment. Present: JOHN KERSHAW & BURWELL BOYKIN, Esq'rs.

Ordered that the Provision made for the support of HENRY KENT at the last February Court be Continued Untill Next February.

SAMUEL GAUNT vs DAVID NICHOLSON. S. P. Judgement Confess'd for L 2 s 9 d 7 with Costs of Suit. Stay Execution to 25th Nov'r 1793.

DAVID BUSH & C'o vs DILLARD COLLINS. S. P. Judgement Confess'd as P Specialty With Costs of Suit Stay Execution 3 Months.

[Page 108] JON'N BELTON vs HENRY GRAGG. Debt. Judgement Confess'd as P Specialty With Costs of Suit Execution to Issue but not Levyed Untill the first of Decem'r Next.

DAVID BUSH & Co vs JESSE COOK. S. P. Judgement Confessed for L 6 s 14 & Interest thereon from the 11th March last Stay Execution Untill the 28 Feby next With Costs of Suit.

JAMES BREEDIN vs NATH'L PACE. S. P. Judgement Confest as Pr Specialty With Costs of Suit Stay Execution Untill 28th Feby 1794.

[30 July 1793]

The Grand Jury Call'd and Impanneld:

1 DAVID BUSH foreman, 2 ISAAC ROSS, 3 JOSEPH THOMPSON, 4 W'M NETTLES, 5 NICHO'S ROBINSON, 6 DAVID MARTIN, 7 WILLIAM SANDERS, 8 JOSHUA ENGLISH, 9 SAM'L BRADFORD, 10 JAMES BROWN JUN'R, 11 SAMUEL LEVY, 12 WILLIAM WARE, 13 HUGH McDOWL.

Ordered that WILLIAM NORRIS be Brought into Court Whereupon the said NORRIS being Brought into Court and Inquired of Whether he Could shew any Cause Why Sentence should not be Passed on him for Petty Larceny of Which he was found GUilty at the last Court and no Cause being Shew, Ordered that he be taken to the Publick Whipping Post immediately after the adjournment of the Court this day there to Receive Twenty Lashes on his Bare Back and pay Costs of Prosecution before discharged.

The State vs ZACHARIAH MARTIN. JOSIAH EVANS Pro's. Cattle Stealing. The Grand Jury return'd a true Bill. DAVID BUSH, foreman.

State vs JOHN PHILLIPS, SHADE PHILLIPS, ISAAC WILLIAMS. Cattle Stealing. JOSHUA ENGLISH, Pro. The Grand Jury Returned a true Bill. DAVID BUSH, foreman.

[Page 109]

[same as previous, GEO. PAYNE, Pro's]

[same as previous, JO McCOY, Pro.]

State vs ZACHARIAH MARTIN. Indictment for Cattle Stealing.

1 REUBIN COLLINS Foreman, 2 ROBERT BARKLEY, 3 AARON ATKINS, 4 GEORGE PAYNE JUN'R, 5 JOHN PAYNE, 6 BERRY ROBINSON, 7 JAMES SHARPLIN, 8 W'M PAYNE, 9 HEZEKIAH LOVE, 10 ISAAC BLANCHARD, 11 WILLIAM ARCHER, 12 ALEX'R ARCHER test.

Ordered that GARDNER FORD Received Letters of Admins'n on ... ISAAC LOVE Deceased the Securities are REUBIN HARRISON and NICHOLAS PEAY.

Ordered that JAMES BROWN A poor Boy be Bound an Apprentice to JAMES THRENTHAM untill he arrive at the age of Eighteen Years.

THOMAS ROACH vs THOMAS SINGLETON. Att. The Garnishee WILLIAM MOUNENCE appeared in Open Court and Declared on Oath that he Ow'd the Defendent the sum of L 3 s 7 or thereabouts Which was to be P'd in trade but he will pay it in three Months in Cash if Therefore Stay Execution three Months.

[Page 110] 30th July 1793

SAM'L MATHIS In'ds of W'M CRAGG vs AARON ADKINS. Debt. Judgement Confess'd for L 10 sterling and Interest from the frst of January last With Costs of Suit. Execution to Issue and Not be Levied Untill the 24th Day of April next.

The Minutes being first Read the Court Adjour'd Untill Tomorrow Ten O'Clock. BUR'L BOYKIN, JOHN KERSHAW.

The Court met agreeable to Adjournment. Present: JOHN KERSHAW, ISAAC DUBOSE, & BURWELL BOYKIN, Esq'rs.

State vs ZACHARIAH MARTIN. Indictment for Stealing Cattle.

[31 July 1793]

The Jury for Yesterday being Call'd into Court brought their Verdict Seal'd up Which being Opened and Read found the Defendent Guilty. REUBIN COLLINS, foreman.

The State vs JOHN PHILLIPS, SHADRACH PHILLIPS, ISAAC WILLIAMS. Indictment Stealing two Cattle from GEORGE PAYNE. The Prisoners being called to the Bar and hearing the Indictment read to

[Page 111]

them in open Court, and being called upon to plead thereto. Confessed Guilty according to the Indictment... except SHADRICK PHILLIPS who pleaded not Guilty.

[Same] Indictment for stealing Six Cattle from BENJAMIN McCOY. JOHN PHILLIPS and ISAAC WILLIAMS pleaded Guilty... SHADRICK PHILLIPS pleaded not Guilty.

The State vs JOHN PHILLIPS, SHADRACH PHILLIPS, ISAAC WILLIAMS. Indictment stealing two Cattle the property of JOSHUA ENGLISH... JOHN PHILLIPS, ISAAC WILLIAMS pleaded guilty... SHADRACH PHILLIPS pleaded not Guilty.

[Page 112]

DAVID HUNTER vs DAVID ORR. On Attachment by Consent of Parties referred to GEORGE MILLER & JAMES COUSART with leave to chuse an Umpire their award returnable to the next intermediate Court to be a Judgment of Court.

State vs SHADRICK PHILLIPS. Indictment for Cattle Stealing.

1 REUBIN COLLINS foreman, 2 ROBERT BARKELY, 3 AARON ATKINS, 4 JAMES SHARPLIN, 5 WILLIAM PAYNE, 6 HEZEKIAH LOVE, 7 ISAAC BLANCHARD, 8 JACOB SHIVER, 9 WILLIAM NETTLES, 10 DAVID PEEBLES, 11 WILLIAM ARCHER, 12 ALEXANDER ARCHER. Verdict Guilty.

SHADRICK PHILLIPS Moved for leave to Withdraw his Plea of Not Guilty on the Indictment for Stealing Six Cattle the Property of BENJAMIN McCOY, also the Indictment for Stealing two Cattle the property of JOSHUA ENGLISH and Plead Guilty thereof. Ordered that his Confession be Recorded.

Ordered that the Estate of WILLIAM HOLMES deceased be sold and a Credit Given untill the first of January next.

[Page 113]

JAMES BROWN & Cᵒ vs DAVID HUNTER. Case. Dismissed Each Party Paying their Own Costs.

State vs ISHAM POWELL & OTHERS. Riot. the same Jury.

SAMUEL TYNES vs FIELDING WOODROFF. Judgement by Default.

SAM'L CLARK vs JOHN JACKSON. S. P. Dismiss'd Each paying half the Costs.

After the Minutes being first Read the Court Adjourned Untill tomorrow Ten OClock. JOHN KERSHAW, IS DUBOSE, BUR'L BOYKIN.

1st August 1793. The Court met agreeable to adjournment. Present JOHN KERSHAW & ISAAC DUBOSE, Esq'rs.

[1 August 1793]

[Page 114] AN'DR LESTER vs F. WOODROFF. Rule Made Absolute.

SAM'L DUNLAP vs WILLIAM CARRACH. S. P. Judgement Confess'd according to Specialty With Costs of Suit.

JAMES BROWN & C'o vs JOHN SWILLA. S. P. Judgement Confessd L 7 s 10 d 7 and Costs of Suit. Stay Execu't to first January Next.

JNO'N BELTON Sur'v of McLEOD vs W'M STARKE. Case. Ordered that ISAAC ALEX'R and JOHN FISHER be appointed Auditers to Compare the Account with the Original Entries, & They are hereby so appointed.

JNO'N BELTON vs W'M STARK. Case. the same order.

State vs ISHAM POWEL, FREDERICK ROBINSON, JAMES HUNTER, JOHN MORGAN, ROBERT FORD. Indictment for a Riot. ISHAM POWELL not guilty. FREDERICK ROBINSON, JAMES HUNTER, JOHN MORGAN, ROBERT FORD. Guilty. REUBIN COLLINS, foreman.

ROBERT FORD moved for a New Trial on Affidavit Granted on paying the Costs.

State vs JAMES COWSAR. Presentment of the Grand Jury and Indictment thereon. Dismiss'd Defend't pay'g costs.

State vs GEORGE MILLER. Presentment of the Grand Jury and Indictment thereon Dismiss'd at Defend'ts Costs.

[Page 115]

State vs ZACHARIAH MARTIN. Sentence to pay a fine of L 40 or Receive Thrity Nine Lashes on his Bare Back at the Publick Whiping Post at Ten O'Clock to Morrow - With Costs.

State vs ISAAC WILLIAMS. Sentence to pay a fine or Receive thirteen Lashes on Each Indictment on his Bare Back at the Publick Whipping Post. three Indictments; at 10 O'Clock to Morrow With Costs.

State vs JOHN PHILLIPS. Sentence to pay the fine or Receive Twenty five Lashes on Each Indictment on his Bare back at the Publick Whipping Post. There is three Indictments at 10 O'Clock to Morrow with Costs.

State vs SHADRICK PHILLIPS. Riot. Sentence to pay the fines on all three Indictments or Receive Twenty Lashes on Each at the Publick Whiping Post on his Bare Back at 10 OClock to Morrow With Costs.

State vs JAMES HUNTER. Riot. Sentence fined the sum of forty shillings and stand Committed Untill the Judgement of the Court be performed With Costs.

State vs JOHN MORGAN. Riot. Sentence fined in the sum of Five Shillings and to pay Costs of suit.

State vs DAVID HUNTER. Presentment of the Grand Jury and Indictment thereon Dismiss'd at Defendent pay costs.

HENRY KENT vs LAZERUS KELLY, JAMES KELLY & ANNE KELLY. Debt. Continued at Pltfs Costs amounting to thirty three shillings and the Plaintiff Shall Peremtorally Come to tryal at the Next Court. and be obliged to pay said Costs before trial and that Witnesses on behalf of the Defendents be Examined before the Clerk of the Court and that their Testimony be Given in Evidence at the Tryal.

[Page 116] 1 August 1793

WILLIS WHITAKER vs JAMES WREN. Debt. Issue. 1 REUBIN COLLINS foreman, 2 ROBERT BARKLEY, 3 AARON ATKINS, 4 JAMES SHARPLIN, 5 WILLIAM PAYNE, 6 HEZEKIAH LOVE, 7 ISAAC BLANCHARD, 8 JACOB SHIVER, 9 WILLIAM NETTLES, 10 DAVID PEEBLES, 11 WILLIAM ARCHER, 12 ALEX'R ARCHER. We find for the Plaintiff agreeable to Specialty With Interest from 1st day of December 1793.

Ordered that Five Shillings paid the Jury by Plaintiffs Attorney be taxed in his bill.

Exo'r of JOSEPH KERSHAW dec'd vs JOHN HOLZENDORF. Att. [same jury as previous case] We find for the Plaintiffs L 42 s 10 with Lawful interest from the first day of Decem'r 1787 and Costs of Suit.

JOHN RUSSEL vs JAMES LOVE. Debt. Judgement Confessed as per Specialty With Costs of Suit. Stay Execution Six Months The Same Jury as above.

FIELDING WOODROOF vs JOHN HOLZENDORF. We find for the Plaintiff L 125 With Interest from the 26th April 1789 allowing the Discount pleaded by the Defendent of L 99 3/2.

[Page 117]

PETER McKINNON vs JAMES RING & Others. Trespass. The Same Jury. We find for the Plaintiff L 5 s 10 value and Defendents Pay Costs of Suit.

State vs JOSEPH McCOY. Presentment of the Grand Jury and Indictment thereon Dismiss'd at the Defend'ts Costs.

Ordered that the Estate of JOHN LEE deceased be sold after the legal time of advertizing on a Credit Untill the First of March Next.

GEORGE GAYDEN appointed as Constible and Sworn Accordingly.

The Minutes being first Read the Court Adjourned Untill To Morrow Ten OClock. IS. DUBOSE, JOHN KERSHAW.

2 Aug't 1793. The Court met agreeable to Adjournment. Present ISAAC DUBOSE, BURWELL BOYKIN, Esq'rs.

ISAAC WILLIAMS & JOHN PHILLIPS appeared in Open Court and Made Oath that they were not able to pay the Jail Fees or Cost of Prosecution.

W'M BROWN Indorser of HENRY HUNTER vs HENRY MOORE. Debt. We find for the Plaintiff 30 Pounds with Lawfull Interest from the first Day of February 1791 With Costs of Suit.

1 REUBIN COLLINS foreman, 2 AARON ATKINS, 3 JAMES SHARPLIN, 4 HEZEKIAH LOVE, 5 WILLIAM PAYNE, 6 ISAAC BLANCHARD, 7 JACOB SHIVER, 8 WILLIAM NETTLES, 9 DAVID PEEBLES, 10 JAMES ROBINSON, 11 WILLIAM ARCHER, 12 ALEX'R ARCHER.

[Page 118] [2 August 1793]

SHADRICK PHILLIPS appeared in Open Court and Made Oath that he was Not able to pay his Jail Fees or Costs of Prosecution.

Ordered that letters of administration Do issue to HENRY KENT ... on DRURY CAMBELL the Securities are SAMUEL McKEE & ROBIN ROBINSON.

WALTER ROWE vs SION COTES. Trover. Dismiss'd at Plaintiffs Costs.

[2 August 1793]

WILLIAM LARGE vs JOHN TAYLOR. Trespass. The Same Jury. We find for the Plaintiff L 6 s 10 With Costs of Suit.

JOSEPH DaCOSTA vs JOSEPH P. McCOY, W'M P. McCOY, D'r THO'S BROWN. Debt. Judgement by Confession agreeable to Bond with Costs the Sail Not to take Place before the first of November Next.

DAVID HUNTER & Wife vs ARCHIBALD McAFFEE & Wife. SLANDER. The Same Jury.

After the Minutes being first Read the Court Adjourned Untill To Morrow Nine O'Clock. IS> DUBOSE, JOHN KERSHAW.

The Court met Agreeable to Adjournment. Present JOHN KERSHAW & ISAAC DUBOSE. Esq'rs.

[Page 119] 3'rd August 1793

GERSHAM CHAPMAN vs PETER McKINNON. Att. Dismiss'd Each paying their Costs Except the Clerk Which the Defendant Pays.

Ordered that all Estrays Within the County that have been advertised the legal time be sold immediately after the adjournment of the Court.

On the Petition of MARY JOHNSON Ordered that the Clerk issue a Warrant against the Parties of Whom she Complains upon her Makeing Proof of the Circumstances set forth in her Petition.

DAVID HUNTER & Wife vs ARCHIBALD McAFEE & Wife. Slander. Jury Return'd the Verdict. We find in Our Verdict on Shilling Damage to the Defendent, that the Platinff Pay Costs of Suit. REUBIN COLLINS, Foreman.

The Same Jury as Yesterday are Sworn to try all Writs of Enquiry.

JOHN DeBUSEY vs ARCHIBALD PAYNE. Case. [entire entry stricken]

LEWIS HUDSON vs HEZEKIAH LOVE. Debt. Judgement Confess'd as P Specialty Stay Execution Untill the first of November Next with Costs of Suit.

PHILLIP G. CHION & JOSEPH DULLIS vs WILLIAM PARKER & WILLIAM WARE. Debt. Judgement Confess'd P Specialty With Costs of Suit Stay Execution first January next.

Ordered that ROBERT WILLIAMS, DILLARD SPRADLEY, ABRAM SHIVER, JAMES HUNTER & JOSEPH PAYNE be appointed Constables for this County until next July term inclusive. ROBERT WILLIAMS, JAMES HUNTER, ABRAM SHIVER & JOSEPH PAYNE appeared & qualified accordingly.

[Page 120]

JOHN MARSHALL vs JAMES GUNN. S. P. Decree according to Specialty With Costs of Suit.

HENRY RUGELEY vs SAM'l BREED. Debt. Judgement Confess'd as P Specialty With Costs of Suit Stay Execution to first of Jan'y next.

SARAH ATKINS vs WILLIAM DOUD. S. P. Decree for Plaintiff as Pr Specialty With Costs of Suit.

JOHN LOCKHART vs JAMES HARRIS. Att. ARCHIBALD WATSON the Garnishee being Call'd and failing to answer on Oath Judgement by Default against the Garnishee.

[3 August 1793]

Ordered that ABRAHAM CHILDERS be No longer a Deputy Sheriff of Kershaw County.

ELIJAH PAYNE being proposed by the Sheriff as a Deputy Was agreed to by the Court Appear and Sworn in Accordingly.

JOHN DeBUSEY vs ROBERT FORD. Case. The Same Jury. We find for the Palintiff L 10 with a full Interest from the 21st December 1792 With costs of Suit. REUBIN COLLINS, Foreman.

JOHN DeBUSEY vs BARVELL EVANS. Case. The Same Jury. We find for the Plaintiff L 10 s 2 d 4 with Lawfull Interest from Jan'y 1792 With Costs of Suit. REUBIN COLLINS, Foreman.

JOHN DeBUSEY vs ARCHIBALD PAYNE. Case. The Same Jury. We find for the Plfts. L 11 2 3 1/2.

HEZEKIAH ALEXANDER vs RICHARD BLANKS. Debt. The Same Jury. We find for the Plaintiff L 17 d 6 with Lawfull Interest from the 25 Sept'r 1792 With Costs of Suit. REUBIN COLLINS, Foreman.

[Page 121]

ABRAHAM KELLY vs JOHN BARRON. S. P. Decree for the Plaintiff L 2 d 7 with Costs of Suit.

BURWELL BOYKIN In'd of SAM'L MATHIS vs MICAJAH CRANSHAW & NATH'L PACE. S. P. Decree for Plaintiff as Pr Specialty With Costs.

JOSEPH MAGOUNE vs Adm'x of JAMES ATHENS. It is ordered by agreement of the Attorneys for both parties that this Petition & Summons be referred to ISAAC DUBOSE Esquire and ZACHARIAH CANTEY who are at liberty to choose an Umpire in Case they cannot agree. It is also agreed by the Atty for both Parties & ordered by the Court that the award of the said Referees or Arbitrators be of the same force and effect as a judgment of this Court. That it be entered of record of the Court & that Execution do issue thereon in the same manner as if a judgment or decree had been obtained in this Court.

JONATHAN DUREN vs JOHN TAYLOR & HENRY HUDSON. Deft. Put off on affidavit by JN'O TAYLOR. Plea a Release. Judicial attachment awarded against HENRY HUDSON.

DAN'L BROWN vs DAN'L BROWN, GIDEON BROCKWAY, BEEMAN BROCKWAY & BERBAN BROCKWAY. Att. The Defendants being solemnly called and failing to appear or make any Defence and the attachment having been duly levied in the hands of BENJAMIN CUDWORTH

[Page 122]

a Guarnishee and also summoned as a Guarnishee and as Attorney for the Defemdant BEEMAN BROCKWAY and makes No Defence. The Court gave a Judgment by Default agreeable to Specialty.

At the request of ISAAC ALEXANDER Esquires, ISHAM POWELL was appointed a Constable for this County whereon he appeared & qualified.

WILLIAM PARKER vs ALEXANDER GOODALL & SAM'L BREED. Debt. Jury sworn. A mistrial. Referred to Dr. ALEXANDER & JOHN McCAW with leave to chuse an umpire their aware to be a rule of Court.

[3 August 1793]

JOHN LOCKHART vs JAMES HARRIS. Att. the Garnishee ARCHIBALD WATSON appeared in Court and made Oath that there is a Certain Grey Stud horse in his Possession and that the said Horse have this Spring been put to three Mares at three Dollars Each and that the said HARRIS is Indebted to the Garnishee Forty Dollars.

TAURENS CONNER vs GEORGE PERRY. Trover. Decree for Plaintiff L 2 with Costs of Suit.

The Court then adjourned untill Monday 10 O'Clock the Minutes being first read. IS. DUBOSE, JOHN KERSHAW.

[Page 123] 5th August 1793

The Court agreeable to Adjournment met. Present ISAAC DUBOSE & BURWELL BOYKIN, Esq'rs.

JOHN LOWRY North C. vs Admix JOHN LOWRY B. C. Case. Ordered that a Commission Do Issue to Examine Witnesses in North Carolina & Georgia.

ROBERT HENRY vs ANDREW LESTER. S. P. Judgement Confess'd as Pr. Specialty With Costs suit Stay Execution first January

SAMUEL MATHIS vs ANDREW LESTER. S. P. Judgement Confess'd as Pr Specialty With Costs Stay Execution first Jan'y.

The Jurors on the Original panal being Deficient it was ordered by the Court & agreed by the Attornies that Talismen be Drawn to fill up the Jury.

Ordered that the following Persons be Summoned as Jurors to Attend this Court Immediately.

The Talismen being Drawn from Box N'o 5 to N'o 6.

1 W'M YOUNG, 2 JOHN CRAVEN, 3 SAMUEL LEVY, 4 W'M OWENS, 5 JAMES BOWLS, 6 ABRAHAM CHILDERS, 7 BEN. CARTER, 8 JN'O ADAMSON, 9 ISAIAH BUSH, 10 JAMES KERSHAW, 11 ROBERT COLEMAN, 12 MATTHEW COLEMAN, 13 THO'S DINKINS, 14 MICHAEL GANTER, 15 DUNCAN McRA, 16 BEN CUDWORTH, 17 JAMES TATE, 18 RICH'D COLEMAN, 19 JOSHUA DINKINS, 20 FIELD WOODROOF.

FREDERICK JOINER vs JOHN R. HUTCHINS. S. P. Decree for Plaintiff Stay Execution to first of Novem'r With Costs of Suit.

JACOB WHITWORTH vs RANSOM STROUD. Debt. Judgement by Default as P Specialty With Costs for Want of Plea.

[Page 124]

DAVID BUSH & Co. vs DAVID HUNTER. S. P. Judgement by Default as P Specialty With Costs of Suit.

CHESNUT BOYKIN & C'o vs W'M GOYEN. S. P. Judgement by Default Decree for Plaintiff L 3 13 6 With Costs of Suit.

ZACHARIAH CANTEY & C'o vs JOHN NORRIMORE. S. P. Judgement by Default Decree for Plaintiff on L 5 s 2 with In't from the first of Jan'y 1790 With Costs of Suit.

THOMAS ROACH vs THOMAS SINGLETON. Decree for Plaintiff for L 4 s 13 d 4 as Garnishee Given in on Oath With Costs.

[5 August 1793]

JOHN SWILLA vs THO'S SMERRILL. Case. Judgement by Default.

W'M PARKER vs ALEX'R GOODALL & SAM'L BREED. Debt. The Arbitrators Award for Plaintiff L 8 s 7 d 8 With Costs of Suit.

JOHN LOCKART vs JAMES HARRIS. Att. Judgement by Default as P Specialty With Costs of Suit.

BENJAMIN CARTER vs HUGH McDOWEL. Case. Judgement Confess'd L 10 s 6 d 3 With Costs of Suit.

JAMES PIERSON vs RICHARD BLANKS. Debt. Judgement Confess'd as P Specialty With Costs.

AARON LOCOCK vs ROGER GIBSON. Debt. Judgement Confess'd as P Specialty With Costs Stay Execution 1 Jan'y.

JOHN COGDALL & C'o vs CHA'S MCGINNEY. Debt. Judgement Confest as P Specialty stay Execution 1 Jan'y.

[Page 125]

FIELDING WOODROFF vs JOHN HOLZENDORF. Att. The Exor of JOSEPH KERSHAW Deceased vs JOHN HOLZENDORF.

Ordered that the Plaintiffs in the above Actions upon attachments Wherein Judgement have been Obtained be allowed to bring suit against the Defendants Debtors upon his Books of Account in their Own Names as Assignees of the Said Defendant to Satisfaction of the Same or as far forth as the Said Book Debts Will extend.

DAN'L BROWN vs BEMAN BROCKWAY & al. Att. BENJAMIN CUDWORTH Garnishee Rendered in an Account on Oath of the Property & Debts in his hands Which was ordered to be filed. And the Court gave Judgment that the same be liable for the Plaintiff Demand agreeable to Law in Case of Judgment on Attachment.

PETER OSGOOD vs HUGH McDOWEL. Debt. Miss Tryal. 1 DUNCAN McRA foreman, 2 WILLIAM YOUNG, 3 JOSIAH BUSH, 4 ROBERT COLEMAN, 5 MAT COLEMAN, 6 FIELDING WOODROOF, 7 WILLIAM NETTLES, 8 W'M OWENS, 9 JA'S ROBINSON, 10 BEN. CUDWORTH, 11 JAMES KERSHAW, 12 MICHAEL GANTER.

W'M WARE and JOHN BAKER vs ISAACK FORD. Replevy. Dismiss'd at Defendants Cost of Suit.

[Page 126]

JOHN BARROW vs JOHN KING. Case. We find for the Defds L 4 d 2 7 d With Costs. DUNCAN McRA foreman. 1 DUNCAN McRA foreman, 2 W'M YOUNG, 3 ISAIAH BUSH, 4 ROBER COLEMAN, 5 MATHEW COLEMAN, 6 BENJ: CUDWORTH, 7 W'M OWEN, 8 W'M NETTLES, 9 JOHN ROBINSON, 10 JAMES ROBINSON, 11 JAMES KERSHAW, 12 MICHAEL GAUNTER.

ZACHARIAH CANTEY & C'o vs SUSANNAH BROWN Adm'x of W'M BROWN deceased. Case. We find for the Plaintiff L 16: 10: 3 With Costs. [same jury as preceding case]

JOHN BLANTON vs Adm'r W'M LECONT. Debt. We find for the Plaintiff L 145 s 12 d 4 With Costs of Suit.

[5 August 1793]

DAVID COTES vs JOHN HARVELL. S. P. Referreed to Arbitration JOHN CHAMPION & FRANCIS BELL are Appointed Arbitrators With Power to Chuse an Umpire PURTIMAN BERRY ENGAGIN that ARNOLD BERRY shall abide by the War and the award be made a Rule of Court.

[Page 127]

DAVID HUNTER & Wife vs ARCH McAFEE & Wife. Slander. The Pltf prayed an appeal to the District Court & Offer to give Security agreeable to Law.

But the Court were of opinion that he was not entitled to an Appeal therefore refused it. In case appeal is granted at the Circuit Court the Pltf agrees to his Errors thence Next Novem'r.

A. F. BRISBANE vs D. BROWN. Commissions to issue to examine Doctor NAT. ALEXANDER & AB. NOTT for Deft.

ISAAC DACOSTA vs W'M BRUMMET. S. P. Discontinued.

After the Minutes being Read the Court Adjourn'd Until the third Monday in October next. BUR'L BOYKIN, IS. DUBOSE.

21 October 1793.

[Page 128]

Agreeable to Adjournment the Hon'ble Court Met. Present JOHN KERSHAW & ISAAC DUBOSE, Esquire.

Ordered that Letters of Administration Do Issue to MARGARET MCDONALD on estate of ARCHIBALD McDONALD Dec'd the Securities are W'M OWEN & JAMES TATE.

Ordered that Letters of Administration Do Issue to JOSEPH THOMPSON on the estate of JAMES CAIN Deceased the Securities are W'M SCOTT & HUGH McGEE.

Ordered that ZACHARIAH NETTLES be taken as a Security in the Place of NICHOLAS PEAY on Estate of ISAAC LOVE Deceased.

Ordered that the Executrix of SAMUEL BELTONs Estate be Allowed to Sell such Part of the Estate as may be Necessary for the Payment of Debts or to Prevent the Loss of Perishable Articles on the 18th day of Novem'r Next at the Plantation on Six Months Credit.

Ordered that the Administrator of ISAAC LOVEs Estate be allowed to Sell such part of the Estate as may be Necessary for the Payment of Debts or to Prevent the Loss of Perishable articles on the 18th Day of November Next at the Plantation Whereon the deceased lately Lived on Twelve Months Credit.

[Page 129]

Ordered that Letters of Administration Do Issue to MARGARET JONES on the Estate of DAVID JONES Deceased the Securities are ABRAHAM BELTON & ARCHIBALD WATSON.

Ordered that Letters of Administration Do Issue to BARVELL EVENS on the Estate of JACOB EVANS Deceased the Securities are PAUL SMITH and AMBROSE BRYANT.

Ordered that Letters of Administration do Issue to MILDRIDGE EVANS on the estate of WILLIAM EVANS Deceased the Securities are PAUL SMITH & BARVELL

EVANS.

The Court Adjourned Untill to Morrow Eleven OClock. JOHN KERSHAW, IS. DUBOSE.

Agreeable to Adjournment the Court Met. Present ISAAC DUBOSE Esquire.

Ordered that the Estrays Which have been Advertized the legal time be sold immediately after the Adjournment of the Court.

[Page 130] October 22nd 1793.

Ordered that ANDREW LESTER & DAVID MARTIN do Chuse a third Person if they Disagree to lay Out a Road from the Ferry downwards through the low Grounds on the West side of the river.

Ordered that the Residue of the Estate of LEMUEL PERRY be sold the Stock of Cattle furniture &c. to be sold at the Plantation the first Monday in December Next and the Negroes on Tuesday following Twelve Months Credit from 1st Jan'y 1794.

Ordered that on MARGARET McDONALD returning an Inventory and appraisement of the Es't of ARCHIBALD McDONALD she be allowed to sell such part of the Personal Property thereunto Belonging as may be Necessary for the Payment of his Debts or to Prevent the Loss or Perishable Articles that she sell at the house Where she resides Within One month after she makes the s'd returns on a credit of three months.

Ordered that ZACHARIAH THOMSON do Receive letters of administration on the estate of ANN BELTON Deceased the securities are FRANCIS BELL & JOSEPH THOMSON.

Ordered that the Administrator of the Estate of ANN BELTON deceased be allowed to sell the Negroe Wench & Child on the first Monday in December Next at Camden and the Remainder of the property the Next Day at the Plantation of SAMUEL BELTON Deceased on a Twelve Month Credit.

[Page 131]

Ordered that the Administrator of JAMES CAINs Estate be Allowed to Sell the Property on Giving three Weeks Notice on the Fifteenth of November Next at Six Month Credit.

Ordered that Letters of Administration Do Issue to JOSHUA ENGLISH on the estate of THOMAS ENGLISH Deceased the Securities are W'M BONDS & RICHARD STRATFORD.

That JAMES CANTEY & THOMAS ENGLISH be Authorized to call upon all the Inhabitants Living between the Black River Road & The Wateree River To assist in opening the new road directed to be laid off by them.

That the Clerk of this Court be Required to Pay the Sum of One Dollar Per Month Untill next court for the relief of Mrs. FLINN a Person in Indigent Circumstances.

That the Clerk Make out an Account of the Monies collected and due the County for fines, forfeitures, Tavern Licences &c since the establishment of this Court, and also an Account of the disposition of such Monies as have been expended and also that the Sheriff furnish the Clerk with an Account of the County tax collected and that the same be brought forward in the Clerks Statement as soon as convenient and at all events by the first day of next Court.

[22 October 1793]

Ordered that the account of the County att'y passed some time ago for about Seven Pounds be Paid out of any Money Not heretofore appropriated, in the Clerks of Sheriffs hands belonging to the County.

Ordered that JOSHUA ENGLISH be Authorized to Sell the estate of THOMAS ENGLISH dec'd on Saturday the 16'th of November Next at the Plantation of the said dec'd on a Credit of one year for all Sums Exceeding forty shillings.

Ordered that MARGARET JONES be Authorized to sell such a Part of the Personal Estate of her dec'd Husband as are Perishable and inconvenient to Keep on a Credit of Twelve Months. The Sale to take Place after due notice on Monday 18th Nov'r next.

GEORGE BARNES and RICHARD RUTLEDGE being approved of a Deputy Sheriffs for this County, appeared and were Qualified.

The Court then Adjourned to the 28th day of February next. IS. DUBOSE, JOHN KERSHAW.

On Friday the 28th February 1794. Grand Jury Drawn from Box N'o 1 to N'o 2.

1 JOHN TRUSDALE, 2 ISAAC KNOX, 3 ANDREW NUT JUN'R, 4 RICH'D CLANTON, 5 W'M STARKE, 6 JOSEPH McCOY, 7 W'M NETTLES near Camden, 8 AARON FERGUSON, 9 JOHN DYE, 10 JON'N BUNCKLEY, 11 SOL OWEN, 12 JOHN ENGLISH, 13 ROB'T MARSHALL, 14 JAMES MARSHALL SEN'R, 15 ALEX'R ARCHER, 16 JAMES NICKLE, 17 W'M PARKER, 18 LUKE GIDBON, 19 ARCH'D OWEN, 20 JOHN McMASTER.

[Page 133]

Petit Jury Drawn from Box N'o 3 to N'o 4.

1 JOSEPH TILLER JUN'R, 2 JAMES LOGAN, 3 DAN'L MAJOR, 4 W'M SHIVER, 5 JOHN PAYNE JUN'R, 6 JOSEPH KNIGHTON, 7 ISAAC FAULKENBURY, 8 JOSEPH LOCKART, 9 JOHN LONG, 10 JAMES CAIN, 11 W'M HUGHS, 12 W'M CRAIG, 13 W'M TILLER, 14 CHARLES SPEARS, 15 GEORGE HAYS, 16 BURWELL CATO, 17 JOHN SWILLA, 18 CHURCH HUGHS, 19 THOMAS SMITH, 20 JOHN SHIVER SEN'R, 21 ALEX'R FLEMING, 22 GEORGE DURIN, 23 SAMUEL LAUGHIN, 24 ROB'T WHITE, 25 EDMUND STRANGE, 26 JOHN BOLAN, 27 STEPHEN BLANDERS, 28 RICH'D WILSON, 29 JOSEPH PERDICUE, 30 BERRY KING.

The Court met agreeable to Adjournment. Present BURWELL BOYKIN, Esq'r.

JOHN ADAMSON vs LEWIS COOK. Debt. Judgement Confess'd for L 47 s 15 with Interest and Costs of Suit.

JON'N BELTON Vs JOHN LONG SEN'R & JOHN LONG JUN'R. Debt. Judgement Confess'd for L 35 and Costs of Suit.

Ordered that the Administratrix of WILLIAM[stricken] EVANS be allowed to Sell a Horse, Rifle, Gun, Whipsaw & ca Stock of Wild Hogs belonging to her Intestate at her house on the third Saturday in Next Month the Gun and Whipsaw on three Months Credit and the Rest on Nine Months Credit Giving Due Notice.

[Page 134]

JONATHAN BELTON vs WALTER SHROPSHIRE & THOMAS SHROPSHIRE. Debt. Judgement Confess'd for the Sum of L 35 Sterling With Interest from the 2 day of Jan'y 1793 with Costs of Suit by WALTER SHROPSHIRE.

[28 February 1794]

DAVID BUSH vs HENRY HUDSON. Debt. Judgement Confess'd for L 35 s 4 d 2 Sterling with Interest thereon from the 15 of Feb'y 1793 With Costs of Suit.

JON'N BELTON vs GEO: BOILSTUN. Debt. Judgment Confess'd for L 35 17/ Stlg. & Costs of Suit.

McRA & CANTEY vs HUGH McGEE. Case. Judgement Confess'd for L 18 5/5 and Costs of Suit.

Ordered that the last Will and Testament of THOMAS VAUGHN be Proven and Recorded. ALEXANDER STEWART appeared in Open Court and was duly Qualified.

Ordered that the Executors of THO'S VAUGHNs last Will and Testament do Receive letters Testamentary, they being Sworn in Open Court.

BRYAN SPRADLEY vs JOSEPH PAYNE. Case. Settled between the Parties. Plaintiff to Pay the Clerk, Sheriff and his Atty's fees and the Defd't to pay his Own Att'y.

JOHN MILLHOUSE Exo'r of JOHN PAYNE vs SAM'L MATHIS Security of JOSEPH KERSHAW Deceased. Debt on Bond. Judgement for the sum of L 433 s 7 d 1 Sterling for the Debt and L 1 s 3 d 8 for the Costs of Suit.

Ordered that letters of Administration Do Issue to Mr's ELIZABETH SCOTT on the estate of JAMES SCOTT Deceased the Securities of ARCHIBALD WATSON and PETER CRIM.

[Page 135]

The Court Adjourned Untill to Morrow Ten OClock. BUR'L BOYKIN.

1 March 1794. The Court met agreeable to Adjournment. Present BURWELL BOYKIN Esq'r.

Ordered that such part of the property of JACOB EVANS Estate as is to be Equally Divided Between the Legatees be Sold at a twelve Months Credit after giving the Legal Notice.

Ordered that PHILIP BURFOOT is appointed as a Deputy Sheriff for the County; he appeared and was Duly Qualify'd.

Ordered that JAMES WILLIAMS be and is hereby appointed as a Deputy Sheriff for the County; appeared and Sworn in Accordingly.

DAVID BUSH & Co. vs BENJAMIN KNOTTS. Case. On Motion, Ordered that the Sheriffs return, of service on the Defend't in this Case, be set aside for irregularity on the affidavit of the Defendant.

Ordered that the Administrator of ISAAC LOVE deceased be allowed to sell some Loose Tobacco, Cotton & Sundry other small articles belonging to said Estate at the House of GARDNER FORD on Saturday the 29th Instant on three Months Credit.

[Page 136]

SUSANNAH BRYANT vs AMBROSE BRYANT. Writ. Slander. Dismissed at the Defendants Costs.

ROBERT HENRY vs JOSHUA DINKINS. S. P. Decreee P Specialty Execution to Issue but not to be Levied Untill the 7th Aug't Next With Costs of Suit.

[1 March 1794]

FRANCIS BOYKIN vs J'O PAYNE & W'M DAVIS. Judgment Confess'd by J'O PAYNE agreeable to Specialty With Costs of Suit Staying Execution Untill the 15'th April Next.

Default as to DAVIS.

DAVID BUSH vs PETER DUNCAN. S. P. Decree as P Specialty With Costs of Suit.

Ordered that the last Will and Testament of LEWIS FRANKLIN BRYANT be proved and Recorded RICH'D MIDDLETON appeared and proved Said Will.

Ordered that WILLIAM MOUNCE Do Receive letters of Administration with the Will annexed on the estate of JAMES DOUGLAS the Securities are

Ordered that the Clerk Pay to LEWIS COOK for Repairing Granies Quarter Creek Bridge Forty Shillings & Three Pence.

[Page 137]

ELIZABETH MICKLE, RACHAEL BELTON and DANIEL PAYNE appeared in Open Court and made Oath to the Substance and effect of the last Will and Testament of SAM'L BELTON JUN'R Deceased Which was made and Nuncupatively Published in his last Sickness in the Presence of the Said Witnesses Who Were Desired to Attest the Same and is in Substance as follows

That it Was his Will and Desire that his Sister CHARLOTTE BELTON Should have & enjoy all his Estate real and Personal excluding thereby his Brother in Law ZACH THOMSON and his Wife MARTHA and that JOHN MICKLE & JON'N BELTON Should act as Exo'rs & Manage and Settle his Estate agreeable to his Will It appeared to the Court that the said THOMPSON had been duly Served With a Process agreeably to Law to Contest said Will and no Cause being Shewn & the Court being Satisfyed with the Probate of Said Will and that the same Was the Will & intent of the Testator.

Ordered that the same be Recorded & Stand in Law as the Last Will & Testament of Said SAM'L BELTON and that Letters Testamentary Issue to JOHN MICKLE as Exo'r the Other declining to Act.

Ordered that Letters Testamentary on the Estate of LEWIS FRANKLIN BRYANT Do Issue to LEWIS BRYANT on all the estate of Said LEWIS F. BRYANT.

Ordered that Letters of administration do Issue to JAMES WILLIAMS on the estate of JAMES TOLAND Deceased the Securites are LEWIS BRYANT & GEORGE EVANS.

[Page 138]

Ordered that RICHARD LLOYD CHAMPION be admitted as Security to MARGARET McDONALD for the due administration of the Estate of ARCHIBALD McDONALD deceased and that the said MARGARET have Letters of Administration upon the said R. L. CHAMPION joining her in a Bond for the due Administration &c.

Ordered that letters of Guardianship Do Issue to DANIEL PAYNE appointing him Guardian of CHARLOTTE BELTON the Securities are ARCHIBALD WATSON & JOHN SWILLA.

The Court Adjourned Untill Monday Next at Ten OClock. BUR. BOYKIN.

3 March 1794. Agreeable to Adjournment the Court Met.   Present BURWELL
BOYKIN Esq'r.

JOHN MILHOUSE Exo'r of JOHN PAYNE vs SAMUEL MATHIS security JOSEPH
KERSHAW dec'd.   Judgement in Debt on Bond.   and now to wit this 3rd day of
March 1794 came the Plaintiff in this case into Court and acknowledged that he
had received of the above named SAMUEL MATHIS full Satisfaction for the Debt
and Costs awarded to him in this Case and so forth.

Ordered that letters of administration do Issue to RICHARD LLOYD CHAMPION
on the estate of JOHN LLOYD CHAMPION the security is JOHN ADAMSON.

[Page 139]

W'M KIRKLAND vs JON'N BARNES, JN'O DIXSON.   Debt.   JONATHAN BARNS
appeared and Confess'd Judgment agreeable as Pr Specialty With a Stay of
Execution Untill the first of January next with Costs of suit.

Ordered that letters of Administration Do Issue to MARGARET LOVE & JOHN
LOVE on the estate of JAMES LOVE Deceased the Securities are EDWARD
ROGERS, ISRAEL MOORE, & JOHN ASHLEY.

SARAH HUTCHINS vs LEWIS & THO'S DINKINS.   The Depositions of NACEY
GILLASPIE & RICHARD COLEMAN in this Case to be taken & Read on the tryal
by Consent in Case they Cant be present.

Ordered that WILLIAM MOUNCE do Receive letters Testamentary in behalf of
his Wife Who Was left Executrix of JAMES DOUGLAS deceased.

A motion was made to Reverse the Probate of the Nuncupitive Will of SAMUEL
BELTON deceased upon the affidavit of ZACHARIAH THOMSON that the Copy of
the Summons issued in this Case Was not left at his house Untill the first Day
of the Present Term as he is told and verily Believes that he was then from
home & did not return Untill late last Night that he had No Notice there of
Untill he did Return & That DANIEL PAYNE & RACHAEL BELTON Who pressed
for the said Probate knew that he was so from home & had no Notice.

The Court refused to grant the said Motion Whereupon the said ZACH'Y
THOMPSON enters an appeal from Said Judgement or Sentence to the Court of
Common Pleas of Camden District.

[Page 140]

DUNCAN McRA & C'o vs ARTHUR MASSY.   Case.   Ordered that a Dedimus Do
Issue to take Examination of FREDERICK FELTS for the Plaintiff and _____
MASSY for the Defendant.

Ordered ZACHARIAH THOMSON Having Retun'd his Citation Duly Published
Moved for letters of Administration on the Estate of SAM'L BELTON JUN'R
Deceased but the same being Cavatted it is therefore, Ordered that the Same Do
Stand Over Untill the Right of Administration Be Determined.

DAVID BUSH & C'o vs JOSEPH MARTIN.   S. P. Ordered that this Writ be
Quashed.

JO. SINGLETON vs JOHN LOCKART.   S. P. Decree as P Specialty With Costs of
Suit.

JAMES PIERSON vs JOSEPH McCOY.   S. P. Decree as Pr Specialty With Costs
of Suit.

Ordered that JOHN COATS be taken as a Security in the room of PETER CRIM
on the administration of JAMES SCOTT's Estate.

[Page 141] 3 March 1794

JOSEPH WADE vs SAMUEL TYNES. S. P. L9:2. the Defendant in this Case Wish'd it to be tryed by a Jury the Following Jurors were Impanel'd and Sworn to wit.

1 ALEXANDER C. CORRUTH, 2 JOHN COATS, 3 PETER CRIM, 4 DAVID RUSSEL, 5 FRANCIS BELL, 6 W'M KEMP, 7 ANTHONY PRESTLES, 8 GEORGE PERRY, 9 JACOB CHAMBERS, 10 JOHN NIXON, 11 DAVID SAUNDERS, 12 JAMES SHARPLIN.

We find for the Plaintiff Nine Pounds two Shillings Sterling With Costs of Suit. ALEX'R C. CARRUTH, Foreman.

Ordered that letters of Administration do Issue to MARTHA NARRIMORE & JOHN NARRIMORE on the estate of EDWARD NARRIMORE the Securities are WILLIAM DEASON and W'M MIRES.

ANDREW BASKINS vs JOHN NARRIMORE. S. P. Decree for Plaintiff as P Specialty With Costs of Suit.

[Page 142]

Ordered that JOHN BROWN, Cap't GEO. ROSS, W'M COOKE & SAMUEL SLOAN or any three of them be appraisers of JAMES LOVEs Estate & That on the appraisement Bill being returned to the Clerk an order issue for the sale of the personal property on a Credit till the 19'th November next the purchasers giving Security for payment.

ANDREW BASKINS vs JAMES ROBINSON. P & S. Trover. Judgment confessed for Costs & the Defendant agrees to give up the Gun immediately on which the process is brought.

The Court Adjourned Untill to Morrow 10 OClock. BUR. BOYKIN.

4 March 1794. Agreeable to Adjournment the Court Met. Present BURWELL BOYKIN Esq'r.

Ordered that letters of Administration Do Issue to FRANCIS BOYKIN on all and Singular the goods and Chattels Rights and Credits of JEFFERSON RAINS.

[Page 143]

Ordered that the Estrays that have been legally advertised be Sold this Day.

Extx ATKINS vs NICHOLAS ROBINSON. S. P. Decree as P Specialty & Account With Costs of Suit Stay Exc't Untill further Orders.

JOSEPH SINGLETON vs W'M INGRAM. S. P. Pr Note. Decree for Seven Pounds With Costs of Suit.

DAVID BUSH vs W'M YOUNG of B. Creek. S. P. Dcree as Pr Specialty With Costs of Suit. Stay Execution two Months.

ABRAM CHILDERS vs BRYAN SPRADLEY et al. S. P. Decree for Plaintiff as Pr Specialty.

Ordered that the Property Distrained in this Case be Sold to Satisfy the Execution.

DAVID HUNTER vs SAMUEL TYNES. S. P. Decree as P Specialty With Costs of Suit.

[4 March 1794]

JESSE REAVES vs JOHN COATS. S. P. Decree as P Specialty the Tobacco to be Valued at 20/ PCt With Int. & Costs of Suit. [entire entry stricken]

THOMAS BALLARD vs JAMES GUNN. S. P. Judgement Confess'd as Pr Specialty Stay of Execution three Months With Costs of Suit.

JOSEPH COATS vs JAMES GUNN & THOMAS SMYRL. S. P. Decree for Plaintiff agreeable to Specialty With Costs of Suit.

[Page 144]

JESSE REAVES vs JOHN COATES. S. P. Judgement for the Pltff. the tobacco assessed @ 20/3 P Cwt. & The Account 5/5 allowed the Discount L3.15 to be deducted & calculation of Int according to the Note & Payment the Pltf to pay the Costs.

Ordered that all Recognizance be laid Over untill the Next Jury Court.

The last Will & testament of WILLIAM WELSH dec'd was proved in Open Court by the Oaths of JACOB GRAY & JESSE HAYES and ordered to be recorded & THO'S WELCH returned a Citation to shew Cause why letters of Administration should not be granted with the Will Annexed. MATHIS in behalf of SHEROD GREY Objected thereto because he the said SHEROD GRAY was Named in the Will as Executor & because as he alledged that the testators Mansion house & last Place of Residence was in the County of Lancaster in Which he meant to Qualify as Executor on behalf of THOMAS WELSH it was objected that SHEROD GREY lived out of this State & Therefore Ought to give Security he further Alledged that the said Mansion house Was Within this County. But the Court thought it a Matter of too great importance to be decided by One Judge and therefore gave no Judgement.

[Page 145]

THOMAS JINKINS vs W'M BRUMMET. S. P. on acco't. Brown for the Pltf: BREVARD for the Def'dt. Decree for the Plaintiff according to the Account With Int. Defendents account of five Dollars to be admitted as a Set off.

DANIEL BROWN vs HUGH McDOWEL. S. P. Judgment by Default.

THOMAS CREIGHTON vs PHILEMON HILLARD, JOHN GREYHAM, ANDREW GRAYHAM & JAMES SIMPSON. Debt. Judgment by Default.

Ordered that the Sherifs Account amounting to Fourteen Pounds thirteen Shillings be paid as P Account Rendered; and the Clerks be paid Ten Pounds as Pr Account.

Ordered that the following Rules and Orders be Established in the County Court of Kershaw Untill altered by the Court & that all Officers of the Court Strictly Observe the same.

1. That the Clerk keep an Execution Docket made Out in proper Form in Which shall be Particularly entered all Executions issuing out of his Office & The returns of the Sheriff of the Same also all Judgement shall be therein entered Whereon Ex'ons are Stayed.

2. the Sheriff shall make his return on Oath at Large of all Executions in his hands to the Clerk two Days before the Meeting of the Court in Order that the Same May be entered on the Ex'on Docket. Which shall each day be brought into Court with the Other Dockets & kept for the Inspection of the Parties.

[Page 146] 4 March 1794

3'rd. There Shall be a Separate Exo'n Docket for State Causes to be Kept in the same manner in Which shall be entered all fines & forfeitures and monies rec'd for Tavern licence, Estrays or Otherwise for the Use of the County.

4. All Causes ended in Court from either of the Dockets shall immediately after the Adjournment thereof be transferred to the Execution Docket Whether Execution issues or Not and in all Causes Where Judgements are Obtained it Shall be the Duty of the Clerk to Issue Exo'n of Course Unless directed to the Contrary by the Party Obtaining Such Judgement or his Attorney.

The Court adjourned Untill the next Court of Course at 10 OClock. BUR. BOYKIN.

The Court Met agreeable to Adjournment. May 7'th 1794. Present. IS. DUBOSE.

[Page 147]

Ordered that letters of Administration With the Will annexed do issue to THOMAS WELSH to execute the Last Will & Testament of W'M WELCH Deceased, the Surviving Exor appointed in the Will having declined Qualifying to Execute the said Will ANDREW BASKINS & JAS. WILLIAMS approved of by the Court as Securitys for THO'S WELSH to Execute said Will.

Ordered that Letters of Administration do issue to M'rs MARY LOWRIE on the estate of HENRY LOWRIE deceased. EDWARD COLLINS & JAMES WHREN approved of by the Court as Securitys.

MARTHA NARRAMORE and JOHN NARRAMORE having Returned the appraisement of the Estate of EDWARD NARRAMORE deceased ordered that the said Be filed. Ordered that Estate of EDWARD NARRAMORE be sold on a Credit till 1'st day of January 1795.

ANDREW BASKINS, THOMAS WELSH & Others having complained to the Court that the Road laid out by order of the Court of Lancaster & since worked on by order of Kershaw Court called MARSHALLS & KIMBALLS Road cannot be made passable as every fresh will Distroy any work that May be put on it & further that two other Roads the one called CANNINGTONS Road Including BELTONS Road & the other called TYNES's road which are now Public Roads, will answer every good purpose intended by the said Road Ordered therefore that the said Road first described shall not be any longer considered as a publick Road.

[Page 148]

Ordered that a Warrant of Appraisement do issue to WILLIAM DOBY, SAMUEL TYNES & SAMUEL JONES & JAMES BASKINS to appraise the estate of WILLIAM WELSH deceased & a due Return thereof be made to our next County Court.

The Court adjournd to Thursday 8'th Ins't at 10 Oclock. IS. DUBOSE.

May 8th. The Court according to Adjournment Present. IS. DUBOSE.

Ordered that JA'S WILLIAMS administrator to the Estate of JAMES TOLAND have Permission to sell the Moveable Property of said Estate on a Credit of Three Months.

Orderd that ARCH'D WATSON Exor do sell the Personal Estate of THO VAUGHAN on a Credit of Two Years.

Orderd that the administratrix of WILLIAM EVANS's Estate do Sell immediately such a Part of the Personal Property of the said dec'd as will satisfye the debts Due by Said Estate on the Credit of Six Months.

The Court adjournd to the 7'th August Next. IS. DUBOSE.

[Page 149] August Term 1794

GRAND JURY. Drawn from Box N'o 1 to N'o 2.

1 JOHN PEACH, 2 JOSEPH THOMSON, 3 DAN'L PEAK, 4 HENRY HUDSON, 5 W'M JONES SEN'R, 6 JAMES PERRY 25 M. C., 7 W'M DUNNAVAN, 8 ROB'T DUNVILE, 9 ARTHUR GREYHAM, 10 SAM'L JONES, 11 W'M DUNLAP, 12 W'M REYNOLDS, 13 W'M CLANTON, 14 JOHN BOYKIN, 15 JOHN O. QUIN, 16 RICH'D HOLLY, 17 SION COATES, 18 JAMES SIMPSON, 19 JOSIAH SAUNDERS, 20 SAM'L SLONE.

PETIT JURY DRAWN FROM BOX N'o to N'o 4.

1 W'M SAUNDERS JUN'R, 2 MOSES AYRES, 3 W'M SCARBOROUGH, 4 W'M GREYHAM, 5 THOMAS MILLS, 6 JOHN TWADDLE, 7 JAMES SHARPLIN, 8 ROB'T GARDNER, 9 JOHN McKEE, 10 ALEX'R McKEE, 11 SAM'L McKEE, 12 W'M MCGILL, 13 AMBROSE BRYANT, 14 JN'O KING, 15 ROBERT FORD, 16 THOMAS DURING, 17 W'M SUTTON, 18 JOHN GRAVES, 19 JAMES WREN, 20 NATH'L JONES, 21 HUGH McLESTER, 22 JN'O ROBINSON B. C., 23 ARTHUR MASSY, 24 JAMES BASKINS, 25 THO'S GARDNER, 26 LEWIS COOK, 27 JOHN KILE, 28 JAMES BELVILE, 29 JACOB SHIVER, 30 JA'S TRANTHAM.

Agreeable to Adjournment the Court Met. Present JOH KERSHAW, ISAAC DUBOSE & BURWELL BOYKIN, Esq'r.

[Page 150]

Ordered that the Following persons be appointed Overseers of the Several Districts of Road Within the County Untill the Next May Court & that all Overseers of the Roads now & hereafter to be appointed do make returns twice in the year viz, to November & May Courts.

DANIEL PEAK vice, JOHN RUTLEDGE, JOHN DINKINS, W'M NETTLES, SAM'L SMITH, THO'S CREIGHTON, JAMES ROSS, BEN'J CARTER, JA'S WILLIAMS, JESSE MINTON, W'M MALONE, JOHN LISSENBY, THO'S KELLY, ARCH'D WATSON, MICHAEL BARNET, WYLY COLLINS, ROBERT MAHAFFY to take all the hands on both Sides hanging Rock late NARRIMORES as well as those before liable, GEORGE KING, DANIEL MONNAHAN hands on East Side of Creek late NARRIMORES in addition to those liable before, JAMES CARN, ALEXANDERR STEWART, ANDERW A. HILL, ISAAC ROSS, JACOB CHERRY, ABRAM SHIVER, THOMAS ENGLISH, THO'S LENORE, THO'S DINKINS, JAMES LOVE, DAVID HUNTER, JAMES COWSART, GEORGE ROSS, MICH'L GANTER, JA'S WILLIAMS, ROB'T FORD, JOHN COOK JUN'R, PATRICK McCAIN, FRANCIS BELL, LEWIS COOK, W'M TWADDLE, LEWIS COLLINS, JOHN LOCKART, BERY KING, W'M CATO, REUBIN PATTERSON, THOMAS VAUGHAN, ANDREW LESTER, WILLIS WHITAKER, DAN'L O.QUIN JUN'R, JACOB SHIVER.

[Page 151]

JAMES TRANTHAM vs LARK SINGLETON & PHILLIP KING. Case.

On Motion Ordered that a Commission do Issue to take the Deposition of JAMES CAMPBELL That the Same be read in Evidence in this case.

Ordered that letters of administration Do Issue to GEORGE BARNES on the estate of FIELDING WOODROOF Deceased, Securities DAVID BUSH & ISAAC ALEXANDER, Esq'rs.

And to WILLIAM MASSEY JUNIOR & JAMES MARSHALL JUN'R on the estate of COL'O JOHN MARSHALL Deceased, Securities ANDREW BAKINS & GEORGE EVANS.

Mr's JOHNSON a Widow Comeing into Court Disguised in Liquor & behaving very insoltently & contemptuous in the face of the Court Was Ordered to be committed to Gaol Untill sun set.

On the Petition of RICHARD DRAKEFORD & ISRAEL MOORE Ordered that ESTHER COOKE Adm'r of JOHN COOK Deceased do appear before this Court on the 10'th ins't to answer their Complaint

[Page 152]

Ordered that letters of Administration Do Issue to DANIEL HORTEN on the estate of AVERET HOUSE Deceased the Securities are JAMES MARSHALL SEN'R Esq'r & JOHN O.QUIN.

DANIEL BROWN appeared and Caveat the Adminstration of GEORGE GARNS on the Estate of FIELDING WOODROOFs.

ORDERED that JOHN PLUNKET, HENRY KENT, HENRY ROTTENBURY & M'rs FLIN Do Receive the Pensions as heretofore allowed by Court Monthly Untill Next May Court.

After the Minutes being Read the Court Adjourn'd Untill toMorrow Nine OClock. BUR'L BOYKIN, JOHN KERSHAW, IS DUBOSE.

8 August 1794. Agreeable to adjournment the Court Met. Present JOHN KERSHAW, BURWELL BOYKIN, ISAAC DUBOSE, Esq'r.

[Page 153]

Ordered that Whenever Returns are hereafter made by Overseers of the Roads, the Clerk shall cause a list of Defaulters to be posted up at the Court house door to continue there during the Setting of the Court, Requiring them to appear at the Next Subsequent Court of Police to Shew Cause Why they should not be fined agreeable to Law, and shall also return to the Court the names of those Overseers Who may have Neglected Making Returns.

And that all Matters & things Relative to Roads & Overseers of them shall in future be Kept in a Seperate book other than the Minuets, Which shall also be read & Signed before adjournment on the several days of holding Court by the presiding Judges & that the Foregoing Orderes be Carried into immediate effect.

Ordered that letters of Administration do Issue to THOMAS PRESTWOOD on the estate of AUGUSTINE PRESTWOOD Deceased, the Securities are JOHN WILLA & BRYAN SPRADLEY.

JACOB CHERRY vs JOHN DINKINS. Debt. Judgement Confess'd agreeable as Pr Specialty With Costs of Suit Stay Exon 1 Decem'r Next.

JONATHAN BARNS vs HENRY VELLENDINGHAM. Debt. Dismiss'd at Defendts Costs by his Consent.

[Page 154]

The Grand Jury being Call'd and Impannel'd are as follows

1 JOHN ADAMSON foreman, 2 JOHN DINKINS, 3 JAMES MARSHALL, 4 WILLIAM NETTLES, 5 WILLIAM PARKER, 6 PHILLIP PLATT, 7 WILLIAM COOK, 8 JAMES BROWN SEN'R, 9 ANDREW NUTT JUN'R, 10 JAMES BROWN JUN'R, 11 ALEX'R ARCHER, 12 MICHAEL GANTER, 13 ISAAC KNOX.

State vs WILLIAM ROBINSON. Assault. A true Bill. JOHN ADAMSON, Foreman.

State vs JOSEPH McCOY. Stealing a Steer. True Bill. JOHN ADAMSON, Foreman.

LION & LEVY vs THOMAS CREIGHTON. Case. Judgement Confess'd for ten Pounds sterling Stay Execution Untill the 1 Jan'y Next.

After the Minutes being Read the Court Adjourn'd Untill Nine OClock. IS. DUBOSE, JOHN KERSHAW, BUR'L BOYKIN.

Agreeable to adjournment the Court Met. Present JOHN KERSHAW, ISAAC DUBOSE, Esq'rs.

[Page 155] 9 August 1794

JOHN NELON vs JOHN BOLEN. Debt. Judgement agreeable as P Specialty Plea With Drawn.

JAMES PEIRSON vs W'M BALLARD. Debt. Judgement Confess'd for teh amount of the Note & In't With Costs of Suit Execution Not to be levied Untill 25 Decem'r next.

JOHN McCAA vs W'M BALLARD. S. P. Judgement Confess'd for L 7 12/11 With In't & Costs of Suit. Exo'n not to be levied untill 25 December next.

THOMAS GARDNER vs W'M BALLARD & THOMAS BALLARD. S. P. Judgment Confess'd as P Specialty with In't. Execution not to be levied untill the 25th Decem'r next.

GABRIEL GUNN vs JOHN PATTERSON. S. P. Decree for Five Pounds and Interest With Costs of Suit.

REUBIN COLLINS vs JAMES GUNN. Debt. Judgement Confessed for Twelve Pounds Sixteen Shillings With Costs of Suit.

State vs GERSHAM CHAPMAN. Felony. [entry stricken]

[Page 156]

Ordered that the Estate of HENRY LOWREY be Sold after a Months Notice on Six Months Credit.

Grand Jury 1 JOHN ADAMSON foreman, 2 JOHN DINKINS, 3 JAMES MARSHALL, 4 W'M NETTLES, 5 WILLIAM PARKER, 6 PHILLIP PLATT, 7 W'M COOK, 8 JAMES BROWN SEN'R, 9 ANDREW NUTT JUN'R, 10 SAMUEL LEVY, 11 ALEX'R ARCHER, 12 MICHAEL GANTER, 13 ISAAC KNOX.

State vs JACOB CHAMPION. Hog Stealing. No Bill. JOHN ADAMSON, foreman.

State vs GURSHAM CHAPMAN. Felony. A True Bill. JOHN ADAMSON, foreman.

DAVID COATES vs JOHN HARVELL. Att. Order'd that award be made Absolute.

ROBERT HENRY vs HENRY MOOES & ISAAC ROSS. Debt. Dismissed at Defd'ts Costs.

HUGH MILLIN vs NICHOLAS ROBINSON. Debt. Judgement as P Specialty With Costs of Suit.

HUGH YOUNG vs ROGER GIBSON. Debt. Dismissed at Defd't Costs.

[9 August 1794]

BURWELL BOYKIN vs BRYANT SPRADLEY. Debt. Dismissed at Defd't Costs.

[Page 157]

JON'N BELTON Surv'r of MCLEOD vs W'M STARKE. Case. Dismissed at Defd'ts Costs.

JON'N BELTON vs W'M STARKE. Case. Dismissed at Def'dts Costs.

JAMES BROWN & C'o vs SAMUEL WELLS. Ass'mt. Dismissed at Def'dts Costs.

JAMES BROWN & C'o vs W'M WELLS. Assm't. Dismissed at Def'dts Costs.

State vs CHARLES PRICE & HUGH McGEE. Hog Stealing. No Bill. JOHN ADAMSON, foreman.

State vs HENRY GREGG. Hog Stealing. A True Bill. JOHN ADAMSON, foreman.

W'M NETTLES In'dse of HELI HOWARD vs GEORGE PETERSON. Debt. Judgement Pr Specialty With Costs of Suit.

DAVID HUNTER vs DAVID ORR. Writ of Attachement. We the above named GEORGE MILLER & JAMES COWSAR Chosen arbitrators Do award to DAVID HUNTER three Pounds Seventeen Shillings & ten Pence N'o Carolina Currency at ten Shillings Pr Dollar or One Pound Sixteen & 3 1/2 d Sterling as appears to us on Evidence to be a Ballance Justly due s'd HUNTER by s'd ORR awarded by us this 20 Aug't 1793. GEORGE MILLER, JAMES COWSAR.

[Page 158]

Petit Jury Impannel'd & Sworn. 1 ZACHARIAH CANTEY foreman, 2 JAMES LOGAN, 3 W'M SHIVER, 4 JOHN PAYNE, 5 W'M CRAIG, 6 WILLIAM TILLER, 7 JOHN SWILLA, 8 JOHN SHIVER SEN'R, 9 JOSHUA DINKINS, 10 SAMUEL DOTY, 11 GEORGE BROWN, 12 JOSEPH TILLER.

State vs GERSHAM CHAPMAN. Felony. Guilty. ZACHARIAH CANTEY, Foreman.

GEORGE PERRY vs DAVID RUSSEL. Case. The Same Jury. We find for the Plaintiff Seven Pounds with Int from Jan'y 1790. Z. CANTEY, Foreman.

JOHN LOWRY N. C. vs Admi'x of JOHN LOWRY. Case. Discontinued.

JOHN LANGSTER vs WILLIAM HUDSON, HUGH BROWN. Case. Settled Plt'f is to pay Att'y & Clerks & Defend't the Rest of the Costs.

JOSIAH CANTEY vs JOSIAH SCOTT. Case.

Ordered that Commission Do Issue to take the Deposition of a Gentleman of the Barr in Charleston.

After the Minutes being Read the Court Adjourn'd Untill Nine OClock on Monday Next. BUR. BOYKIN, IS. DUBOSE, JOHN KERSHAW.

[Page 159]

11 August 1794. Agreeable to Adjournment the Court Met. Present JOHN KERSHAW, ISAAC DUBOSE, BURWELL BOYKIN, Esq'rs.

McRA & CANTEY vs JOSEPH SINGLETON. Judgement Confessed for L 15 s 2 d 9 with Costs of Suit Execution to Stay for three Months.

[11 August 1794]

Exor's of JOSEPH KERSHAW Vs JEFFRY HUDSON. Debt. Judgement Confessed for Ten Pounds with In't from the 27 March 1786 & Costs Execution to stay in the Sheriffs hands to the first of January Next allowing a payment made the 27 Sept'r 1786 on the Note for L 4 s 4 to be deducted.

HUGH YOUNG VS JAMES GUNN. S. P. Judgement for the amount of Note & Interest With Costs of Suit. Execution not to be levied for three months.

Exo'r CH'S McCAY vs JOSEPH McCOY. Debt. Judgement Confessed for L 237 Old Currency With Interest from the 1'st day of January 1777 With Costs of Suit.

1 ZACHARIAH CANTEY Foreman, 2 JAMES LOGAN, 3 WILLIAM SHIVER, 4 JOHN PAYNE, 5 SAM'L BREED, 6 WILLIAM TILLER, 7 JOHN SWILLA, 8 JOHN SHIVER SEN'R, 9 JOSHUA DINKINS, 10 SAMUEL DOTY, 11 GEORGE BROWN, 12 JOSEPH TILLER.

JAMES BROWN vs W'M YOUNG. G. Q. Case. We find for Plaintiff L 13 4/3 With Interest from the first of January 1793. ZAC'H CANTEY, foreman.

[Page 160]

State vs HENRY GREGG. Hogstealing. Ordered that the Defd't do Enter into Security of L 40 and two Securities of L 20 each.

The State vs SARAH JOHNSON. Bastardy. Ordered that Sciera Facias do Issue against her and Securities to appear at Next Court.

The State vs DORIS NEES. Hog Stealing. Recognizance to be Continued untill next Court REUBIN STARKE is Requested to bind Over the Witnesses.

The State vs JOSEPH McCOY. Stealing Steer.

Recognizance of the Prosecutor, Defendent & Security be Continued Untill Next Court.

DAVID BUSH vs W'M RANDOLPH. Writ. Att. Same Jury. We find for the Plaintiff L 30 5/ With Interest from the first of Jan'y 1794. ZAC'H CANTEY, foreman.

HUGH MCDOWL vs HENRY MOORE. Case. Same Jury. We find for the Plaintiff thirty six 8/ With In't from first of Jan'y 1793. Z. CANTEY, Foreman.

JAMES BROWN & C'o vs WILLIAM DOUD. Assm't. Same Jury. We find for the Plaintiff Eight pounds 14/4 With Interest from first of Jan'y on acco't 1793. Z. CANTEY, Foreman.

[Page 161]

ISAAC ROSS vs FREDERICK LAMB. Nonsuit for the Defendent With Costs of Suit.

JOHN BALLARD vs JOHN TAYLOR, DAVID RUSSELL. Debt. Judgement Confessed as Pr Specialty With Costs of Suit.

HENRY KENT vs LAZERUS KELLY, JAMES KELLY, ANNE KELLY. Debt. We find for Defendnets. ZACHARIAH CANTEY, Foreman.

DANIEL MCMILLAN vs JOHN NARROWMORE. S. P. Decree according to Specialty Six pounds and Interest from the first of January 1791 with Costs of Suit.

[11 August 1794]

DAVID BUSH & C'o vs WILLIAM DOUD, STEPHEN RIEVES. Case. We find for the Plaintiff L 31 10/5. Z. CANTEY, Foreman.

HAMPTON STROUD vs ZACHARIAH THOMSON. Trover. Dismissed at Pltfs. Costs.

DAVID BUSH vs JOHN TAYLOR. Debt. Judgement Confessed as P Specialty With Costs of Suit.

JOHN CHESNUT vs W'M WARE. Debt. The Same Jury. We find for the Plaintiff Twenty Guineas With Int. from the 11 Feb'y 1794. Z. CANTEY, Foreman.

[Page 162]

DAVID BUSH vs TAURENCE CONNER. Debt. Judgement by Default.

JOHN CHESNUT vs JOHN HOOD. Debt. Settled at the Defendents Costs.

DAVID BUSH vs JA'S RUSSELL. Debt. Judgement by Default.

JOHN FRANCIS WOLFE vs SAM'L DOTY. Debt. Judgement Confessed as P Specialty With Costs of suit.

ISAAC ALEXANDER vs PETER McKERNAN. Att. Dismissed.

BURWELL BOYKIN vs W'M MIRES. Debt. Dismissed at the Defendents Costs.

W'M McKEE vs WALTER SHROPSHIRE. Debt. We find for the Plaintiff L 17 s 6 With Interest from the first of Nov'r 1785. Z. CANTEY, Foreman.

JAMES BROWN & C'o vs HEZ. LOVE. Ass'mt. We find for the Plaintiff L 2 14/10. Z. CANTEY, Foreman.

JON'N BELTON vs WILLIAM DUNNAVANT. S. P. Decree as P Specialty With Costs.

[Page 163]

Camden O. Society vs RICHARD KING. Appeal. S. MATHIS on the part of th Plaintiff Suggests that two of the Judges of this Court are members of the Camden Orphan Society. therefore interested in the Event of this Suit & incompetent to try the same and thereupon prays that he may be allowed to carry the said Appeal up to the District Court. Ordered that the same be granted.

The Minutes being read the Court adjourned untill tomorrow morning Nine OClock. JOHN KERSHAW, IS. DUBOSE. BUR. BOYKIN.

12 Aug't 1794. Agreeable to Adjournment the Court met. Present JOHN KERSHAW, ISAAC DUBOSE, BURWELL BOYKIN, Esq'rs.

Ordered that letters of Administration With the Will annexed on the Estate of SAMUEL BELTON JUN'R Do Issue to DANIEL PAYNE he having been Qualified According to Law to Execute Said Will the Securities approved of by the Court for his faithful Administration are ARCHIBALD WATSON & JOHN SWILLEY.

[Page 164] 12 August 1794

1 ZACHARIAH CANTEY Foreman, 2 JAMES LOGAN, 3 WILLIAM SHIVER, 4 JOHN PAYNE, 5 SAM'L BREED, 6 WILLIAM TILLER, 7 JOHN SWILLEY, 8 JOHN SHIVER SEN'R, 9 JOSHUA DINKINS, 10 SAMUEL DOTY, 11 GEORGE BROWN, 12 WILLIAM CRAIG.

JOHN RUSSEL vs JOHN SANGSTER. Att. We find for the Plaintiff L 43. Z. CANTEY, Foreman.

WILLIAM RICHARDSON appeared in Open Court and Qualified as Executor to the last Will & Testament of WILLIAM RICHARDSON late of the High hills Deceased Which Will has been Proved and Recorded in the Office of the Ordinary of the District of Camden.

DAN'L CARPENTER vs JAMES BROWN JU'R &C. S. P. Dismissed at Defd'ts Costs.

LION & LEVY vs THOMAS WHITAKER. Appeal. Dismissed at the Defendents Costs Except the Plaintiffs paying his Attorney.

Ordered that JOHN SAUNDERS, WILLIAM NETTLES and ARCHIBALD WATSON be taken as Securities on the administration of ESTHER COOK in the Room of RICHARD DRAKEFORD & ISRAEL MORE and that the Bond of Said Drakeford & Moore be given up.

[Page 165]

JOHN LOCKHART vs JAMES HARRIS. On attachment. In this case the attachment was levied on a stud horse in the custody and keeping of Mr. ARCHIBALD WATSON. On Motion in behalf of said WATSON it was permitted him go into Evidence before the Jury to prove his account against said HARRIS. And the Jury having found that said HARRIS is indebted to the said WATSON the sum of L 7 s 19 d 6 for keeping the said horse, previously to the attachment levied on him. It was Ordered that the Sheriff do keep in his hands out of the proceeds arising from the sale of the said horse, the said sum of L 7 s 19 d 6 to be subject to the future order and direction of this Court.

1 SAM'L DOTY foreman, 2 GEORGE BROWN, 3 JOHN SWILLEY, 4 SAM'L BREED, 5 W'M SHIVER, 6 W'M CRAIG, 7 JOHN SHIVER, 8 JOHN PAYNE, 9 W'M TILLER, 10 JOSEPH TILLER, 11 JOSHUA DINKINS, 12 JAMES LOGAN.

PETER OSGOOD vs HUGH McDOWL. Debt. We find for the Defendent With costs of Suit. SAM'L DOTY, Foreman.

[Page 166]

REA & DaCOSTA Sur'vrs of NELSON vs WILLIAM BRUMMET. S. P. Dismissed at Plaintiffs Costs.

ISAAC DaCOSTA Vs WILLIAM BRUMMET. S. P. Dismissed at Plaintiffs Costs.

JOHN ROBINSON vs W'm VELLINDINGHAM. Debt. Dismissed at Defendents Costs.

W'M KIRKLAND vs REUBIN HARRISON. S. P. Ordered that the Deposition of MOSELEY COLLINS be taken and the same be Allowed in Evidence on this Tryal.

GEORGE WAIN vs ARCH'D WATSON. S. P. Dismissed the Defendent to pay his Attorney the Plaintiff pay the Remaining Costs.

[12 August 1794]

WILLIAM COWSAR vs WILLIAM BRUMMETT. S. P. Decree for Plaintiff as P Specialty the Tobacco at 9/4 P C't to Draw Interest from the 1 Decem'r 1792 With Costs of Suit.

JAMES HUNTER vs LAZERUS KELLY. Judgement by Default as pr Specialty With Costs of Suit.

JOHN SANDERS vs HENRY HUDSON. Appeal. Judgement Reversed.

JOHN STARKE vs HARTWELL MEKIN. S. P. Ordered that a Commission Do Issue to take the Deposition of JAMES MUNTFORD in Georgia.

HUGH YOUNG vs JOSHUA WATSON. S. P. Decree as Pr Specialty With Costs of Suit.

[Page 167]

ZACHARIAH HESTER vs JAMES GUNN. S. P. Decree as P Specialty With Costs of Suit the Tobacco at 10/ P Ct.

WILLIAM DANZA vs JESSE MINTON. S. P. Decree as P Specialty With Costs of Suit. Stay Exo'n three months.

ROBERT DOVE vs CHARLES McGINNEY. S. P. Decree as P Specialty With Costs of Suit. Stay of Execution three Months.

JAMES PIERSON vs JESSE MINTON. S. P. Decree as Pr Specialty With Costs of Suit. Stay of Exo'n three Months.

JON'N BELTON vs RUSH HUDSON. S. P. Judgement by Default.

The Court then adjourned untill tomorrow at Nine O'Clock. JOHN KERSHAW, IS. DUBOSE.

Agreeable to Adjournment the Court met. Present ISAAC DUBOSE, BURWELL BOYKIN, Esq'rs.

Ordered that the Estate of AUGUSTINE PRIESTWOOD be Sold after Due Notice and a Credit given Until the first of Next April.

[Page 168] 13 August 1794.

1 ZACHARIAH CANTEY foreman, 2 GEORGE BROWN, 3 SAMUEL DOTY, 4 JOSEPH TILLER, 5 SAM'L BREED, 6 W'M SHIVER, 7 JOHN PAYNE JUN'R, 8 JAMES LOGAN, 9 W'M TILLER, 10 WILLIAM CRAIG, 11 JOHN SHIVER, 12 JOSHUA DINKINS.

JOHN McKINNIE vs Ex'or of JOHN BELTON. Case. We find for the Plaintiff Sixteen pounds 16/ With In't from 26th March 1794. Z. CANTEY, foreman.

State vs GERSHAM CHAPMAN. Felony. On Motion Ordered that the Verdict in this Case be Set Aside and a New Tryal Granted.

W'M HIDE vs JOHN HOLZENDORF. Att. Discontinued.

BRYANT SPRADLEY vs JOHN WILSON. Att. It is the Opinion of the Court that the Order for the Sale of the land levied on is illegal Since the Establishment of this County several other cases of a similar Nature have Occurred, in not one of Which any appearance has been entered & From the Want of a proper investigation of the Subject Before, the Court have on all of them given Judgement & an Order for the sale of the Land, they now are of Opinion the Judgement be Reversed.

[13 August 1794]

1 ZACHARIAH CANTEY foreman, 2 GEORGE BROWN, 3 SAMUEL DOTY, 4 JOSEPH TILLER, 5 SAM'L BREED,6 W'M SHIVER, 7 JOHN PAYNE JUN'R, 8 JAMES LOGAN, 9 WILLIAM TILLER, 10 WILLIAM CRAIG, 11 JOHN SHIVER, 12 JOHN SWILLA.

SARAH HUTCHINS vs LEWIS & THO'S DINKINS. Trespass. We find for the Plaintiff s 40 & costs of Suit. Z. CANTEY, foreman.

[Page 169]

In the Case of the Securities to the Administration of COOKEs Estate. ARCHIBALD WATSON not haveing entered Security Yesterday to relieve the former Securities, Ordered that the Administration to the WIDOW COOKE be revoked & committed to RICHARD DRAKEFORD & That he take Possession of the Estate of the Deceased & Make sale thereof on a Credit till the 1st of Jan'y Next giveing three Weeks publick Notice of such sale in the most publick places in the County & That he be Sworn in before the Clerk.

This Order to be Void on Condition that the WIDOW COOKE Within Six Days enter two Good Securities to be approved by the Clerk & One of the Judges for her faithful Administration and in that Case the Bond of MOORE & DRAKEFORD to be Given up.

Ordered that the following persons be & they are hereby appointed Constibles for the ensuing twelve months: GEORGE BROWN, THOMAS PRESTWOOD, JAMES BOWLES & WILLIAM NETTLES JUN'R.

The minutes being read the Court adjourned untill tomorrow Nine O'Clock. JOHN KERSHAW, IS. DUBOSE.

The Court met agreeable to adjournment. Present JOHN KERSHAW, ISAAC DUBOSE & BURWELL BOYKIN, Esq'rs.

[Page 170] 14 August 1794.

JOHN McKINNEY Vs Exo'r of JOHN BELTON. Case. On Motion of the Defd'ts Attorney for a New Tryal, a New Tryal Granted on the Defendents paying the Costs of Suit.

WILLIAM LANG vs FREDERICK ROBINSON. Case. We find for the Plaintiff L 8 d 6 with Costs of Suit. Z. CANTEY, foreman.

THOMAS GARDNER vs WILLIAM BALLARD, THOMAS BALLARD. S. P. Judgement Confessed as P Specialty With In't the Tobacco to be Valued at s 10 with Costs of Suit.

JOSHUA ENGLISH vs THOMAS SMYRL. S. P. Judgement by Default as Pr Specialty With Costs of Suit.

JON'N BELTON vs SAM'L HOWZE. S. P. Judgement by Defaultas P Specialty With Costs of Suit.

Exors JOSEPH KERSHAW vs JAMES BROWN and SAMUEL BREED. Debt. Judgment by Confession. Note L 36.16.7 Interest from the 25th June 1787, to the 15 Feby 1791. ll:18:10. Discount admitted, Account 14.8.1. Interest on the Ballance. L 34: 7:4.

FRANCIS BOYKIN vs WILLIAM BRYANT, TURNER STARKE. Debt. We find for the Plaintiff L 35 with Interest from the 24th Novem'r 1793. Z. CANTEY, foreman.

[Page 171] 14 August 1794

MARY LEE vs WILLIAM LEE. Att: Judgement by Default according to Specialty. JOHN RASBERRY Was also Cal'd and Made Default Ordered that the Plaintiff have Judgement against him and that the personal Property be Sold.

Whereas the Order of Court made the 1st August 1792 Requiring persons haveing Estrays to Produce them on the first day of the Court at Which they ought to be Sold has been found Productive of too much expence, it is Ordered that hereafter the persons in Whose Possession they are Shall produce them on the last day of the Court.

1 SAMUEL DOTY foreman, 2 GEORGE BROWN, 3 JOSEPH TILLER, 4 SAM'L BREED, 5 W'M SHIVER, 6 JOHN PAYNE JUN'R, 7 JAMES LOGAN, 8 WILLIAM TILLER, 9 WILLIAM CRAIG, 10 JOHN SHIVER SEN'R, 11 JOHN SWILLEY, 12 WILLIAM YOUNG.

DUNCAN McRA & C'o vs ARTHUR MASSAY. Case. We find for the Plaintiff L 12 7/10 with In't from 1st Jan'y 1786. SAM'L DOTY, foreman.

1 ZACHARIAH CANTEY foreman, 2 GEORGE BROWN, 3 JOSEPH TILLER, 4 SAM'L BREED, 5 W'M SHIVER, 6 JOHN PAYN JUN'R, 7 JAMES LOGAN, 8 WILLIAM TILLER, 9 WILLIAM CRAIG, 10 JOHN SHIVER, 11 JOHN SWILLEY, 12 SAMUEL DOTY.

JAMES TRANTHAM vs LARK SINGLETON, PHILLIP KING. Case. We find for the Plaintiff L 16 6/8 With Interest from March 1793. Z. CANTEY, Foreman.

[Page 172]

WHITNEY WEST vs JOHN McCAA. S. P. Settled the Defendent paying his Attorney, the Plaintiff pays the remaining Costs.

SAMUEL TYNES vs JAMES HANNAH. Att. Judgement by Default, An Order of Sale for Personal Property.

The Exors of JOSEPH KERSHAW vs NICHOLAS ROBINSON. Judgement confessed on 4 Notes 1st dated Sept. 19, '89. 13. 11.10. Interest from date. 2nd dated Sept'r 19, 1789. Interest from date 13.11.10. 3rd dated Sep. 19, 1789. Interest from date 13.11.10. 4th dated Sep. 19, 1789. Interest from date 13.11.10. Payable at different times, the last payment to be four years after date.

JAMES TRANTHAM vs LARK SINGLETON, PHILLIP KING. Case. On motion of BENJAMIN PERKINS Ordered that an appeal be Granted on the Usual Terms.

In Consequence of the Extraordinary expence attending the Keeping of Estrays, liable to be sold on the last day of the Court, it is Ordered that all those Which are brought in be sold this day at four OClock & The Estray Cow in the Possession of DORIS NEES. The Remainder to be Sold to morrow at One OClock.

Ordered that the Orphan Child of JAMES CONDON Dec'd be allowed the same sum for Subsistance Pr. Month as formerly & That it Commence from the time the former Order Expired & Continue Untill next May Court.

RICHARD BERRY, GEORGE BROWN, & THOMAS PRESTWOOD appeared and were Sworn in Constibles for the Ensuing Year.

[Page 173]

The Minutes being first read the Court adjourned untill tomorrow ten O'Clock. BUR. BOYKIN, JOHN KERSHAW, IS. DUBOSE.

[15 August 1794]

The Court met according to adjournment. Present JOHN KERSHAW, ISAAC DUBOSE, Esq'r.

JAMES ROCHEL vs EDWARD COLLINS. S. P. Dismissed at Defendents Costs.

JOHN SWILLEY vs THOMAS SMIRREL. Case. Settled Costs equally Divided.

Ordered that JOHN PLUNKET, HENRY ROTTENBURY, HENRY KENT & Mrs FLIN [entry stricken]

DAVID BUSH vs JEREMIAH PARISH. Debt. Judgement by Default as Pr Specialty.

W'M CRAIG vs JAMES AYRES. Debt. Judgement by Default as Pr Specialty.

[Page 174]

The Sheriff of this County appointed JAMES BOWERS as One of his Deputies in the Office of Sheriff Which Said JAMES BOWLES was approved by the Court and Appeared & in Open Court took the Oath Prescribed by Law.

The Court adjourned Until the Seventh of November Next at 10 Oclock. IS. DUBOSE, JOHN KERSHAW.

November 7'th 1794. The Court met according to adjournment. Present JOHN KERSHAW, BURWELL BOYKIN, Esq'rs.

REBECCA, ELIZABETH, & FRANCES LEE, Infants the two former being upwards of fourteen years of Age came into Corut & Chose HENRY HORTON their Guardian as also for their Sister FRANCES LEE she being within the age of discretion. He was approved of by the Court. Whereupon it is ordered that he give bond in the Sum of L 120 Sterling for the faithful discharge of his trust.

[Page 175]

JAMES KERSHAW having by his Petition set forth that the present Landing on the South side of Camden Ferry is not so proper as if changed to about three hundred yards lower down the River.

Ordered thereon that THOMAS WHITAKER, ISAAC ROSS & JOSEPH KERSHAW be appointed Commissioners to fix on a place more porper than the present for a landing, and also for laying out the Road therefrom the nearest & Most convenient way to cross WRIGHTs branch agreeably to the prayer of the Petition.

Ordered that the sum of Eleven shillings per Month be allowed & paid to MARGARET WOODS, untill the next Court for the County for assisting in the maintenance of her two Children.

It being represented to the Court that two Estray Cattle in the Possession of PETER DUNLAP, cannot be brought before the Court House for Sale, Ordered thereon that the said PETER DUNLAP be considered the purchaser of them, on his giving a Note with security for the Ammount of the Sum to which they were appraised.

The Court then adjourned untill tomorrow ten O'Clock. JOHN KERSHAW, BUR. BOYKIN.

[Page 176] 8'th November 1794

Agreeable to Adjournment the Court Met. Present JOHN KERSHAW, ISAAC DUBOSE. Esq'rs.

Ordered that the Personal Estate, the Negroe Excepted, of SAMUEL BELTON JUN'R be sold after due Notice being Given on the Second Monday in December Next on a Credit of twelve Months.

JOSEPH THOMSON Administrator of the Estate of JAMES CAIN Deceased Rendered in an Account of Monies Received & Paid by him as Administrator it appears that the Property Sold for L 40: 1: 10. Amount of Debts due by the Estate 32: 01: 11. Ballance Remaining in his hands. 7: 19: 11. From Which Deduct Maintenance of the Child.

Ordered that the Estrays Which have been advertised the legal time be sold this afterNoon at four OClock.

It being represented to the Court by Several Respectable inhabitants of the County that the Estate of JOHN ALLEN Deceased has been & Still continued to be improperly & illegally Squandered & Destroyed to the great injury of his Children & That they are so destitute of Friends as not to be able to procure one Who is capable of Acting as a Guardian for them. Ordered that the Clerk of the Court be requested to apply to the County Attorney for his Advice and Assistance and that he take every legal Method in behalf of the Children to Preserve the Remaining Property and to Recover if Possible What has been improperly & Unlawfully applied and Disposed of & make a Report thereof at the Next Court.

[Page 177]

The Court then adjourned to February 7'th Next. IS. DUBOSE, JOHN KERSHAW.

FEBRUARY TERM 1795

Grand Jury Drawn from Box N'o 1 to N'o 2.

1 CHARLES McGINNEY, 2 JAMES RUSSELL, 3 JAMES CANTEY, 4 WILLIAM WARE, 5 GEORGE SANDER JUN'R, 6 ARCHIBALD McFEE, 7 MOSES FERGUSON, 8 JAMES DOUGLAS, 9 THOMAS SHROPSHIRE, 10 ELY KERSHAW, 11 ANDREW BASKINS, 12 JOSHUA ENGLISH SEN'R, 13 THOMAS STRICKLAND, 14 WILLIAM ANDERSON, 15 JOHN BALLARD, 16 CHARLES McLELAND, 17 HUGH McLESTER, 18 DAVID MARTIN, 19 FRANCIS WATTS, 20 JOHN RUSSELL.

Petit Jury Drawn from Box N'o 3 to N'o 4.

1 BURWELL EVANS, 2 NICHOLAS THOMSON, 3 JOHN TRANTHAM, 4 PATRICK LAYTON, 5 EPHRAIM CLANTON, 6 WALTER ROWE, 7 JOHN DENNIS, 8 JOHN JONES, 9 DILLARD COLLINS, 10 MOSES SANDERS big pond, 11 REUBIN ROBERTS, 12 LEWIS PERRY, 13 BENJAMIN MAJOR, 14 CHARLES PRESTLEY, 15 ARCHIBALD CARUTH, 16 WILLIAM PAYNE, 17 JOHN SUTTON, 18 RICHARD DRAKEFORD, 19 DRURY GOYEN, 20 JOHN GAYDEN, 21 ROB'T TRANTHAM, 22 W'M COOK G. Q., 23 ZACH DENSDILL, 24 ROB'T McCAIN, 25 JOHN RIDDLE, 26 ROB'T BARKLEY, 27 JOHN CHAMBERS, 28 SAM'L BRADFORD, 29 JN'O DICKSON, 30 BEN PARNELL.

[Page 178]

7th Feby 1795. Agreeable to Adjournment the Court Met. Present ISAAC DUBOSE Esq'r.

ISAAC KNOX vs READ HUTT. S. P. Judgement Confess'd for Ten Pounds Stay of Execution Two Months With Costs of Suit.

[7 February 1795]

JOHN ADAMSON vs BRYAN SPRADLEY & THOMAS SMERRIL. S. P. Judgement Confessed for L 7 s 10 d 6 with Costs of Suit.

JOHN RUSSELL vs THOMAS BRADFORD. S. P. Judgement Confessed for the Note & Interest With Costs of Suit.

Ordered that JOHN OQUIN do Receive letters of Administration on the estate of DANIEL HORTON Deceased the Securities are ANDREW SHIVER & JEREMIAH PARISH SEN'R.

Ordered that MARY HORTEN Do Receive letters of Administration on the estate of AVERET HOUSE Deceased the Securities are ANDREW SHERER and JEREMIAH PARISH SEN'R.

The Court Adjourned Untill Monday Next at 10 O'clock.. IS. DUBOSE.

Agreeable to Court Met. Present JOHN KERSHAW, ISAAC DUBOSE, Esq'rs.

[Page 179] 9 Feby 1795.

Ordered that letters Testamenry Do Issue to CATHARINE SMITH Executrix of JAMES SMITH Deceased.

WILLIAM CRAIG vs JOHN RUSSELL, HENRY HUDSON. Debt. Judgement Confessed for the amount of the Note & Interest with One half of the Cost of Suit.

JON'N BARNS vs EPHRAIM CLANTON, JOHN CLANTON. Debt. Judgement Confessd for the amount of Note & Int With Costs of Suit.

JOHN NAUDEN vs THOMAS HAWFIELD. Case. Judgement Confess'd for L 16 d 1 With Costs of Suit.

HUGH YOUNG vs ARCH'D WATSON. Case. Dismis't at Defend'ts Costs.

NATHANIEL RUSSELL vs JORDAN ASHLEY. Debt. Judgement Confess'd for L 16 s 2 d 11 with Costs of Suit.

DAVID BUSH vs RICHARD WILSON. Debt. Judgement Confess'd for the amount Note & Interest & Costs of Suit Deducting three Pounds P'd the 7th Jan'y 1795.

JOHN ADAMSON vs MATHEW BOWEN. Case. Judgement confess'd for L 12 s 11 d 9 With Costs of Suit.

JAMES TATE vs JACOB SHANDY. S. P. Dismiss'd at Defendents Costs.

SARAH YANCEY ex'ix JAMES YANCEY vs SAM'L TYNES. Debt. Judgement Confess't as Pr Specialty With Costs of Suit.

[Page 180]

BRYAN SPRADLEY vs DAVID LOGAN. Judgement Confess't for the amount of Note & In't With Costs of Suit.

Ordered that Letters of Administration Do Issue to DANIEL BROWN on the estate of THOMAS POLK Within this State Unadministered the Securities are BENJAMIN PERKINS & JOSEPH BREVARD.

Ordered that Letters of Administration Do Issue to ELIZABETH DOTY on the estate of SAMUEL DOTY Deceased.

[9 February 1795]

State vs GERSHAM CHAPMAN. Felony. The County Attorney has leave to Enter a Nole Presequi Upon the Defendents Paying the Costs.

W'M KIRKLAND vs REUBEN HARRISON. S. P. Decree for the Defendant With Costs.

W'M NETTLES vs GEORGE PETERSON. fi fa. Ordered that a Rule do Issue against the Sheriff to Shew Cause Why the Money levied in this Case should not be paid Over to Plaintiff.

McRA & CANTEY vs WILLIAM LAYTON. Debt. Judgement Confess't for L 24 s 18 With Interest from the first day of January last & Costs of Suit.

McRA & CANTEY & C'o vs W'M WATSON Ex'or of PETER CASITY deceased. Debt. Judgement Confess't for L 55 4/4 with Costs of Suit.

[Page 181]

McRA & CANTEY vs JESSE MINTON. Debt. Judgement Confess't for L 39 d 16 d 2 & Costs.

The Court Adjourned Untill To Morrow Ten OClock. BUR. BOYKIN, IS. DUBOSE.

Agreeable to Adjournment the Court Met. Present ISAAC DUBOSE, BURWELL BOYKIN, Esq'r.

The Copy of the last Will & Testament of JOHN DOUGHTY being produced in Open Court and approved of by the Court the Original being Destroyed Since the Death of the Testator, and the Destruction of Said Will being Proved to the Court, Ordered that the Copy thereof be Recorded, and that letters Testamentary do Issue to JOSHUA ENGLISH the Nominated Executor and JUDITH DOHERTY Ex'x of the Original, on all and Singular the goods & Chattels Rights & Credits of the said JOHN DOUGHERTY.

The Sheriff appeared to Shew Cause on the Rule Granted yesterday, and it appearing to the Court that two Elder Executions are in the hands of the Destrict Shf. One in favour of HUGH McDOWL & One in favour of JAMES CORBET; Ordered that they be first Satisfied according to their Priority, and the Ballance if any, be p'd Over to WILLIAM NETTLES against GEORGE PETERSON.

[Page 182]

Ordered that all the Recognizances Bound Over to this Court be laid Over Untill Next Court.

RICHARD LLOYD CHAMPION to whom was granted at the last Court Letters of Administration on the Estate of JOHN LLOYD CHAMPION deceased having since that time found a Will, appeared personally in Court and delivered up his Letters of Administration and prayed leave to qualify as Executor under the Will. Ordered that the Letters be received that the Bond given by him for the due administration of the sd. Estate be returned, and that he qualify as Executor under the Will.

JOHN McKINNIE vs Ex'or of JOHN BELTON. Fi fa. Ordered that the Execution be taken up and a New tryal Granted at the Next Court the fees being Paid.

JAMES P COOKE vs DOCT. JA'S MARTIN. Upon Motion heading the affid't of the Defendant Order'd that the Deposition of Col. WADE HAMPTON be taken de bene esse & to be read in Evidence at the Trial of this Cause in case the

Witness does not personally attend.

[Page 183] 10 Feb'y 1795.

Ordered that letters of administration do Issue to JOHN MAXWELL on the estate of WILLIAM MAXWELL, the Securities THOMAS DICKSON.

Ordered that letters of Administration do Issue to ANN BROWN on the Estate of DOCTOR THOMAS BROWN and that the Clerk Administer the Oath and take Security for One hundred Pounds.

Ordered that JACOB LEWIS PERRY and DANIEL HARKINS be & they are hereby appointed Appraisers to appraise the estate of JOHN DOUGHERTY deceased; and also that the Cattle belonging to the said Estate be sold on the second Monday in May next, on a Credit of three months. And that all the rest of the personal estate of the said deceased, except such part as is Specifically devised by the Will, be sold on Wednesday the third day of March next on a Credit of three months.

Ordered that letters of Administration do Issue to DANIEL BROWN on FIELDING WOODROOFs Estate the Securities are ISAAC ALEXANDER & DAVID BUSH.

NATHANIEL RUSSELL vs JOHN ASHLEY. On Motion of the Plaintiffs Attorney, Ordered that the Defendent do give Special Bail.

NATHANIEL RUSSEL vs W'M STOKES. S. P. Judgement Confess'd for L 5 s 2 d 16 & Interest from 1st July last With Costs of Suit.

[Page 184]

NATH'L RUSSELL Indorsee of DAVID BUSH vs W'M KIRKLAND. Debt. Judgement Confess'd for L 9 s 11 Sterling and Interest from 28th May 1792 stay Ex'tion Until 7th Augt 1795.

ADAM THOMSON vs JAMES RUSSELL. S. P. Decree for the Note and Interest With Costs.

The Court then Adjourned Untill Tomorrow Ten O'Clock. JOHN KERSHAW, BUR. BOYKIN., IS. DUBOSE.

Agreeable to adjournment the Court met. Present ISAAC DUBOSE.

JOHN REID vs ARCH'D WATSON. S. P. Judgement by Default for L 6 and Interest from 27th March 1793 With Costs of Suit.

WILLIAM AGLENTON vs JEREMIAH SIMMONS. Ordered that a reule do issue on the Defendant to shew cause here at Next Court why the Judgment he has obtained against BRYAN SPRADLEY upon the Pltffs note should not belong to the Defendant and the note delivered up. And it is also Ord'd that in the Mean time the execution be stayed, and that BRYAN SPRADLEY be forbidden to pay the Note & Judgment to said SIMMONS.

[Pgae 185] 11 Feby 1795

NATHANIEL RUSSELL vs ELIJAH PAYNE. S. P. Judgement by Default.

DAVID BUSH & C'o vs JOHN BALLARD. Debt. Judgement by Default.

NATHANIEL RUSSELL vs W'M AGLETON. S. P. Judgment Confess'd as P Specialty With Costs of Suit.

NATHANIEL RUSSELL vs WALTER SHROPSHIRE. Debt. Judgement by Default.

[11 February 1795]

NATHANIEL RUSSELL vs W'M SANDERS. Debt. Judgement by Default.

NATHANIEL RUSSELL vs WILLIAM NETTLES SEN'R. Debt. Judgement by Default.

NATHANIEL RUSSELL vs W'M HUDSON. Debt. Judgement by Default.

DAVID BUSH vs JOHN NARRIMORE. Debt. Judgement by Default agreeable to Specialty.

GARDNER FORD vs JAMES GUNN & JOHN COATES. S. P. Judgement by Default agreeable to Specialty one Months stay of Execution in the Sheriffs Office.

GARDNER FORD vs JAMES GUNN & THOMAS SMIRL. S. P. Judgement by Default agreeable to Specialty One Months Stay of Execution in the Shffs. Office.

JACOB CHERRY Adm'or of JOSHUA CHERRY vs JOSHUA DINKINS. Debt. Judgement by Default agreeable to Specialty.

[Page 186]

MOSES HOLLIS vs FRANCIS WREN. Debt. Judgment by Default agreeable to Specialty.

REUBIN HARRISON & NICHOLAS PEAY vs W'M CLANTON. Debt. Judgment by Default agreeable to Specialty.

Ordered that the Estrays Which have been advertized the legal time be sold this after noon a 4 OClock.

W'M AGLESTON vs JAMES CAMPBELL. Appeal from the Judg't of ANDREW BASKINS Esq'r. It being suggested to the court that the Magistrate would not send up the Appeal because the Costs were not paid & the said AGLETON not being liable to pay the Costs before a final Decision, Ordered that the Magistrate do stay Proceedings on his Judgment & certify the appeal to the Next Court or Shew Cause to the Contrary.

Ordered that letters Testamentary do Issue to PHILEMON HILLARD one of the Nominated Executors of the last Will & Testament of DAWSON VALENDINGHAM the Will being approved of by the Court & Proven.

Ordered that ROBERT FORD be allowed the Sum of Ten Pounds for building the bridge over little Lynches Creek.

[Page 187]

Ordered that JOHN KERSHAW and THOMAS BROWN be and they are hereby appointed Commissions for Repairing Pine Tree Creek Bridge and that the Sum of Ten Pounds be allowed for that Purpose.

Ordered that RICHARD L. CHAMPION and THOMAS KELLY be and they are hereby appointee Commissioners for repairing the bridge over Sander's Creek and that the Sum of Six Pounds be allowed for that Purpose.

That JAMES COUSART and GEORGE ROSS are appointed Commissions for building a bridge over Graneys Quarter Creek great North Road, and that Ten Pounds be allowed for that Purpose.

That MICHAEL BARNETT and FRANCIS BELL are appointed Commissions for Repairing the bridge over Graneys Quarter Creek, Rockymount Road, and that five Pounds be allowed for that Purpose.

That JOHN McWILLIE Surveyor, be authorized to run the upper line of this County from GEORGE MILLERS to Harrisons for on Great Linches Creek, and have the same Plainly blazed and Marked, and that he return a Plat thereof with the Names of the Settlements Near & on the line.

[Page 188]

Orderd That the Sheriffs Acc't amounting to Twelve Pounds Ten Shillings and the Clerks to Ten Pounds be Paid.

Ordered that the sum of L 21 s 16 d 3 public Money in the Sheriffs hands be paid by him to the Clerk of the Court.

Ordered that one twelfth part of the amount of the General Tax of this County be Collected for the use of the County by the general Tax Collector, he having consented to Make the Collection.

The Court proceeded to the Election of a Sheriff when JOHN FISHER was duly Elected.

The Court then Adjournd to the seventh day of May Next. IS. DUBOSE, JOHN KERSHAW, BUR. BOYKIN.

[Page 189] 7th May 1795

The Court met according to Adjournment. Present JOHN KERSHAW Esquire.

Mr. JOHN FISHER the Sheriff Elect, appeared and took the Oath of Office as Prescribed by Law.

WILLIAM KIRKLAND Was approved of as a Deputy Sheriff for the County, he appeared and being approved of Was Duly Elected.

The Court then Adjourned untill tomorrow Ten O'Clock. JOHN KERSHAW.

The Court met According to Adjournment. Present JOHN KERSHAW, ISAAC DUBOSE, BURWELL BOYKIN, Esq'r.

Ordered that Letters of Administration Do Issue to THOMAS CURRY on the estate of JOHN POTTER deceased, the Securities are GEORGE ROSS & HUGH McGEE.

CHARITY STRATFORD Wife of RICHARD STRADFORD came into Court & acknowledged her Total Renunciation of Dower to a Tract or Plantation of Land containing 510 acres lying on both sides of Great Lynches Creek Sold by the said RICHARD & herself to JAMES MARSHALL.

[Page 190] 8 May 1795

MARY HORTEN Administratrix of the Estate of EVERET HOUSE, Returned to the Court an Inventory & Appraisement of the said Estate, Whereupon she was Required to give an additional Security to those approved of last February Court.

Her Security JAMES MARSHALL was approved, Ordered that the above Named MARY HORTEN administratrix of EVERET HOUSE Deceased be authorized to Sell the Stock of Cattle after giveing three Weeks Notice by advertisements on a Credit Untill the first day of January next.

[8 May 1795]

JOHN OQUIN Administrator of the Estate of DANIEL HORTON Deceased Returned to the Court an Inventory and appraisement of the Estate of the Said Deceased he Was Required to give an additional Security to those approved of last February Court.

A Petition from Sundry Inhabitants of Beaver Creek was Presented, Praying that a Road Might be laid Out from the Hanging Rock to Mickles Ferry by Archers Mill.

Ordered that ARTHUR CUNNINGHAM, JOS CARRUTH, WILLIAM BALLARD & EDWARD COLLINS be appointed Commissioners to ascertain the Distance, the advantages & disadvantages attending laying Out the said Road, & Make a Report thereof to Next Court.

HESTER COOK administratrix of the Estate of JOHN COOK deceased returned to the Court an Inventory & appraisement of the Estate of the said Deceased. Ordered that the Personal Estate be sold on a Credit to the 1st day of Januuary Next after giveing Due Notice, Purchasers giving bonds with good Security.

[Page 191]

Ordered that Letters of Administration of the Effects of JOSHUA RHOADES Deceased be Granted ₊o JOHN RUTLEDGE Junior his Securities are Wᴹ KIRKLAND & EDWARD RUTLEDGE.

The Court then Adjourned untill Tomorrow Nine O'Clock. JOHN KERSHAW, B. BOYKIN, IS. DUBOSE.

Agreeable to Adjournment the Court Met. Present JOHN KERSHAW, B. BOYKIN, IS DUBOSE, Esqʳs.

Ordered JOHN MAXWELL Administrator of the Estate of WILLIAM MAXWELL returned to the Court an Inventory & appraisement of the Effects of the deceased. Ordered that the same be Sold, after giving legal Notice of the Sale, on a Credit to the first of January next, Purchasers giving bonds with Good Security.

Mʳ FRANCIS BOYKIN having petitioned the Court for Opening a Road into his Plantation on the River from the great Road-

Ordered that JOHN ENGLISH & MALACHI MURPHEY be Authorized to lay Out the Most convenient Way for the said Road, so as not to Injure any Cultivated or enclosed lands belonging to the Adjoining Plantations see Minutes 12'th August posted.

[Page 192]

Ordered that the Plat of that Part of the Line between this County & Lancaster as Returned by ADAM McWILLIE, be Recorded in the Clerks Office. Also that his Account by Paid by the Clerk.

Ordered that the following persons be appointed Overseers of the several Districts of Road Within the County for the ensuing Year.

From Pinetree Creek to Town Creek. JOHN CASE Vice. WILLIAM BRACEY, WILLIAM PARKER, SAMUEL SMITH, GEORGE MILLER, JEFFRY HUDSON, JAMES BROWN JUNʳR, THOMAS LANKFORD, ROBERT FORD, JOHN MARSHAL, GEORGE EVANS, THOMAS KELLY, WILLIAM DANIEL JUNʳR, SAMUEL WEBB, REUBIN COLLINS, SAMʟ JONES, WILLIAM JONES, JOHN CATO, WILLIAM BOND, PETER CRIM, WILLIAM MACKEY, THOMAS WHITAKER, JOSIAH SCOTT, JOHN SWILLEY, JOHN BETHENY, JOHN RUTLEDGE, JOHN DINKINS, WILLIAM NETTLES, SAMUEL SMITH, THOMAS CREIGHTON, JAMES ROSS, BENJAMIN

CARTER, JAMES WILLIAMS, JESSE MINTON, WILLIAM MALONE, JOHN LISSENBY, THOMAS KELLY, ARCH'D WATSON, MICHAEL BARNET, WYLY COLLINS, ROBERT MEHAFFEY, GEORGE KING, DANIEL MONNAHAN, JAMES CAIN, ALEX'R STEWART, ANDREW A. HILL, ISAAC ROSS, JACOB CHERRY, ABRAM SHIVER.

[Page 193] 9th May 1795

The Clerk shall Immediately Make Out Lists of defaulters on the Publick Roads and send them to each Overseer in the Different Road Districts, that they may be put up at some Publick Place in each district, Which Notice on each list that all Defaulters Who Do Not Within two Months give in an Excuse on Oath to the Clerk of the Court, shall have Execution against them Immediately after the Expiration of Said time, And that Notice be also given to the late Overseers Who have not made Returns, that they Will be proceeded against according to Law Unless they, Within the Same time render their excuses to the Clerk of the Court on Oath.

Ordered that THOMAS GARDNER Esq'r be Authorized to sell the Estray Steer in the Possession of JOHN COATS at Publicks Auction, after giving ten Days Publick Notice of Such Sale, and taking a Note with good Security payable to the Clerk in Six Months.

Ordered that the fine of Two shillings & four pence Pr Day for each White Person and two Shillings Pr Day for each Negroes be Executed for all Defaulters in Working on Roads Who Shall not Make Sufficient Excuse Within the time Notified.

[Page 194]

Ordered That all Persons haveing Estrays Horses in their Possession Which have been advertised for three Courts be prosecuted, for not produceing them for sale at the Court House Aggreeable to the Law, & Orders of this Court, & that the Clerk furnish the County Attorney with a list of the Defaulters & Description of the Hoses Tolled.

Ordered that the sales of Estray Cattle Hogs &C Which cannot be conveniently brought to Court, be hereafter Made by the Sheriff at such places as he may think Most Convenient, and for the benefit of the County allways giving due Publick Notice of Such Sale.

Ordered that ____ ASHLEY, ELY K. ROSS, JOHN RUTLEDGE JUN'R, SAMUEL BROWN, JACOB CHAMBERS, & LEWIS DINKINS be and they are hereby appointed Constables for the County the Ensuing year.

JAMES BOWLES Was Approved as a Deputy Sheriff, and appeared and took Oath prescribed by Law.

The Court then Adjourned to the seventh day of August Next. IS. DUBOSE, JOHN KERSHAW, B. BOYKIN.

[Page 195]

AUGUST TERM 1795

Grand Jury Drawn from Box N'o 1 to N'o 2.

1 JAMES WILLIAMS, 2 THOMAS WATTS, 3 STARKE HUNTER, 4 DAVID PEEBLES, 5 ABRAHAM KELLY, 6 DANIEL HARKINS 25 M. C., 7 W'M PEACH B. C., 8 ABRAM BELTON, 9 FRANCIS WREN, 10 SAMUEL TYNES, 11 JAMES FLEMING, 12 JAMES CUNNINGHAM, 13 WILLIAM BOND, 14 DAVID COATS, 15 DAN'L GARDNER W. O., 16 REUBIN PATTERSON, 17 FRANCIS BRIMES, 18 THOMAS ENGLISH, 19 JAMES ROBINSON SEN'R L. C., 20 DENNIS QUINLAND.

AUGUST TERM 1795

Petit Jury Drawn from Box N'3 to N'o 4.

1 WALTER SHROPSHIRE, 2 CHARLES ROBINSON L. C., 3 THO'S KELLY, 4 MICHAEL BARNET, 5 ENOCH ANDERSON, 6 JAMES DICKSON, 7 ADAM McWILLIE, 8 ROBERT FAULKINBERRY, 9 ROBERT HOOD, 10 JEFFRY HUDSON, 13 WILLIAM GRIFFIN, 14 JOHN DRAKEFORD, 15 WILLOUGHBY WINCHESTER, 16 JOHN NEILSON, 17 ARC'D WATSON, 18 JOHN SANDERS G. Q., 19 REUBIN BRASSFIELD, 20 WILLIAM CAMPBELL, 21 HENRY KENT JUN'R, 22 CORNELIUS MALONE, 23 ELY K. ROSS, 24 MATTHEW BOWEN, 25 REUBIN BROWN, 26 JAMES TERRY, 27 JOHN ASHLEY G. Q., 28 ROBERT MEHAFFEY, 29 JOHN CREIGHTON, 30 ROBERT TURNER.

Agreeable to Adjournment The Court Met. Present JOHN KERSHAW, ISAAC DUBOSE, Esq'rs.

McCREDICK & YOUNG vs SAMUEL JONES. S. P. Dismiss'd Defd'ts haveing P'd the Debt & Costs.

[Page 196]

HUGH YOUNG vs GEORGE SANDERS. ss. Judgment Confess'd for the amount of the note with In't & Costs of Suit.

NATHAN'L RUSSELL vs SAMUEL WEBB. Judgement Confess'd for the Amount of Note & Interest With Costs of Suit.

NATH'L RUSSELL vs PHILLIP PAYNE. Judgment Cofness'd for L 6 s 1 d 6.

Tales Men for the Grand Jury from Box N'o 5 to N'o 6.

1 ISAAC ALEXANDER, 2 ROBERT COLEMAN, 3 SAMUEL BREED, 4 JOHN ADAMSON, 5 ZACHARIAH CANTEY, 6 WILLIAM ADAMSON.

DOCTER JOHN TRENT vs ABRAHAM KELLY. SP. Dismiss'd at Defendants Costs.

MICAJAH VAUGHN vs SAMUEL WELLS. Sci: fa. Confess'd Judgement for Debt & Costs.

JOHN L. DeBUSEY vs MICAJAH VAUGHN. Sci: fa. Judgment for Debt and Costs.

Ordered that letters of Administration Do Issue to GEORGE EVANS & JOHN MIDDLETON on the Estate of RICHARD MIDDLETON Deceased. The Securities are SAMUEL JONES & JAMES BASKINS.

THOMAS MICKLE vs JOHN TWADDLE, WILLIAM TWADDLE. Debt. Discontinued at the Defendants Costs.

[Page 197] 7 August 1795

McCREDICK & YOUNG vs PAUL SMITH. S. P. Judgment Confess'd.

JAMES PIERSON vs ROBERT McCAIN. Debt. Judgment Confess'd.

JEREMIAH SIMMONS vs EDWARD ROGERS. Debt. Judgment Confess'd.

HUGH & W'M YOUNG vs HINSON DAVIS. S. P. Judgment Confess'd.

NATHANIEL RUSSELL vs WILLIAM DUNNAVANT. S. P. Judgment Confess'd.

[7 August 1795]

HUGH & W'M YOUNG vs SILAS CAMPBELL. Debt. Judgment Confess'd.

State vs SAMUEL MARTIN, MATHEW BOWEN, WILLIAM BOWEN. The Defendants Acknowledge the takeing up of an Estray Bull Which they did not tole agreeable to Law but Killed the Same and Submitted to the Court to be fined Whereupon Ordered that they Pay a fine of five Pounds to the County & Costs of Prosecution.

[Page 198]

Ordered that the Personal Estate of DANIEL HORTEN be Sold the Twenty Ninth Instant at the Plantation of DANIEL HORTEN Deceased on a Credit of Six Months giving 3 weeks public Notice.

NATHANIEL RUSSELL vs JOHN ASHLEY. Debt. Judgment Confess'd for L 31 19/1 Stel'g & Costs of Suit.

JONATHAN BELTON vs WILLIAM TWADELL, JOHN TWADDELL. Debt. Judgment Confess'd.

Ordered that letters Testamentary Do Issue to JAMES ENGLISH one of the Executors Nominated in the Last Will and Testament of JOSHUA ENGLISH Deceased. the Will haveing been Produced in Open Court and Proved according to Law.

Ordered that the Property of RICHARD MIDDLETON Deceased be sold the last Saturday in August Giveing three Weeks Notice on a Credit to the first of January Next.

It appearing to the Court the ROBERT COOK, who was bound over to appear at this Court to answer a charge exhibited against him by JOSIAH CANTEY for a larceny is dead whereupon ordered that the recognizances be discharged.

The Court then adjourned untill tomorrow 10 O'Clock. JOHN KERSHAW, IS. DUBOSE.

[Page 199]

Agreeable to adjournment the Court Met. Present JOHN KERSHAW, ISAAC DUBOSE, BURWELL BOYKIN, Esq'rs.

NATH'L RUSSELL vs JOHN BOLDING. S. P. Judgment Confess'd.

JOHN ADAMSON vs HUGH BROWN, SAM'L WEBB. Judgment Confess'd.

McRA & CANTEY vs ROBERT FORD. Debt. BREVARD. Judgment Confess'd for L 37 5/ Sterling With In't from the 10th day of Feb'y 1795 & Costs.

McRA, CANTEY & C'o vs JAMES MAN. BREVARD. Judgment confessed for L 38 2/9 With Costs.

McRA, CANTEY & C'o vs JOHN COATES, JOHN PATTERSON. BREVARD. Debt on Note Judgment Confessed for L 24 s 19 d 6 with Costs.

ROBERT MARSHALL vs WILLIAM KIRKLAND. Debt on Note. BREVARD. Judgment confessed for L 10 with Interest from the 1st day of January 1793 and Costs of Suit. Execution to be stayed Six Months.

[8 August 1795]

The Grand Jury Call'd and Impannel'd as follows.

1 ZACH CANTEY foreman, 2 SAMUEL BREED, 3 JOHN RUSSELL, 4 CHARLES McGINNEY, 5 CHARLES McLELAND, 6 THOMAS STRIPLING, [no number 7], 8 ANDREW BASKINS, 9 ARCHIBALD McAFEE, 10 GEORGE SAUNDERS JUN'R, 11 JAMES CANTEY, 12 JOHN BALLARD, 13 JOHN ADAMSON, 14 ROBERT COLEMAN, 15 HUGH McLESTER, 16 MOSES FERGUSON affirms.

[Page 200]

The State vs BRYAN SPRADLEY. Cattle Stealing. a true bill. ZACH CANTEY, Foreman.

The State vs WILLIAM NARRIMORE. Hog Stealing. a true Bill. ZACH. CANTEY, foreman.

JOHN McKINNEY vs Ex'or JOHN BELTON. Abated by the Death of Defd't.

JN'O & ALEX'R PURVIS vs JEREMIAH SIMMONS. Debt. Judgment by Default. Plea With Drawn.

DAVID BUSH vs BAILEY FLEMING. Debt. Judgment by Default. Stay of Exeuctino 3 Months.

NATHANIEL RUSSELL vs ROGER GIBSON. Abated by the Death of Defendant.

BRYAN SPRADLEY vs RICHARD CAIN. Dismiss'd at the Plaintiffs Costs.

RICHARD CAMPBELL vs THOMAS DOHERTY. Ordered for Judgment.

JONATHAN BELTON vs EX'ors ISAAC PIDGEON. Judgment by Default.

PHILLIP HART vs MIDDLETON McDONALD. Debt. Judgment by Default.

Exo'r of HENRY SPRY vs Administrators of DANIEL BRITON. S. P. Decree for the Plaintiff as Pr Specialty. Execution to Issue against the Asets of the Deceased Not to Charge the Admo'r De Bonis Propris.

[Page 201]

A Petit Jury Impaneld and Sworn. 1 ALEXANDER CARRUTH foreman, 2 BARVELL EVANS, 3 PATRICK LAYTON, 4 APHRAIM CLANTON, 5 DILLARD COLLINS, 6 WILLIAM PAYNE, 7 RICHARD DRAKFORD, ROBERT TRANTHAM [stricken], 8 WILLIAM COOK, 9 JOHN RIDDLE, 10 ROBERT BARKLEY, 11 JOHN CHAMBERS, 12 JOHN DIXON.

JOHN SUTTON vs JAMES GUNN. Case. We find for the Plaintiff L 20 With Interest from the 25th December 1793. ALEXANDER C. CARRUTH, foreman.

EDWARD MORTIMER & C'o vs ABRAM CHILDERS. Sci fa. Ordered that Judgement be Revived.

BENJAMIN CUDWORTH In'dse of DANIEL BROWN vs JOSEPH McADAM. Judgment Confess'd as P Specialty With Costs.

JAMES PIERSON vs WILLIAM NETTLES S. C. Judgment by Confession. Stay of Execution to the first of January next.

The State vs HUGH McGEE. Asslt & Battery. A True Bill. ZACH CANTEY, foreman.

[8 August 1795]

The State vs JOSEPH McADAMS. Assault & Battery. No Bill. ZACH. CANTEY, foreman.

The State vs ROBERT BAIRD. Assault & Battery. No Bill. ZACH. CANTEY, foreman.

HUGH & W'M YOUNG vs W'M NETTLES S.C. S.P. Judgment by Confession. Stay of Execution to the first of January Next as P Specialty.

[Page 202]

Ordered that Letters Testamentary Do Issue to ZACHARIAH CANTEY & ISAAC ROSS SEN'R the two Nominated Executors in the last will and Testament of ROGER GIBSON Deceased the Will being first Produced in Open Court and Proved According to Law.

Ordered that all the Personal Estate of ROGER GIBSON Deceased be Sold at the Plantation of the Deceased the 2nd Tuesday in September next giving three Weeks Previous Notice.

The State vs ISHAM POWEL. Larceny. A true Bill. Z. CANTEY, foreman [entry stricken]

JAMES TRANTHAM vs LARK SINGLETON. Ordered that the Execution do Issue Immediately.

State vs WILLIAM NARRIMORE. Hog Stealing. Lays Over.

The State vs JOHN RUSSELL. Assault & Battery. No Bill. ZACH CANTEY, foreman.

The State vs ISHAM POWEL. Larceny. a true Bill. ZACH CANTEY, foreman.

THOMAS SMYRL vs SAMUEL THOMSON. Appeal. Judgment Confess'd by THOMAS SMYRL for 48 Shillings & 4 Pence With Costs.

The State vs JAMES ESTER. Discharged Witness Not Attending.

[Page 203] 8 August 1796

The State vs BENJAMIN PARNELL [stricken]

Exo'r VALENDINGHAM vs HENRY VALENDINGHAM. Case. The Defendent Personally appeared and Confess'd Judgment for L 11 s 5 d 6 Stlg & Costs of Suit. Stay of Execution Six Months.

The State vs JOSEPH McCOY & PATRICK McCAIN. The Recognizance Forfeited.

The State vs WILLIAM NARRIMORE. Hog Stealing. Dismiss'd. Nol: Prosequi.

The State vs JOSEPH LOCKART. Assault & Battery. Ordered that ANDREW BASKINS Esquire Bind Over the Prosecutor to the Next Court and the Recognizance be continued.

The State vs BENJAMIN PARNELL. Larceny. No Bill. ZACH CANTEY, foreman.

Ordered that Notice be given W'M BROWN BROOM That the Grand Jury has present as a Grievance that the two Bridges across the Mill Races Below Pinetree Creek are now entirely rotten & very dangerous for Waggons & other carriages and that he be Required to put them in immediate repair.

The Court then adjourned untill Monday ten OClock. JOHN KERSHAW, IS. DUBOSE, B. BOYKIN.

[Page 204] 10 August 1795

Agreeable to adjournment the Court Met. Present JOHN KERSHAW, ISAAC DUBOSE, Esq'rs.

WILLIAM LANGLEY vs JAMES ONEAL. Att. Dismiss'd.

JO: MIDDLETON vs SOLO LIZENBEA. Att. Dismiss'd.

ANCRUM Sur'vr of LOOCOCK vs ROGER GIBSON. S. P. Abates by the Death of Defd't.

Ex'or of JOSEPH KERSHAW vs GEORGE DUREN. Case. Settled.

JAMES SPRADLEY vs MARY ANN BUTIT. Settled at the Defendants Costs.

The State vs WILLIAM ROBINSON. Assault. Continued Over.

The State vs HENRY GRIG, GIDEON LOWRY. Recognizance Forfeited.

The State vs JOHN GRIG. Recognizance Forfeited. See Minuets 12'th Instant.

[Page 205]

DAVID CARWELL vs JOHN TRANTHAM SEN'R. S. P. Judgment Confess'd for L 4 Stay Exon Six Months With Costs.

JAMES PIERSON vs JOHN COATES & JAMES GUNN. Judgment by default against JOHN COATES. Judgment by Confession vs JAMES GUNN.

STEPHEN DUKE vs WILLIAM MOUNCE. Judgment by Default.

ADAM F. BRISBANE vs DANIEL BROWN. Debt on Note Ballance L 31:2:4 In't from 8th July 1791.

By consent of Parties the Defendants account filed is admitted to the sum of L 32 12/9. The Plaintiff has also an Account against the Defendant for carpenters work done, which is to be brought in by the Plaintiff and liquidated and the Defendant confesses Judgment for the balance & in case any dispute arises in liquidating the Account the matter is referred to Col'o CANTEY to liquidate whose Award shall be final & become a Rule of Court.

JOHN P. COCKE vs JAMES MARTIN. Debt.

ALEX'R CARRUTH foreman, BARWELL EVANS, PATRICK LAYTON, EPHRAIM CLANTON, DILLARD COLLINS, WILLIAM PAYNE, RICHARD DRAKEFORD, ROBERT TRANTHAM, W'M COOK, ROBERT McCAIN, JOHN RIDDLE, JOHN CHAMBERS.

[Page 206]

CHARLES STERNS vs WILLIAM BRACEY JUN'R. S. P. Dismiss'd at Defend'ts Costs.

DAVID HUNTER In'ds of SAMUEL SLOAN vs PATRICK SLOAN. S. P. The Deft Withdraws his Plea & allows Judg't to be given having Nothing to say against it.

JONATHAN DUREN vs JOHN TAYLOR & HENRY HUDSON. Debt. Judgment Confess'd by JOHN TAYLOR (alias Writ vs HUDSON)

[10 August 1795]

ADAM McWILLIE vs TURNER STARKE. S. P. Decree for L 7 with Costs.

JOHN NARRIMORE vs NICHOL'S ROBINSON. S. P. Dismiss'd at Pltfs Costs.

JOHN STARKE vs HARTWELL MEKIN. S. P. Decree for the Plaintiff for L 4 s 11 d 8 With Costs of Suit.

DAVID BUSH & C'o vs JOSEPH MARTIN. S. P. Dismiss'd.

JOSEPH PAYNE [DAVID LOGAN stricken] vs JOSEPH MARTIN. S. P. Decree for the Defendt With Liberty to appeal to the District Court.

The Court then adjourned untill tomorrow ten O'Clock. JOHN KERSHAW, IS. DUBOSE, B. BOYKIN.

[Page 207] 11 August 1795

Agreeable to Adjournment the Court met. Present JOHN KERSHAW, BURWELL BOYKIN, ISAAC DUBOSE, Esq'rs.

Ordered that letters of Administration do Issue to MARTHA CASE on the Estate of JOHN CASE Deceased the Securities are JOHN SWILLEY & JOHN CHAMBERS.

GARDNER FORD vs JAMES GUNN, JOHN COATS. S. P. Judgment Confess'd by JAMES GUNN With Interest and Costs. Judgment by Default against JOHN COATS.

GARDNER FORD vs JAMES GUNN & THOMAS SMIRL. S. P. Judgment Confess'd according to Note with In't & Costs by JAMES GUNN. Judgment by Default against THOMAS SMIRL.

SARAH BROWN vs DAVID COLLINS, MILLY COLLINS, GEORGE COLLINS. Trover. Dismiss'd the Plaintiff pays all the Costs Except the Defendants Att'y.

WILLIAM PARKER vs ANDREW HAVIS. Writ. Slanter. Dismiss'd.

NATHANIEL RUSSELL vs AARON ADKINS. S. P. Decree as Pr Specialty With Costs. 3 Months Stay of Exon.

[Page 208] 11 August 1795

JAMES P. COOKE vs JAMES MARTIN. Debt. Verdict. We find for the Defendent With Costs.

JOHN ROBINSON & C'o vs JAMES GUNN. S. P. Judgment Confess'd for L 5 11/8 Sterling & Costs.

McCREDIE & YOUNG vs JOSHUA WATSON. S. P. Judgment Confess'd for L 6 s 14 d 2 With Costs of Suit.

The State vs BRYAN SPRADLEY. Cattle Stealing. Verdict. We find the Defendant Not Guilty. ALEX'R C. CARRUTH.

ALEXANDER C. CARRUTH foreman, BARWELL EVANS, PATRICK LAYTON, EPHRAIM CLANTON, DILLARD COLLINS, WILLIAM PAYNE, RICHARD DRAKEFORD, ROBERT TRANTHAM, WILLIAM COOK, ROBERT McCAIN, JOHN RIDDLE, JOHN CHAMBERS.

WILLIAM ODANIEL vs JOHN RUSSELL. Debt on Bond.

[11 August 1795]

The Defendant being ruled to Special Bail RUSH HUDSON and the said Defendant acknowledged themselves bound in Special Bail for the Debt....

Ordered that DUNCAN McRA & Docter JAMES MARTIN, ISAAC ALEXANDER are hereby appointed Commissioners to Ascertain the proper place for a road to leave to the Old Ware house at the mouth of Pinetree Creek to Serve as a Private road to the Plantations of Colo KERSHAW & DANIEL PAYNE and Should the above named Commissioners disagree in their Opinion Respecting the same, then they are to fix on a Disinterested third person Who shall finally decide so as to fix the said Road, and Whose Opinion shall become a Rule of Court.

[Page 209]

SUSANNAH BROWN Adm'x of WILLIAM HOLMES vs JESSE GILES & HENRY HUDSON. Debt. Settled.

SARAH MAXWELL vs EDWARD WATSON. S. P. Decree Two Guineas for the Plaintiff with Costs of Suit.

JOSEPH BURROWS & JAMES KIRKPATRICK Administrators of SAMUEL BURROWS vs JOHN LOCKART. Debt. Verdict. We find for the Plaintiff L 9 with lawful Interest & Costs of Suit. ALEX'R C CARRUTH, foreman.

FRANCIS BOYKIN vs WILLIAM BRUMMET. Att. Verdict. We find for the Plaintiff L 20 s 6 With Interest from 23rd July 1793 and Costs of Suit. ALEX'R C CARRUTH, foreman.

JAMES PEIRSON vs JOHN GRAHAM. Debt. Judgment Confess'd agreeable to Specialty. Stay of Exo'n two Months with Costs of Suit.

JOHN McNEIL vs EDWARD ROGERS. Case. Dismiss'd.

MATHIS PEIRSON & C'o vs JESSE MINTON. Debt. Judgment Confess'd for the Ballance. Stay Execution for Six Months by paying the Costs.

[Page 210]

JAMES PEIRSON vs JOHN GRAHAM, FRANCIS GRAHAM. Debt. Judgment according to Note With Costs.

ZACHARIAH HESTER vs JEFFRY HUDSON & SAMUEL SLONE. Judgment according to Note With Costs.

DAVID DRENNAN vs WILL'M McGILL. Appeal. Dismissed.

MATTHEW BROWN vs WILLIAM McKEY. Continued at Plfts Costs.

Exo'r McKEE vs DAVID DRENNAN. Att. Decree for Plaintiff five Pouinds With Costs.

SUSANNAH MILLS vs FRANCIS GENO. Settled by Arbitration Each Party to pay their Own Costs.

The Court then Adjourned Untill Tomorrow Ten O'Clock. JOHN KERSHAW, IS. DUBOSE, B. BOYKIN.

[Page 211]

Agreeable to Adjournment the Court Met. Present JOHN KERSHAW, ISAAC DUBOSE, BURWELL BOYKIN, Esq'rs.

[12 August 1795]

Exo'r JASPER SUTTON vs LEWIS COOK & THOMAS SMIRL. S. P. Judgment by Confession of LEWIS COOᴋ. Judgment by Default of THOMAS SMIRL. Exo'n stay three Months.

JOHN BROWN G. Q. vs JOHN GAYDEN, GEORGE GAYDEN. Debt. Dismiss'd.

Ordered that M'r THOMAS LENORE be appointed in the Room of M'r MURPHEY for laying Out a Road to FRANCIS BOYKINS Plantation. See 9'th May last.

Ordered that the Clerk do purchase two Ink Stands for the use of the Court.

JAMES HAMILTON vs JESSE MINTON. S. P. Judgment Confess'd for amount of Note with Interest & Costs of Suit With Stay of Exo'n One Month.

NANCEY EVANS vs JESSE MINTON, JA'S ROCHELL. S. P:. Judgment Confess'd for the Amount of Note With Interest & Costs of Suit by JESSE MINTON.

GEORGE MILLER vs WILLIAM PARKER. Debt. Verdict. We find for the Plaintiff Eleven Guineas With Interest and Costs of Suit.

NATHA'L RUSSELL vs THOMAS CREIGHTON. S. P. Judgment the Defendent having Nothing to say against it as Pr Specialty.

[Page 212]

Ordered that a Road be laid Out from Hanging Rock by Archers Mill to Mickles Ferry.

RAWLEY HAMMOND is appointed Overseer from Hanging Rock to WILLIAM BALLARDS and ALEXANDER ARCHER is appointed Overseer from WILLIAM BALLARD's to Rocky Mount Road and JOHN MICKLE is appointed Overseer from Rocky Mount Road to said MICKLEs ferry.

HUGH McGEE vs JOHN RUSSELL. Writ. Assault & Battery. We find for the Plaintiff one Shilling With Costs. ALEX'R CARRUTH, foreman.

JOHN GREG appeared in Court and Shewed sufficient cause Why his recognizance should not be forfeited as entered on the Minutes of this Court the 10'th Instant.

WILLIAM YOUNG vs ROBERT FORD. S. P. Decree as Pr Specialty With Costs. Stay Ex'on Untill the first of Jan'y next.

SAM'L WEBB vs HUGH BROWN, AGNESS BROWN. S. P. Decree for Plaintiff L 5 with Interest from the first of Jan'y 1794 & Costs of Suit.

Same vs Same. S. P. Decree as Pr Specialty With Costs of Suit.

DAVID BUSH vs ROBERT FORD. Debt. Judgment by Default Plea Withdrawn. Stay Ex'on to the first of January next with Costs.

NATH'L RUSSELL vs SAM'L THOMSON. Debt. Judgment Non Sum.

McCREDIE & YOUNG vs JESSE MINTON. Case. Judgment Confessed for L 18 8/7. Stay Ex'on untill the 10th March Next With Costs.

[Page 203; error in pagination beginning here]

NATHANIEL RUSSELL vs JOHN WEBB. S. P. Dcree for Plaintiff as Pr ᴜpecialty. Stay of Execution three Months with Costs.

NATH'L RUSSELL vs RUSH HUDSON. Debt. We find for the Plaintiff L 41 s . d 4 With Interest & Costs of Suit. ALEX C. CARRUTH, foreman.

JAMES COUSART vs JOHN HOOD. Case. We find for the Plaintiff L 15 with Interest & Costs of Suit. ALEX'R C. CARRUTH, Foreman.

NATH'L RUSSELL vs JESSE MINTON. Debt. Judgment Confess'd as P Specialty With Costs. Stay Exo'n to the 1 Jany 1796.

DAVID BUSH vs BENJ. EVANS. Att. We find for the Plaintiff L20:3:10 and we find the property of the Within named Negro JACK to be the property of CHARLES EVANS. ALEX'R C. CARRUTH, foreman.

THOMAS DUREN vs JOHN GRAHAM. S. P. Ordered that an appeal be Granted in this Case. Settled at Def'dts Costs.

NATH'L RUSSELL vs WILLIAM McDOWELL. Debt. Judgment according to Specialty def'dt having Northing to Say ag't it.

JAMES COWSER In'drse of ALEX'R CAMMERON vs THOMAS SMIRL. Debt. Judgment (the Def'dt having Nothing to say against it) as Pr Specialty.

NATHANIEL RUSSELL vs HUGH BROWN. Debt. Judgment according to Specialty. Stay Ex'on three months.

[Page 204]

NATHANIEL RUSSELL vs HUGH BIRD. Debt. Judgment according to Specialty. Stay Ex'on three Months with cost.

NATHANIEL RUSSELL vs JOHN TWADDLE, W'M TWADDLE. Debt. Judgment according to Specialty. Stay Ex'on three Months With Costs.

NATH'L RUSSELL vs WILLIAM LAYTON. Debt.

Ordered that a Commission Do Issue to take the Deposition of HENRY SINCLAIR.

ISAAC ROBERTS vs JEREMIAH PARISH. Case. Judgment Confess'd as P Specialty With Costs.

ISAAC ROBERTS vs MELDRIDGE EVANS admin'ix of WM EVANS. Judgment by Default. a Writ of Enquiry.

RICHARD CAMBELL vs THOMAS DAUGHERTY. Att. We find for the Plaintiff L 17:10 With Lawfull Interest on the Different notes of hand With Costs of Suit. ALEX'R C. CARRUTH, foreman.

JAMES PEIRSON vs HULON VAUGHN. Judg't on Specialty.

The Same vs JOHN GAYDEN. Decree on Specialty for Pllf.

DAVID BUSH vs JERE. SIMMONS. Judg't by Default on Specialty.

[Page 205]

HUGH & W'M YOUNG vs RICH'D CLANTON. Judg't by Default on Specialty.

JOSHUA DINKINS vs Exor PETER CASSITY. Judg't by Default.

THOMAS CASSITY vs Exor PETER CASSITY. Default & Writ of Inquirey.

JOSEPH PAYNE vs JOHN BLAKENEY. Dismissed each party pays his own Costs.

[12 August 1795]

NAT. RUSSELL vs ED REYNOLDS. Judg't by Default.

SAM MATHIS vs GARDNER FORD Admor ISAAC LOVE. Decree for Pltf. on note and acco't.

BENJAMIN CUDWORTH In'ds of D. BROWN vs GIDEON LOWRY. S. P. Decree for Pltf. according to Specialty With Costs.

HUGH & W'M YOUNG vs DILLARD COLLINS. S. P. Decree for the Plaintiff according to Specialty Stay of Execution 3 Months.

JOHN RUSSELL vs WILLIAM JONES. Att. Decree for L 8 s 6. Ordered that the Property attached be Sold.

[Page 206]

BENJAMIN PARNELL vs JAMES EASTER. Slander. Dismissed at Defend'ts Costs.

The Court adjourned untill tomorrow Nine O'Clock. JOHN KERSHAW, IS DUBOSE.

Agreeable to adjournment the Court Met. Present ISAAC DUBOSE, JOHN KERSHAW.

WILLIAM AGLENTON vs JEREMIAH SIMMONS. Case on Petition.

It appearing to the court that the Deft. Received from the Plaintiff a note of hand on BRYAN SPRADLEY for More than the demdn SIMMONS had on him, as Security to pay said demand, which note the said SIMMONS has sued in his Own Right against SPRADLEY.

Ordered that the Justice of the Peace proceed to give Judgment against SPRADLEY, and direct the Constible Who is Ordered to Levy the amount of the Debt against SPRADLEY, and in the first Place Pay the amount of the demand SIMMONS has against AGLENTON to SIMMONS, deducting the Costs of this Application and the Remainder Pay Unto the said AGLENTON.

[Page 207]

ALEXANDER McKEE vs ROBERT FORD. Debt. Judgment by Default according to Specialty With Costs.

WILLIAM TWADDLE vs SAMUEL WEBB. Debt. Judgment Confess'd for L 15 sterling and Interest from 1st January last.

NATHANIEL RUSSELL vs JOHN REYNOLDS, SHADRICK ANDERSON. S. P. Judgment Confess'd for amount of Note & Interest With Costs.

JOHN ROBINSON & C'o vs JOHN ROBERTSON. S. P. Decree for L 8 s 10 d 8 Stay Execution Six Months with Costs.

JOHN ROBINSON & C'o vs JAMES STEWART. S. P. Decree for L 3 s 2 d 2 Stay of Execution four Months With Costs.

BURWELL BUGE vs Ex'or SAM'L BOYKIN. Debt. Dismiss'd Each party paying their Own Costs.

WILLIAM BRUMMET vs MATHEW COLEMAN. S. P. Discontinued.

JOHN ROBINSON & C'o vs MATHEW COLEMAN. S. P. Decree for L 5 s 13 d 1 Subject to a Discount. Stay Ex'on three Months.

[Page 208] 13 August 1795

HEZEKIAH ALEXANDER vs JOHN SWILLA. Bail for RICHARD BLANKS. Judgment according to Specialty the Debt & Costs in the former action against the Principal & Costs of this action.

HUGH & W'M YOUNG vs MICHAEL GAUNTER. S. P. Decree for L 6 13/7. Stay Execution three Months With Costs.

IIUGII & WILLIAM YOUNG vs JOHN ASHLEY. S. P. Decree as P Specialty with Costs.

JAMES PEIRSON vs JAMES CANTEY. S. P. Decree as P Specialty With Costs of Suit. Stay Ex'on four Months.

ROBERT TRANTHAM vs MATHEW NUTT. Appeal. Judgment Reversed.

DAVID BUSH vs BENJN EVANS [CHARLES EVANS stricken]. Appeal to District Court. Ordered the Deposition of ISAIAH BUSH be taken de bene esse.

The Court Then Adjourned untill the Seventh Day of November Next, at 10 O'Clock. JOHN KERSHAW, IS. DUBOSE.

[Page 209] 7th November 1795

Agreeable to adjournment the Court Met. Present JOHN KERSHAW.

Ordered that the Administrator of THOMAS POTTER Estate Sell the Property, on the Last Saturday in this Month giving four Months Credit.

Then the Court Adjourned untill Monday Ten OClock. JOHN KERSHAW.

Agreeable to Adjournment the Court Met. Present ISAAC DUBOSE & BURWELL BOYKIN.

WILLIAM DOBY being Recommended to the Court by the Sheriff as a Deputy, and being Approved of by the Court, Was Sworn Accordingly.

On Motion of BENJAMIN PERKINS Esqr Ordered that a Rule Do issue against the Administrator & Administratrix of WILLIAM EVANS deceased to shew cause why the Letters of Administration should not be revoked.

Whereas the law directs that all Sales made by the County Sheriffs by Virtue of Executions in their hands Shall be at the Court House Except the Judges Shall Direct Other Places for the Said Sales.

[Page 210] 9th November 1795

and whereas great inconveniences have arised in this county for Want of Such Direction

It is therefore hereby Ordered and directed that the Sheriff of the Said County May sell any Tobacco, Provisions, Forage, House-hold Furniture and Other goods and Chattels Which are too Bulky or cumtersome for removal or Would be attended With considerable Expence also Cattle, Hogs, Sheep, Goats and Poultry, and also Colts & Fillies or other Horse kind not capable of being brought to the Court House by reason of their being too Wild, too old, Weak or Otherwise that is to say that the said Sheriff May Sell or cause to be sold any of the said Articles at the Respective Plantations Whereon they are seized or at some other place Near and convenient to the same so as to be as Publick as Possible consistent With the Principles of Economy.

Then the Court adjourned to Tuesday Ten OClock. IS. DUBOSE, B. BOYKIN.

Agreeable to Adjournment the Court Met. Present ISAAC DUBOSE Esqr.

Ordered that JAMES COWSART be paid ten pounds allowed by the County for building a bridge Over Graneys Quarter Creek, he as one of the Commissioners having made Report to the Court that the bridge is compleated by the Workman With Whom he contracted.

[Page 211] November 10th 1795

Ordered that the Clerk do Issue Orders immediately to the Overseers of the District of Road Next above & below the said bridge to clear & Make good the Road to the Bridge each on the side Within his District.

Ordered that M'r CHAMPION one of the Commissioners for building a bridge over Sanders Creek be authorized to receive from the Clerk the Sum allowed for that purpose as soon as the Work is compleated agreeable to his contract.

That the Estrays Which have been advertised the legal time be sold immediately after the adjournment of the Court.

The Court Then Adjourn'd untill the 7'th of February next. IS. DUBOSE.

Feb'y Term 1796

Grand Jury Drawn from Box N'o 1 to N'o 2.

1 ALEX'R STEWART S. C., 2 THOMAS LENORE, 3 ARTHUR CUNNINGHAM, 4 WYLY COLLINS, 5 ARTHUR B. ROSS, 6 LEWIS PEEBLES, 7 WILLIAM JONES JUN'R, 8 JAMES SOWELL, 9 REUBIN STARKE, 10 DANIEL KIRKLAND, 11 SAM'L SMITH, 12 GEORGE MILLER, 13 DANIEL OQUIN SEN'R, 14 JOHN RUTLEDGE SEN'R, 15 JOHN TEAKLE, 16 JAMES INGRAM, 17 GEORGE ROSS, 18 JACOB GREY, 19 RICHARD STRATFORD, 20 WILLIAM NETTLES, G. S.

[Page 212] 8 Feby 1796

Petit Jury Drawn from Box N'o 3 to N'o 4.

1 PATRICK MCCAIN, 2 MARTIN TRANTHAM, 3 JOHN KILE, 4 ALEXANDER CRUMPTON, 5 WILLIAM JONES W. O., 6 JOSEPH CAMPBELL, 7 TYDY LAYTON, 8 JOHN MOTLEY Bell Branch, 9 PATRICK McFADDIN, 10 JOHN BROWN B. C., 11 JOHN PRESTLY, 12 W'M MIDDLETON, 13 CHARLES SPEARS JUN'R, 14 WILLIAM NUTT, 15 JAMES RIDDLE, 16 DAVID FAULKINBERRY, 17 ISAAC BLANCHARD, 18 ADAM TAMSON, 19 TYRE BRASWELL, 20 STERLING CLANTON, 21 W'M MELONE, 22 JOHN ABBOTT S. C., 23 PRESTLY REEVES, 24 JAMES ENGLISH, 25 W'M NUXT, 26 W'M WILLIAMS H. Rock, 27 JOHN PAYNE SEN'R, 28 W'M WIMBERLY, 29 SAM'L THOMPSON, 30 LEWIS COLLINS.

Agreeable to Adjournment the Court Met. Present ISAAC DUBOSE, BURWELL BOYKIN, JOHN KERSHAW.

JOHN REID vs THOMAS SMYRL. Debt. Judgment Confes'd for L 10 Sterling with Interest from 1st Jany last and Costs.

CANTEY & Others vs HUDSON & Others. Debt. Dismiss'd at the Defendants Costs.

ROBERT FORD vs GEORGE KING. Slander.

Ordered that the Plantiff do Shew Cause To Morrow why the Bail in this Case Should not be Discharged.

[Page 213] 8 Feby 1796

JOHN ADAMSON vs JAMES PERRY. Debt. Judgment Confes'd for L 33 s 2 & Interest.

SAMUEL MATHIS appeared in Open Court and took the Oath of allegiance to this State and the United States and also the Oath of Office as a Justice of the Peace for this County.

JOHN ADAMSON vs JOHN MARTIN. Debt. Judgment confess'd for L 30 1/9 Sterling With Interest thereon from the 12 January 1795 & Costs.

HEZEKIAH ALEXANDER assignee &c vs JOHN ADAMSON [& JOHN SWILLA stricken] Debt. Settled at the Defendants Costs.

ZACH HESTER vs JEFFRY HUDSON, SAM'L SLONE. Case. Judgment Confessd for L 18 With Interest from the 25th day of December 1793 & Costs of Suit.

[Page 214]

JOHN SWILLA vs EDWARD CALVERT. Settled.

Ordered that Letters of Administration Do Issue to SARAH BROWN & JAMES BROWN on the Estate of JAMES BROWN deceased the Securities to be given before the adjournment of the Court to next Term.

Petit Jurors Impaneled & Sworn accordingly.

1 MICHAEL BARNET foreman, 2 JOHN DRAKEFORD, 3 ELY K. ROSS, 4 HENRY KENT JUN'R, 5 JOHN HOOD, 6 JEFFRY HUDSON, 7 JOHN ASHLEY, 8 JOHN NEILSON, 9 MATHEW BOWEN, 10 JOHN CRAIEHGONT A, 11 ROBERT HOOD A, WILLOUGHBY WINCHESTER A.

THOMAS CASITY vs W'M WATSON Executor of PETER CASITY. Case. We find for the Plaintiff L 17 s 10 with Interest from the date of the note.

GREEN RIVES vs JOHN MARTIN. S. P. Judgment Confess'd as Pr Specialty With Costs.

Ordered that GEORGE SCOTT & ANN SCOTT Do Receive Letters of Administration on the estate of JOHN SCOTT SEN'R Deceased the securities are DANIEL OQUIN & W'M FOX.

BENJAMIN ALEXANDER vs THOMAS COLLIER. Writ. Settled at the Pltffs Costs.

State vs WILLIAM ROBINSON. Dismissed at the Defendants Costs.

MARY GLAZE vs WILLIAM MOUNCE, JAMES PURDY. S. P. Dismissed the Defendant having paid the debt & Costs.

Then the Court adjourned Untill To Morrow ten OClock. IS. DUBOSE, B. BOYKIN, JOHN KERSHAW.

Agreeable to Adjournment the Court Met. Present ISAAC DUBOSE, BURWELL BOYKIN, JOHN KERSHAW.

JAMES PEIRSON vs THOMAS BALLARD. S. P. Dismiss'd

JAMES PEIRSON vs HENRY HUDSON. S. P. Judgment Confess'd for the Ballance of the Note With Interest & Costs.

[Page 216] 9'th Feby 1796

McRA & CANTEY Vs WILLIAM NETTLES. Judgment Confess'd for L 34 s 9 d 8 and Costs of Suit. Ex'on to Stay in Sheriffs hands Untill next August Court.

JONATHAN BELTON vs THOMAS WATTS SEN'R. Debt. Judgment Confess'd agreeable to Specialty with Costs of Suit With Stay of Ex'on Untill August next.

McRA & CANTEY vs RICHARD DUMVILLE. Debt. Judgment Confess'd for L 15 & Interest from the first day of November last with Costs of Suit.

WILLIAM WHITAKER vs THOMAS SMYRL. S. P. Settled Each Party to Pay their Own Costs.

THOMAS SMYRL vs WILLIAM WHITAKER. S. P. Settled Each Party to pay their Own Costs.

Ordered that WILLIAM KIRKLAND and WILLIAM NUTT together with any third person they may appoint shall proceed to examine the new Road that leads from the hanging rock to Mickles ferry and if found Practible & proper to alter such part or parts of it as may be found injurious to any of the Inhabitants near the said Road, & report thereon.

[Page 217]

JOHN ADAMSON vs JAMES WILLIAMS. S. P. Dismiss'd at the Plaintiffs Costs.

NATHANIEL RUSSELL vs JOHN ASHLEY. Debt. THOMAS SMYRL & JOHN HOOD Special Bail of the Defendant.

Came into Court and Surrender'd the Body of his Principal and Mov'd to be Discharge from his Bail Bond Which the Court Ordered accordingly and that the shff do take him into Custody.

JOHN REID vs GEORGE BROWN, JANE BROWN. S. P. Judgment Confess'd by GEORGE BROWN & JANE BROWN his Wife but a Sole and Seperate dealer duly appointed and authorized do jointly & Severally Confess Judgment on the Within process for L 8 s 8 d 8 Sterling with Interest from this Date but no Execution is to be levied in Consequence thereof before the 1st January Next (this 19th Jany 1796 for the debt Confess'd).

SAMUEL MATHIS Sur'vr vs JESSE MINTON. Judgment Confess'd for L 16 s 3 & Costs. Exo'n to be lodge to bind the Property but not to be levied for Six Months.

[Page 218]

JOSIAH CANTEY vs JOSIAH SCOTT. Case. Dismiss'd at the Plaintiffs Costs for Want of his Prosecuting his Suit.

The State vs JESSE MINTON. Assault & Battery. Not a true Bill. SAM'L TYNES, Foreman.

1 SAMUEL TYNES foreman, 2 JAMES WILLIAMS, 3 THOMAS WATTS JUN'R, 4 ABRAM KELLY, 5 W'M PEACH, 6 ABRAM BELTON, 7 JAMES CUNNINGHAM, 8 W'M BOND, 9 DAVID COATS, 10 DAN'L GARDNER, 11 REUBIN PATTERSON, 12 THOMAS ENGLISH, 13 JAMES ROBINSON SEN'R.

W'M BROWN VS HENRY HUNTER. Debt. We find for the Plaintiff one shilling damages with costs of Suit. MICHAEL BARNET, foreman.

[9 February 1796]

1 MICHAEL BARNET foreman, 2 JOHN DRAKEFORD, 3 ELY K. ROSS, 4 HENRY KENT JUNR [JOHN HOOD stricken], 5 JEFFRY HUDSON, 6 JOHN NEILSON, 7 ARCHIBALD WATSON, 8 JOHN SANDERS, 9 MATHEW BOWEN, 10 JOHN CREIGHTON, 11 ROBERT HOOD, 12 WILLOUGHBY WINCHESTER.

The State vs WILLIAM SKIPPER. Assault & Battery. Not a true Bill. SAM'L TYNES Foreman.

DAVID COLLINS vs DAVID REES. Assault. Dismiss'd at the Defd't Costs.

[Page 219]

WILLIAM ANCRUM Sur'vr vs DANIEL OQUIN. Case.

FRANCIS BOYKIN vs BRYAN SPRADLEY. S. P. Judgment Confess'd as Pr Specialty With Costs of Suit.

WILLIAM ANCRUM Sur'vr of ARON LOCOCK vs CHARLES McGINNEY. S. P. Ordered that the Plaintiff be Nonsuited. Tis Therefore Considered that the Said CHARLES do recover against the said WILLIAM his Costs thereon.

Adm'r of JOHN LEE vs Adm'x of ROBERT LEE. Case. Dismiss'd at the Defendants Costs.

EDWARD WATSON In'dse of ARCHELUS PAYNE vs JOHN VAUN. S. P. Dcree against M'rs SARAH MAXWELL Garnishee for four Pounds.

On Motion of BENJAMIN PERKINS Esq'r Ordered that a Rule Do Issue to Cite BARWELL EVANS to Shew Cause if any he Can Why the administration of JACOB EVANS Should Not be Revoked.

[Page 220]

JOHN REID vs THOMAS SMYRL. Debt. Judgment Confess'd as Pr Specialty With Costs of Suit.

PHILLEMON HILLIARD vs LITTLE RAINS & MATTHEW NUTT. Debt. Judgment by Default.

WILLIAM ANCRUM Sur'vr &c vs DANIEL QUIN. Case. We find a Verdict for the Defendant Four Pounds Seven Shillings & 8d.

THOMAS ENGLISH vs JOSEPH COLE. Att. Case. Writ of Enquity Executed. Verdict as follows Viz.

ELIZABETH SCOTT vs DAVID COATS & JOHN COATS. S. P. Case. Decree on Note the Tobacco Valued at 16 s & d 4 with Interest & Costs of Suit.

[Page 221]

The State vs JAMES HESTER, JONATHAN LIGGETT. Trespass & Misdemeanor. True Bill against JAMES HESTER. No bill against JONATHAN LIGGETT. SAM'L TYNES, Foreman.

The Court Adjourned Untill To Morrow Ten OClock. B. BOYKIN, JOHN KERSHAW.

Agreeable to Adjournment the Court Met. Present JOHN KERSHAW, BURWELL BOYKIN.

HUGH & W'M YOUNG vs JONATHAN COOK. S. P. Decree as Pr Specialty With Costs.

[10 February 1796]

McCREDIE & YOUNG vs JONATHAN COOK. S. P. Decree for L 6 s 14 d 5 with Costs.

JAMES PIERSON vs HENRY HUDSON. S. P. Judgment Confes't as Pr Specialty.... [entire entry stricken]

[Page 222] 10 Feby 1796

LEWIS & THO'S DINKINS vs W'M SCOTT Ex'r of JN'O SCOTT SEN'R. Abates by Death of the Defendant.

THOMAS ENGLISH vs JOSEPH COLE. Att. Case. Write of Enquity Executed. Verdict as follows Viz:

We Find a Verdict for the Plaintiff Sixteen pounds With Costs of Suit. MICHAEL BARNET, foreman.

In Compliance with the Petition of sundry persons respecting the appropriation of public monies within the County

Ordered That the Clerk do exhibit at the Court House door at every Court to be hereafter held a Copy of the several orders of this Court made or which may be made at any future time, laying a tax, & that he do also render an account clearly & fairly stated of all the public Moneys by him received or expended from time to time on account of the County, which shall ever during Court be placed at the Court House door & at other times be placed at his Office in a conspicuous manner for the information of all persons concerned.

[Page 223]

JAMES SPRUNT vs W'M BALLARD, THO'S CREIGHTON. Debt. Dismiss'd at Plaintiffs Costs.

JOHN G. GUIGNARD vs DILLARD COLLINS. Case. We find a Verdict for the Plaintiff for L 10 6/2 with Costs of Suit. MICHAEL BARNET, foreman.

On the Petition of Sundry Inhabitants on the South side of the Wateree River, ORDERED that WILLIS WHITAKER, ARTHUR BROWN ROSS, JOSIAH SCOTT & DANIEL OQUIN be & they are hereby appointed to cause such alteration to be Made in the Road leading from Camden to McCords Ferry as they shall think Most for the Benefit of the County & the Petitioners & That the Overseer of the Present Road be Required to attend at a Convenient time With the hands liable to Work thereon to carry the alteration of the above Named Commissioners into effect.

NATHANIEL RUSSELL vs DAVID BALLARD. Debt. Judgment Confess'd for L 22 18/1 Sterling & Costs.

MATHEW BOWEN vs WILLIAM MACKEY. S. P. Dismiss'd at the Plaintiffs Costs.

[Page 224]

ISAAC ROBERTS vs MILDRIDGE EVANS, Adm'x of W'M EVANS. Writ on the Case. Judgment by Default as Pr Specialty With Costs of Suit.

JAMES COWSAR In'dsee of ALEX'R CAMERON vs THOMAS SMYRL. Sci: fi: for RICH'D L. CHAMPION bail.

The State vs WILLIAM NARRIMORE. Hog Stealing. We find the Defendant Guilty. MICHAEL BARNET, foreman.

[10 February 1796]

1 MICHAEL BARNETT foreman, 2 JOHN DRAKEFORD, 3 ELY K. ROSS, 4 HENRY KENT JUN'R, 5 JEFFRY HUDSON, 6 JOHN NEILSON, 7 ARCHIBALD WATSON, 8 JOHN SANDERS, 9 MATHEW BOWEN, 10 JOHN CREIGHTON, 11 ROBERT HOOD, 12 WILLOUGHBY WINCHESTER.

Ordered that DILLARD COLLINS appointed overseer of the Road leading from the main Charleston Road to English Ferry Untill Next Court in the Room of ARON FERGUSON Whose age exempts him from Serving. And that ISAAC UNDERWOOD be appointed in the room of JOHN CASE Deceased Untill Next Court.

MOSES HOLLIS vs REED HUTT & SUSANNAH HUTT. Debt. Dismiss'd at the Defend'ts Costs.

[Page 225]

JONATHAN BELTON vs JAMES MAN. Debt. Judgment for Plaintiff Defen'dts Atty Not being Instructed of any Defence.

PHILLIMON HILLARD vs LITTLETON RAINS, MATTHEW NUTT. Debt. The defendant in this Case Came into Court and Entered an appearance by his Attorney.

ROBERT MATHIS vs THOMAS SMYRL. S. P. Judgment by Default agreeable to Specialty With Costs of Suit.

JAMES PEIRSON vs THOMAS JONES. S.P. Judgment by default agreeable to Specialty With Costs of Suit.

[Page 226]

DAVID BUSH vs TAURENS CONNER. Writ of Sci: Fa. Ordered that the Judgment be Revived and that he Plaintiff do have his Execution Revived.

NATH'L RUSSELL vs DAVID PEEBLES. Debt. on Note. Judgment Confess'd as P Specialty With Costs of Suit.

JOHN ENGLISH vs BRYAN SPRADLEY JUN'R, BRYAN SPRADLEY SEN'R. S. P. on Note. Judgment by Default according to Specialty With Costs.

HUGH & W'M YOUNG vs DENNIS BURNS. S. P. Judgment by Default according to Specialty With Costs of Suit.

JOHN MAXWELL vs HENRY ROWE [THOMAS KELLY stricken] S. P. Decree as P Specialty With Costs of Suit.

WILLIAM NETTLES vs BRYAN SPRADLEY. S. P. Decree as Pr Specialty With Costs of Suit.

[Page 227]

EDWARD HULIN vs W'M PARKER. Mal. Proston. We find for the Plaintiff two pounds With Costs of Suit. MICHAEL BARNET, foreman.

JAMES PERKINS a Minor having appeared at the last Court & Prayed that DAVID PERKINS his Uncle May be apppointed a Guardian for him. Thereupon Ordered that the said DAVID PERKINS be appointed his Guardian & be Vested with the Property of the said JAMES PERKINS as his Guardian.

ZACHARIAH CANTEY vs JOHN RUTLEDGE. S. P.

[10 February 1796]

Ordered that a Commission do Issue to Georgia to take the Deposition of LEWIS JOHNSON for the Plaintiff.

MOSES LAVZEDAR vs DILLARD SPRADLEY. S. P. Decree according to Specialty With Costs of Suit.

MOSES LAVZEDAS vs W'M CHAMBERS. S. P. Decree according to Specialty With Costs of Suit.

The Court Adjourned untill to Morrow ten OClock. JOHN KERSHAW, B. BOYKIN.

[Page 228] 11 Feby 1796

The Court met agreeable to Adjournment. Present JOHN KERSHAW, BURWELL BOYKIN.

MOSES LAVZEDAR vs MOSES BEARD. S. P. Decree for Plaintiff as Pr Specialty.

CHARLES BARBER vs GEORGE PERRY, DAVID RUSSELL. Debt. Dismiss'd

HUGH YOUNG vs MICHAEL GANTER. Settled between the parties.

It appearing to the Court the BARWELL EVANS administrator of JACOB EVANS is Wasting the goods and Effects of the deceased: It is therefore Ordered that the administration granted to the said BARWELL EVANS be revoked and that AMBROS BRIANT and PAUL SMITH the said BARWELL EVANS two Securities for his faithful administration be appointed administrators on said Estate. WILLIAM TILLER is approved of as their Security.

WILLIAM McDONALD vs JOHN GRAHAM. Debt. Judgment for amount of the Note and Interest With Costs of Suit. The Defendants Atty having No Instruction of any Defence.

[Page 229]

DAVID BUSH vs BEN: EVANS, CHARLES EVANS Guarnashee. Att.

Ordered that a Commission do Issue to the State of Georgia to take the Depositions of RUAL EVANS and FREDERICK EVANS: and that DAVID PERKINS be announced de bene esse.

ARTHUR INGRAM vs THOMAS BALLARD, DAVID BALLARD. Case. THOMAS BALLARD Came into Court and Confess'd Judgment agreeable to the Specialty. The Tobacco Settled at Fourteen Shillings Pr Hundred Weight. Stay of Execution Untill the first of August.

MOSELEY COLLINS vs WILLIAM BALLARD, BLAN BALLARD. S. P. Decree for Plaintiff for L 5 & Interest thereon from the 9th of Decemr 1793 With Costs of Suit.

Exo'r ISRAEL MATHIS vs FRANCIS BOYKIN, JAMES MARTIN. S. P. Decree for the Defendants.

NATH'L RUSSELL vs JAMES PERRY. Debt. Judgment agreeable to Specialty the Def'dts Atty having Nothing to Say; with costs of suit.

[Page 230] 11 Feby 1796

JAMES PEIRSON vs PHILLIP BURFORD. Debt. Judgment as P Specialty the defendants Atty having With Drawn his Plea.

[11 February 1796]

SAMUEL WEBB vs WILLIAM KIRKLAND. Debt. Verdict for the Plaintiff. We find a Verdict of L 2 s 2 d 4 with Interest thereon. MICHAEL BARNAT, foreman.

NATHAN'L RUSSELL vs JAMES PERRY, JOSIAH PERRY. Debt. Judgment agreeable to Specialty With Costs of Suit the defendants Att'y having no Defence.

JAMES PEIRSON vs ROBERT FORD. Debt. Judgment agreeable to Specialtys With Costs of Suit. The Defendants Att'y having no Defence.

JAMES PEIRSON vs THOMAS BALLARD. Debt. Judgment agreeable to Specialties With Costs of Suit. The defendants Att'y having no defence.

[Page 231]

WILLIAM ODANIEL vs JOHN RUSSELL. Debt. Judgment agreeable to Specialty With Costs of Suit With Stay of Ex'on in the Shff Office three Months. The defendts Att'y having no defence.

JAMES ESTHERS vs JAMES BROWN JUN'R. Debt. Judgment agreeable to Specialty With Costs of Suit. The defendants Att'y having no defence.

REUBIN HARRISON & NICHOLAS PEAY vs HENRY HUNTER. Debt. Judgment agreeable to Specialty With Costs of Suit. The Defendants Att'y having no defence.

On Motion made at the request of SAMUEL MILHOUS son of JOHN MILHOUS & at the request & by the consent of JOHN MAXWELL, Ordered that the said SAMUEL MILHOUS be admitted an Administrator jointly with the said JOHN MAXWELL on the estate of WILLIAM MAXWELL deceased & that JOHN MICKLE be approved of as his Security. The said SAM MILHOUS took the usual Oath in this Case &c.

[Page 232]

JAMES ROBINSON vs JOSIAH CANTEY. Case. The Plaintiff came to trial, and was nonsuited.

CHARLES POLK vs LION & LEVY. S. P. Ordered that A Commission do Issue to Examine Witnesses in the State of North Carolina.

JOSEPH BELL vs JOSEPH TILER SEN'R.

MOSES HOLLIS vs HUGH BROWN & SAM'L WEBB. Debt. Judgment agreeable to Specialty With Costs. The Defendents Att'y having no defence.

HUGH YOUNG vs BRYAN SPRADLEY. Case. Judgment for L 11 s 4 with Costs of Suit.

FRANCIS BOYKIN vs WILLIAM BRUMMITT. Debt on Attach't. Judgment being obtained, ordered that the property attached and replevied in this Case be returned & delivered up to the Sheriff to be sold in Satisfaction of this Judgment.

[Page 233]

JONATHAN DUREN vs HENRY HUDSON. Debt. Judgment by default According to Specialty.

[11 February 1796]

Ordered that JAMES SOWEL be received as Security and Enter into a bond for the due administration of MELDRIDGE EVANS as Administratrix of the Estate of WILLIAM EVANS in the place of PAUL SMITH one of the Securities.

Ordered that all the Recognizances of Persons Bound Over to this Court Stand Over Untill the Next Court.

WILLIAM ANCRUM Surv'r & c vs ISAAC ROSS JUN'R. Case. Dismiss'd at the Plaintiffs Costs.

JOSEPH McADAMS appeared in Open Court and Took the Oath as a Constable for this County.

MOSES SARZEDAS vs TURNER STARKE. S. P. Decree as Pr Specialty the Pork Valued at four Dollars Pr hundred With Costs of Suit.

JOSEPH BELL vs JOSEPH TILLER SEN'R. Case. We find for the Defendant with Costs of Suit. MICHAEL BARNET, foreman.

The Court adjourned untill tomorrow Eleven OClock. JOHN KERSHAW, B. BOYKIN.

[Page 234] 12 Feby 1796

The Court agreeable to Adjournment Met. Present BURWELL BOYKIN, JOHN KERSHAW.

SAMUEL MATHIS vs MATHEW BOWEN. Debt. Judgment Confess'd for Ten Guineas & Interest With Costs.

DAVID RUSH vs BENJ'N EVANS. CHARLES EVANS Guar'ee & Claimant of the Property Attached.

By Consent of parties the Deposition of ISAIAH BUSH on behalf of the Pltf to be taken de bene esse in this Cause.

JAMES COWSAR Ind'ee ALEX CAMERON vs RICHARD L. CHAMPION Bail for THOMAS SMURREL the principal. Sci facias. BROWN for Pltf. BREVARD for Deft.

On hearing the Cause on the part of the Pltff and Defendant it is adjudged by the Court that the Defendant hath now Shewn sufficient causy why & ca. therefore it is considered that the Pltf have judgment .... from which Decision the Deft craves and appeal to the next Dist. Court. Ordered that the same be granted on his complying with the Law in Such Cases.

[Page 235]

SAMUEL HARRISON vs JOHN RUSSELL. S. P. Decree for the Defendant with the Costs.

Ordered that all the Estrays that have been advertised the legal time be immediately Sold after the adjournment of the Court.

JOHN BRANNUM vs HUGH FEARFIELD. S. P. for Damage. Decree for the Plaintiff Five Pounds With Costs of Suit.

ROBERT FORD vs GEORGE KING. Writ on slander. Ordered that the Bail be Discharged from the Bail Bond Given in this Case.

HENRY HUGHES vs JOSEPH TILLER. Debt. Judg't by Default agreeable to Specialty With Costs.

[12 February 1796]

Ordered that the Sheriff do receive of the Clerk as Pr his Account L 12 s 10 and that the Clerk do receive L 10 in like Manner.

DAVID DAVIS vs ROBERT WOOD, SAM'L TOMSON. Att. in Debt. Ordered that the Bay Mare attached in this Case be sold at Next Sale Day unless she be replyved before the Day of Sale.

[Page 236]

JAMES BROWN & SARAH BROWN not having their Security ready for their Administration on JA'S BROWN SEN'R's estate Ordered that when they give Security to be approved by two of the Judges of the Court they be qualified before the Clerk & that Letters of Adm'n issued.

Ordered that MICHAEL BARNET & LEWIS COLLINS be authorised on behalf of the County to contract With any Workman to rebuild the Bridge over Graneys Quarter Creek on the Rocky Mount Road the Bridge to be erected two feet highter than the Present and that an adequate sum be provided for defraying the Expence not to exceed Fifteen pounds.

It having been represented to the Court that the Bridge undertaken to be built over Saunders Creek on said road is by no Means done either in a strong or Workman like Manner. Ord'd that the Clerk do not pay the sum allowed for it, untill the Court shall be satisfied then with and order otherwise.

Court adjourn'd untill the 7th May next. JOHN KERSHAW, B. BOYKIN.

Agreeable to Adjournment the Court Met. Present ISAAC DUBOSE, BURWELL BOYKIN, Esq'rs.

The Commissioners WILLIAM KIRKLAND and WILLIAM NUTT Not having Reported on the Propriety of Continuing or altering the Road leading from Hanging Rock to Mickles Fery agreeable to Order dated 9th Feby 1796, Ordered that CHARLES BARBER is hereby added to the other two Commissioners and that they do Make Report to the Court at their Next Sitting.

[Page 237]

The Court adjourn'd Untill Monday ten Oclock. IS. DUBOSE, B. BOYKIN.

Agreeable to Adjournment the Court Met. Present ISAAC DUBOSE, BURWELL BOYKIN, Esq'rs.

Ordered that the following Persons are appointed overseers of the several districts of roads within this County for the ensuing year, each overseer to appoint a summoner for his district,

JOHN BETHANY, ISAAC UNDERWOOD, THO'S BROOM, W'M COOK, JOHN ROBINSON, JA'S COWSAR, MATTHEW COLEMAN, JA'S WILLIAMS, ROB'T FORD, JOHN BETHENY, JOHN CASE, W'M BRACEY, W'M NETTLES, SAM'L SMITH, GEO. MILLER, JA BROWN JUN., THO. LANGFORD, ROB'T FORD

[Page 238] 9 May 1796

W'M MALONE, JOHN KING, ARCH'D WATSON, JACOB CHAMPION, FRAN'C WREN, ROB'T MAHAFFEY, SAM'L TINES, JACOB FALKENBERRY, ROB'T WILLIAMS, JA. CAIN, THO. WATTS, IS'C ROSS JUN'R, JOHN OQUIN, JOSEPH PAYNE, JACOB CHAMBERS, JA'S ENGLISH from English Ferry to McCords ferry Road, JOHN MARSHALL, THO. KELLY, W'M DANIEL JUN'R, SAMUEL WEBB, REUBEN COLLINS, SAM'L JONES, W'M JONES, JOHN CATO, W'M BOND, PETER CRIMM, W'M McKEY, THO WHITAKER for lower road to Columbia, JOSIAH SCOT, JOHN SWILLEY, DILLARD COLLINS.

[9 May 1796]

Mr. CHAMPION having reported that the Bridge Built over Saunders Creek is now well and compleatly finished, Ordered that the Money appropriated by the Court for that Purpose be paid to THO'S KELLY for the Same.

[Page 329]

Ordered that ARCHIBALD WATSON be and he is hereby Permitted to sell at Public Auction the remaining part Stock of Cattle Horses & Hogs of the Est. of SAMUEL BELTON dec'd on a Credit of 12 Months and that a return of the Sale be MAde to the Clks Office to be Recorded.

Ordered that the Letters of guardianship granted to DAN'L PAYNE of CHARLOTTE BELTON be Revoked and that ALEXANDER STEWART be Appointed Guardian of the s'd CHARLOTTE BELTON in her Stead the Securities of ALEX'R STEWART are ARCHIBALD WATSON & LEWIS COLLINS.

Ordered that Letters Testamentory do Issue to SARAH ROY Executrix of the Goods & Chattels of WILLIAM ROY deceased, the Last Will & Testament of said WILLIAM ROY being Produced and Proven in Open Court.

Ordered that Letters of Administration do Issue to FRANCIS WREN on the estate of ROBERT WREN deceased the Securities are JAMES WREN & JOHN RUTLEDGE JUN'R.

The Court then adjourned to the 8th day of August Next. IS. DUBOSE, B. BOYKIN.

[Page 330] AUGUST TERM 1796

Grand Jurors Drawn from Box N'o 1 to N'o 2.

1 PHILEMON HILLIARD, 2 WILLIAM RUSSELL B.C., 3 REUBIN COLLINS, 4 RICHARD MARR, 5 LOVICK ROCHELL, 6 WILLIS WHITAKER, 7 WILLIAM DANIEL, 8 JOHN CATO, 9 WILLIAM ARCHER, 10 JAMES MARSHALL SEN'R, 11 DOUGLAS STARKE, 12 SAMUEL HELTON, 13 WILLIAM CATO, 14 JOHN FLETCHER, 15 DANIEL McMULLIN, 16 WILLIAM WALDEN, 17 ROBERT TOMSON, 18 GEORGE EVANS [JAMES SCOTT stricken], 19 GEORGE RICHARDSON, 20 PETER TURLEY.

Petit Jurors Drawn from Box N'o 3 to N'o 4.

1 ELIAS JONES, 2 THOMAS LILLEY, 3 GEORGE PYLAND, 4 JOHN OWEN, 5 JAMES McCORKEL, 6 DANIEL HOLLIDAY, 7 TOUSON GENO, 8 WILLIAM ELKINS Saw. C., 9 JACOB CHERRY, 10 REUBIN COOK, 11 JOSEPH ROBERTS, 12 JOHN WHEAT, 13 ISAAC WILLIAMS, 14 JAMES NIPPER, 15 JAMES HESTER, 16 WILLIAM WELLS, 17 JOHN BRADLEY JUN'R, 18 ABRAM SHIVER, 19 HENRY KING, 20 EDWARD WATSON, 21 JOHN LOCKART, 22 RICHARD GARNER, 23 LEWIS GRANT 25 m Creek, 24 JACOB FAULKENBERRY, 25 DAVID McMULLEN, 26 JOHN BROWN G.Q., 27 JAMES HOLLEY, 28 JAMES ROBINSON JUN'R, 29 FRANCIS ADAMS B.C., 30 BENJ. WATTS.

8 August 1796

Agreeable to Adjournment the Court met. Present ISAAC DUBOSE, BURWELL BOYKIN, esq'rs.

JESSE LEE appeared in Open Court and took the Necessary Oaths as Deputy Sheriff for the County of Kershaw.

[Page 231] 8th August 1796

Ordered that Letters of Administration do Issue to SUSANNAH GARDNER on the estate of DANIEL GARDNER deceased the securities are THOMAS GARDNER & JOHN KILE.

GEORGE ASHFORD vs W'M BRUMMITT. Debt. Judgment Confess'd by Defendant for L 11 s 11 d 3 sterling and Costs of suit.

HUGH FEARFIELD vs ISAAC BLANCHARD. S.P. Settled Between the Parties the Plaintiff to Pay the Costs.

JAMES MARTIN vs GEORGE ROSS. S.P. Dismiss'd the Defendant having Paid the Debts and Costs in both these Cases.

MARTIN & TRENT vs the Same. S.P.

JAMES PERISON vs Admo'r W'M MAXWELL. Debt. Judgment Confess'd by JOHN MAXWELL One of the Defendants for L 16 sd 7 sterling & costs of Suit.

HUGH YOUNG Surv'r vs ROBERT McKAIN. S.P. on Note. Judgment Confess'd by the Defendant for the amount of the Note & Interest.

[Page 232]

HUGH YOUNG vs Adm'x of ARCH'D McDONALD. S.P. on Note. Judgment Confess'd by the Defendant for the Ballance of the Note & Interest...

HUGH YOUNG vs the Same. S.P. on an open Acco't. Judgment Confess'd by the Defendant for L 3 s 11 d 4....

SAM'L MATHIS In'ds of W'M CRAIG vs JOHN RUSSELL. Debt. Judgment Confess'd by the Defendant for L 13 s 5 d 4 sterling.

An Order having Passed the Court October 17th 1791 for Opening a Road from JOSEPH McCOYS to Little Lynches Creek at PATRICK McCAINES Bridge &c and Whereas it has been found that a much Nearer Way can be Laid Out for Said Road therefore Ordered that the Said Road shall be laid Out the Nearest & best Way from PATRICK McCAINS bridge on Little Lynches Creek to Camden and that GEO: EVANS is Appointed Overseer to Carry the Same into Effect.

The Court then adjourn to to Morrow 10 OClock. IS. DUBOSE, B. BOYKIN.

[Page 233]

9th August 1796. Agreeable to Adjournment the Court Met. Present BURWELL BOYKIN, ISAAC DUBOSE, Esq'rs.

JOHN OQUIN Administrator of the estate of DANIEL HORTEN returned an account which was examined and approved of By the Court and Ordered to be filed in the Records of this Court.

The State vs JAMES HESTER. Misdemeanor. Petit Jury Sworn & Impanel'd.

1 JAMES KERSHAW foreman, 2 PATRICK McCAIN, 3 JOHN KILE, 4 WILLIAM JONES JUN'R, 5 JOHN MOTLEY, 6 ISAAC BLANCHARD, 7 ADAM TOMSON, 8 LEWIS COLLINS, 9 JOSHUA DINKINS, 10 GEORGE BROWN, 11 JAMES BUCKHANAN, 12 MICHAEL GANTER. We find the Defendant Guilty. JAMES KERSHAW, foreman.

JOHN MICKLE vs JOHN MAXWELL, SAM'L MILHOUSE Adm'or W'M MAXWELL. Debt. Judgment Confess'd for the amount of the Note & Interest with Costs of Suit.

[Page 234] 9th August 1796.

The State vs JOHN BUNT. Assault. No Bill. GEORGE ROSS, foreman.

Grand Jury Sworn and Impanneld

1 GEORGE ROSS foreman, 2 WYLY COLLINS, 3 WILLIAM JONES, 4 JAMES SOWEL, 5 REUBIN STARKE, 6 DANIEL KIRKLAND, 7 GEORGE MILLER, 8 JOHN RUTLEDGE SEN'R, 9 JACOB GREY, 10 RICHARD STRATFORD, 11 WILLIAM NETTLES SEN'R, 12 LEWIS PEEBLES, 13 ARTHUR CUNNINGHAM.

LAZERUS KELLY vs JOHN TWADDLE. S.P. Judgment Confess'd agreeable to Specialty With Costs of Suit. Stay of Ex'on in the Shffs hands three Months.

McRA CANTEY & C'o vs PETER TWITTY. Debt. Judgment Confess'd for L 40 s 4 d 5 with Costs of Suit.

GEORGE GAYDEN vs DAVID DRENNAN & JOHN HOOD. Debt. Judgment Confess'd for L 7 s 15 d 8 With Costs of Suit. Ex'on to Stay in the Shffs hands for five Months.

JOHN CRAIG vs JOSEPH GASTON. S.P. Decree as Pr Specialty With Interest & Costs of Suit Stay Exo'n three Months.

[Page 235]

WILLIAM FAIRFIELD vs JOHN LAWRENCE. S.P. Settled.

THOMAS JONES vs JAMES GUNN. S.P. Judgment by Default agreeable to Specialty With Int. & Costs of Suit.

NATHANIEL RUSSELL vs JOHN OWEN. S.P. Judgment by Default agreeable to Specialty With Interest & Costs of Suit.

DANIEL OQUIN SEN'R vs JESSE MINTON. Debt. Judgment Confess'd for L 15 & Interest from the 23rd April 1796. Stay of Exo'n in the Shffs hands to 23 April 1797 With Costs.

The State vs BURWELL MILLS. Larceny. True Bill. GEORGE ROSS, Foreman.

State vs DANIEL LANDON. Assault. True Bill. GEORGE ROSS, Foreman.

[Page 236]

HUGH YOUNG vs JONATHAN COOK. Case. Writ of Inquirey. Verdict. WE find for the Plaintiff L 16 15/7. JAMES KERSHAW, foreman.

ZACHARIAH HESTER vs JOHN RUTLEDGE JUN'R. S.P. Decree for the Plaintiff for L 6 s 3 with costs of Suit.

The State vs JAMES HESTER. Guilty. Sentence to pay Twenty Shillings and fess and be Confined for One Month on the Common Gaol of the County and to be continued in Confinement after the end of the Month till his fines & fees are paid.

The Court then adjourned to toMorrow Ten OClock. IS. DUBOSE, B. BOYKIN.

Agreeable to Adjournment the Court Met. Present ISAAC DUBOSE, BURWELL BOYKIN, Esq'r.

LEWIS COOK vs DANIEL PAYNE. Appeal. Settled by Plaintiff.

Ordered that the Estate of WILLIAM ROY be Sold by the Executrix after giving Legal Notice on a Credit Untill the first of January next.

[Page 237] 10th August 1796

JOHN ADAMSON vs JOHN HOOD.   S.P.   Judgment Confess'd for L 7 s 19 sterling.

The State vs BURWELL MILLS.   Larceny.   Not Guilty.   JAMES KERSHAW, foreman.

1 JAMES KERSHAW foreman, 2 PATRICK McCAIN, 3 JOHN KILE, 4 WILLIAM JONES, 5 JOHN MOTLEY, 6 ISAAC BLANCHARD, 7 ADAM TOMSON, 8 LEWIS COLLINS, 9 JOSHUA DINKINS, 10 GEORGE BROWN, 11 JAMES BUCKHANNAN, 12 MICHAEL GANTER.

Ordered that the above named BURWELL MILLS be Released from Confinement.

The State vs JAMES NORTON.   Ordered that JAMES NORTEN be Bound Over to the Superior Court in the Sum of L 50 and One Security in L 25 and that JOHN RUTLEDGE JUN'R the Prosecutor & Wintess be Bound Over to appear at the same court.

JOSEPH KERSHAW vs JN'O NARRIMORE, W'M KEMP SEN'R.   Debt on Bond. WILLIAM KEMP appeared in Open Court and Confessd Judgment agreeable to Specialty.

[Page 238]

JAMES WILLIAMS vs THOMAS BRADDUM.   S.P.   Settled at the Defendants Costs.

JAMES BELL Vs SAM'L THOMSON.   S.P.   Decree by Default as Pr Specialty With Costs of Suit.

JOHN ROBINSON & C'o vs JOSEPH PAYNE.   Case.   Verdict for the Plaintiff for L 15 s 7.

DAVID RUSSELL vs JOHN ROBINSON.   Debt.   Plea Withdrawn and Judgement by Default according to Specialty With Costs of Suit.

JOHN RUSSELL vs MARTIN TRANTHAM.   Trover.   Verdict for Defendant.

Ordered that the Estate of ARCHIBALD McDONALD be Sold by the Administratrix One Negro Boy to be sold for Cash the Remainder of the Property to be Sold on a Credit Untill the first of March Next after giving Legal Notice.

[Page 239]

GEORGE PERRY vs WILLIAM LANGLEY & GEORGE MORRIS.   Case.   Ordered that the Deposition of ELIZABETH STEWART be taken De bene esse.

The State vs REUBIN BROWN.   Larceny.   Ordered that the Recognizance in this Case be laid over Untill Next Court.

The Court then adjourn to tomorrow Ten OClock. IS. DUBOSE, B. BOYKIN.

Agreeable to Adjournment the Court met.   Present ISAAC DUBOSE, BURWELL BOYKIN, Esq'rs.

JOHN McCAA vs BRYAN SPRADLEY.   S.P.   The defendant appeared in Open Court and Confess'd Judgment agreeable to Specialty.

JAMES BOWLES & Ex'rs vs JOHN GREGG.   S.P.   Judgment by Default agreeable to Specialty with Costs of Suit.

[Page 240] 11th August 1796

ZACH CANTEY vs JOHN RUTLEDGE SEN'R. S.P. Upon hearing the Cause the Court were Devided in Opinion and referd it to the determination of the Jury. The Plaintiff having moved for the same Which the Defendant Objected to but was Over Ruled. The Following Jury were Sworn:

1 JAMES KERSHAW foreman, 2 PATRICK McCAIN, 3 JOHN KILE, 4 WILLIAM JONES, 5 JOHN MOTLEY, 6 ISAAC BLANCHARD, 7 THOMAS DINKINS, 8 LEWIS COLLINS, 9 JOSHUA DINKINS, 10 GEORGE BROWN, 11 JAMES BUCHANNAN, 12 MICHAEL GANTER.

We find for the Plaintiff 53 Bushels Corn 3/6 Nine Pounds five Shillings & Six Pence. JAMES KERSHAW, foreman.

ROBERT FORD vs GEORGE KING. Slander. Dismiss'd.

JONATHAN BELTON vs HENRU RUGELY. S.P. Decree for L 7.17.2. Execution to Stay till 1st day next Feby Court to whatever Judg't the defen't may then Establish.

The Court then adjournd till tomorrow ten OClk. B. BOYKIN, IS. DUBOSE.

[Pgae 241] 12th August 1796

Agreeable to Adjournment the Court Met. Present ISAAC DUBOSE, Esquire.

Ordered that DANIEL PAYNE Guardian of CHARLOTT BELTON Do Receive his Bond from the Clerk of the Court he having Produced his Accounts and properly Attested.

ROBERT McCREDIE Surviver vs JOHN OWEN. S.P. Decree for L 3 d 2.

REUBIN STARK Stark vs ELIZABETH SCOTT Adm'x of JAMES SCOTT dec. Dismiss'd at the Defd't Costs.

DAVID DUNCAN vs The Executrix of JAMES SMITH dec'd. S.P. Judgment by Default agreeable to Specialty With Costs.

JOHN ROBINSON & C'o vs JAMES BROWN JUN'R. S.P. Judgment Confess'd for L 2 s 14.

[Pgae 242]

JESSE MINTON vs MARTIN TRANTHAM. Trover. We find for the Defendant. JAMES KERSHAW, foreman.

1 JAMES KERSHAW foreman, 2 PATRICK McCAIN, 3 JOHN KILE, 4 WILLIAM JONES, 5 JOHN MOTELY, 6 ISAAC BLANCHARD, 7 ADAM TOMSON, 8 LEWIS COLLINS, 9 JOSHUA DINKINS, 10 GEORGE BROWN, 11 JAMES BUCKHANNAN, 12 MICHAEL GANTER.

It was agreed by Mutual Consent that this Case should be tryed with One Judge Presiding.

DAVID BUSH vs WILLIAM MASSY. On Motion of the Plaintiffs Atty Ordered that the Defendant be held to Special Bail.

JAMES WILLIAMS vs WILLIAM DOBY. Debt. On Motion of Plff's Atty Ordered that the Pltf have leave to amend his Process in this Case.

CHARLES POLK vs LION & LEVY. S.P. DANIEL BROWN appears in Court and Consents to be Security for the Costs and Says that he will pay the same if the Pltff. is Cast.

FRANCIS BOYKIN vs JOHN RUTLEDGE & WILLIAM NETTLES. Case. On Motion of Plff's Atty Ordered that the Pltf have leave to amend his Process in this Case.

[Page 243] 12 August 1796

CHARLES POLK vs LION & LEVY. S.P. The Defendant Prayed a Jury. The following Jury was Sworn.

1 JAMES KERSHAW foreman, 2 PATRICK McCAIN, 3 JOHN KILE, 4 WILLIAM JONES, 5 JOHN MOTELY, 6 ISAAC BLANCHARD, 7 ADAM TOMSON, 8 LEWIS COLLINS, 9 JOSHUA DINKINS, 10 MARTIN TRANTHAM, 11 JAMES BUCKHANNAN, 12 MICHAEL GANTER.

We find for the Plaintiff L 7 s 10 d 10. JAMES KERSHAW, foreman.

FREDERICK JOINER vs JOSEPH PAYNE. Case. Dismiss'd at the Plaintiffs Costs.

The Court then adjournd till to Morrow Ten OClock. IS. DUBOSE.

Agreeable to Adjournment the Court met. Present ISAAC DUBOSE, Esq'r.

WILLIAM ANCRUM & Others Trustees of J'O K'S Estate vs ISAAC ALEXANDER. Debt. Judgment Confes'd for L 8 d 6 with Interest from 2nd Feby 1796.

WILLIAM BRACEY JUN'R vs THOMAS HAWFIELD. S.P. Decree according to Specialty Ex'on not to Issue Untill Next Feby Court.

[Page 244]

McRA CANTEY & C'o vs DANIEL WILLIAMS. Debt. Settled at Defendants Costs.

DAVID BUSH vs WILLIAM MASSEY JUN'R. Debt. Judgment by Default on Note.

W'M STEEL vs LEWIS HUDSON. Case. Judgment by Default.

ARCHIBALD WATSON vs JOHN JACKSON. Settled at Defendants Costs.

DAVID BUSH vs DANIEL PAYNE. Case. It was Mutually agreed by the Parties that this Case should be tryed With One Judge Presiding.

FRANCIS BOYKIN vs JOHN RUTLEDGE SEN'R. Case. A Motion made by the Defenant to Quash the Writ. Ordered that the Cause Do Stand Over Untill the next Court in the Same Situation that it is now is to be then Argued before a fuller Bench.

JESSE MINTON vs W'M SKIPPER. Trespass. [stricken]

[Page 245] 13th August 1796

ISHAM MOORE vs JOSIAH SCOTT. Debt. The Plaintiffs Atty in this Case Notice that THOMAS HOOPER Esq'r is the Real Pltfs the Def't having produced a Receipt in full from him to said Deft & an Order on the Said Atty for the Note.

DUNCAN McRA & ZACHARIAH CANTEY vs JOHN SANDERS. Debt. Ordered that the Defendant give Special Bail in this Case.

HUGH TEMPLETON & MATTHEW ROGERS vs RICHARD DUMVILLE. Case. Judgment by Default.

The State vs JOSEPH McCOY. Indictment. Ordered Peremtorily that this tryal come on at the Next February Court.

Ordered that the Sheriff do procure a list of the inhabitants of the County liable to serve in Juries to be laid before the next Court for the purpose of having a New Jury list Made Out according to Law.

[Page 246] 14th August 1796.

The Court Adjourn'd Untill the Seventh of November next. IS. DUBOSE.

7th November 1796. Agreeable to Adjournment the Court Met. Present BURWELL BOYKIN, ISAAC DUBOSE, Esq'rs.

Ordered that ISAAC ALEXANDER Do Receive Letters of Administration on the estate of MICHAEL CURRENT deceased, the Security is ARTHUR BROWN ROSS.

Ordered that Letters of Administration do Issue to JOHN ROBINSON SEN'R on the estate of ROBERT ROBINSON Deceased, the Security is JOHN ADAMSON.

Ordered that the Administratrix of DANIEL GARDNER Deceased do keep the Property of the estate in her hands Until Otherwise Ordered by Court.

Ordered that letters of Administration do Issue to SARAH BROWN and JAMES BROWN on the estate of JAMES BROWN deceased, the Security is SAMUEL BREED.

The Court adjournd to tomorrow 10 OClock. IS. DUBOSE, B. BOYKIN.

[Page 247] 8 November 1796

Agreeable to Adjournment the Court Met. Present ISAAC DUBOSE & BURWELL BOYKIN, Esq'rs.

Ordered that WILLIAM ODANIEL do Receive letters Testamentary on the last Will & Testament of WILLIAM ODANIEL Deceased, he being first Sworn in Open Court.

SAMUEL MATHIS late of the Commissioners of the Poor of this County having brought in and returned an Account of the Monies received and Paid by the late Commissioners for the use of the Poor of the said County & also an Account of the Names of the persons & Estates from Whom Money and Taxes have been received together with the Vouchers supporting the said Accounts. The same after due examinatoin are found to be just and right and are approved.

Ordered that they be filed With the Clerk of this Court and Preserved among the Records. It is also ordered that the sum of Three pounds 8/ 4 1/2 (the balance appearing in thier hands) be paid over to the Clerk of this Court. and SAMUEL MATHIS paid the same to the Clerk accordingly.

Ordered that letters of Administration do issue to GRACE FLECTHER on the estate of JOHN FLETCHER Deceased, the Securities are THOMAS BRADFORD and GEORGE MILLER.

[Page 248]

Ordered that GRACE FLETCHER Administratrix have leave to Sell Part of the Property of the Estate of JOHN FLETCHER dec'd and make a Return to the Next Court (say part of the Stock).

Ordered that the Clerk do pay Monthly to each of the following Persons the Sum opposite to each Name as far as the Money arising from the Poor Tax which he now has in his hands will go Viz't

[8 November 1796]

PLUNKETs 2 Idiot Children each	10/.
HENRY ROTTENBURRY	10/.
CONDONs Child MARGARET	7/.
WIDOW SCOT	5/.
JACOB SUMMERFORD	5/.

Ordered the letters of Administration do Issue to ZACHARIAH CANTEY on the estate of WILLIAM BROWN deceased, the Security is DUNCAN McRA.

Ordered that the Administrator of the Estate of WILLIAM BROWN deceased be permitted to ₋ell all such parts of said Estate as he May think proper. Payable the first of January next.

[Page 249]

Ordered that the Clerk do apply to the County Tax Collector for an Acc't of Monies Rec'd by him on Acc't of the County tax since his last settlement before the Court. Also an acc't of Strays sold by him as Sheriff during the time he was in Office.

The Court then Adjourned to the Seventh Day of February Next. IS. DUBOSE, B. BOYKIN.

Feby Term 1797

Grand Jury Drawn from Box N'o to N'o 2.

1 JOSIAH SCOTT, 2 ARTHUR CUNNINGHAM, 3 JACOB GREY, 4 JAMES ROCHELL, 5 DANIEL GARDNER, 6 WILLIAM NETTLES S.C., 7 LEWIS COLLINS, 8 ARTHUR B. ROSS, 9 THOMAS ROACH, 10 ALEXANDER ARCHER, 11 SAMUEL BROWN, 12 RICHARD GARDNER, 13 DANIEL PAYNE, 14 RICHARD STRATFORD, 15 THOMAS BALLARD, 16 JOHN CHESNUT Esq'r, 17 SHEROD SIMS, 18 WILLIAM COLLINS, 19 JAMES ENGLISH, 20 JAMES CARRUTH.

Ordered that WILLIAM DUNLAP & ROBERT DUNLAP Executors of the last Will & Testament of CATHARINE SMITH do receive letters Testamentary the Will being first Proved in Open Court.

[Page 250] 7 Feb 1797

Petit Jury Drawn from Box N'o 3 to N'o 4.

1 SOLOMON ASBELL, 2 ABRAM SCOTT, 3 CHARLES RALEY, 4 WILLIS WINDHAM, 5 WILLIAM BETHANY, 6 JOHN ESAL, 7 JOHN BRADLEY, 8 JOSIAH PARKER, 9 JOHN TEKLE, 10 JONATHAN ARCHER, 11 JOHN HORTON, 12 JONATHAN BUNCKLEY, 13 WILLIAM HOOD, 14 THOMAS CURRY, 15 JOHN PARKINS, 16 JOHN RUTLEDGE JUN'R, 17 JOHN PAYNE, 18 ALEXANDER CARRUTH, 19 ARON ARKINS, 20 JOHN HOOD, 21 RICHARD MAN, 22 DAVID TOD, 23 ROBERT DUNLAP, 24 THOMAS DICKSON, 25 ARCHIBALD OWENS, 26 LEWIS BRYANT, 27 JACOB FAULKINBERRY, 28 LEWIS PEEBLES, 29 SIMON BECKHAM, 30 FRANCIS BELL.

Agreeable to Adjournment the Court met. Present JOHN KERSHAW, ISAAC DUBOSE, BURWELL BOYKIN, Esq'rs.

Ordered that PRESTLY REEVES and JESSE REEVES do Receive letters of administration on the estate of MOSES REEVES deceased: DANIEL PAYNE and THOMAS COLLIER are the Securities.

Ordered that WILLIAM ODANIEL do Receive letters of administration on the estate of JOHN ODANIEL deceased. the Securities are ROBERT DUNLAP & WILLIAM DUNLAP.

[7 February 1797]

M'r JAMES SPARKS was appointed a Deputy Sheriff of this County with the approbation of the Court & appeared in open Court & took the Oath pointed out by the Constitution & also the Oath of Office directed by the County Court Law of this State in such case made & provided.

[Page 251]

Ordered that letters of Administration do Issue to JOHN CRAVEN on the estate of PHILLIP PLATT deceased. The security is JOHN McCAA.

JOHN ADAMSON vs SAMUEL TYNES, W'M DOBY. Debt on Note. Judgment Confessed by SAM'L TYNES for the amo't of the Note & Interest.

JOHN ADAMSON vs WILLIAM BRACEY. Settled Between the Parties and Costs Paid.

HUGH YOUNG vs ZACH'Y NETTLES. Discontinued, Deft having paid Debt & Costs.

SAMUEL MATHIS vs WILLIAM CRAIG. Debt on Bond. Judgment confessed for L 78 18/11 and Interest thereon from 1st Jany 1796.

JOHN KERSHAW, IS. DUBOSE, B. BOYKIN.

Agreeable to Adjournment the Court met. Present JOHN KERSHAW, ISAAC DUBOSE, Esq'rs.

Ordered that letters Testamentary do Issue to WILLIAM SOWDEN of the estate of WILLIAM PERKINS decd.

[Page 254] 8 February 1797

Ordered that the Property of ROBERT ROBINSON deceased be Sold by the Administrator on the first Saturday in March giving Nine Months Credit advertising agreeable to Law.

The Grand Jury Sworn & Impaneled are as Follows.

1 WILLIS WHITAKER foreman, 2 PHILEMON HILLARD, 3 WILLIAM RUSSELL, 4 REUBIN COLLINS, 5 LOVICK ROCHELL, 6 WILLIAM ODANIEL, 7 JAMES MARSHALL SEN'R, 8 DANIEL MACMULLIN, 9 WILLIAM CATO, 10 WILLIAM WALDEN, 11 ROBERT THOMSON, 12 GEORGE EVANS, 13 WILLIAM ARCHER.

Ordered that Letters Testamentary do Issue to BURWELL BOYKIN and JAMES CANTEY the Nominated Executors of the last WIll & Testament of JOHN DYE Deceased the Will being Produced in Court and Proven.

JOHN ADAMSON vs LOVICK ROCHELL. Debt. Judgment Confess'd for Amount of Note & Interest. Execution to be lodged but not levied untill 8th August next & Then for half the Debt & Interest & on the 1st Jany next for the remainder.

HUGH TEMPLETON & MATHEW ROGERS vs RICHARD DUMVILLE. Case. We find for the Plaintiff L 18. ZACH CANTEY, foreman.

Petit Jury Sworn & Impaneld.

1 ZACHARIAH CANTEY foreman, 2 JAMES McCORKLE, 3 JACOB CHERY, 4 JOHN WHEAT, 5 JAMES NIPPER, 6 W'M WELLS, 7 ABRAM SHIVER, 8 JOHN LOCKHART, 9 LEWIS GRANT, 10 MICHAEL GANTER, 11 DAVID McMULLIN, 12 FRANCIS ADAMS.

[Page 253] 8 February 1797

DUNCAN McRA, ZACH CANTEY, & ROBERT HENRY vs REUBIN COLLINS. Debt. Judgment Confess'd for L 50 s 9 With Interest accordint to Note & Costs of Suit.

WILLIAM STEEL vs LEWIS HUDSON. Case. We find for the Plaintiff L 9 s 7 d 1. ZACH CANTEY, foreman.

ALEX'R IRWIN vs WILLIAM BRUMMETT. Debt. We find for the Plaintiff L 30 s 6 d 2. ZACH CANTEY, foreman.

DAVID DAVIS vs ROBERT HOOD & SAM'L THOMSON. Att. Debt. Dismiss'd Each Party paying their Own costs. ARTHUR CUNNINGHAM is the Real Plaintiff in this Case.

MATHEW BOWEN vs WILLIAM BOWEN. ISAAC ROSS Surrenderd the Body of the Defendant in Discharge of himself as Bail to the Action and Agrees to become Special Bail. ISAAC ROSS JUN'R.

DUNCAN McRA, ZACH CANTEY vs JOHN SANDERS. Debt. We find for the Plaintiff the amount of note With Interest. I. BUSH, foreman.

1 ISAIAH BUSH foreman, 2 JAMES McCORKLE, 3 JACOB CHERY, 4 JOHN WHEAT, 5 JAMES NIPPER, 6 W'M WELLS, 7 ABRAM SHIVER, 8 JOHN LOCKHART, 9 LEWIS GRANT, 10 MICHAEL GANTER, 11 DAVID McMULLIN, 12 FRANCIS ADAMS.

[Page 254]

ROBRT HENRY Ind'se of JOHN SWILLY vs DANIEL PAYNE. Debt. Settled at Defd'ts Costs.

GEORGE SMITH vs JESSE MINTON. S.P. Stand on a Peremtory Rule to come to tryal at next Court a Commission to Issue to North Carolina to Qualify GILES JONES a Witness for the Defendant.

PHILLEMON HILLIARD vs MATTHEW NUTT. Debt. Issue Tried. Verdict. We find for the Plaintiff L 15 s 14 d 3. ZACH CANTEY, foreman.

JAMES PEIRSON vs RAWLIEGH HAMMOND. Debt. Dismiss'd the Defen'dt having Paid Shff. FISHER Debt and Costs.

ALEXANDER WORK vs SAM'L TYNES. Debt. Plea With drawn Judgment by Nihil Dicit.

The State vs STEPHEN DUKE. Misdimianor. True Bill. WILLIS WHITAKER, foreman.

DAVID BUSH vs WILLIAM MASSEY JUN'R. Debt. Judgement by Default.

FRANCIS WREN vs STARKE HUNTER. Debt. Dismiss'd the Defendt Costs.

ALEX'R STEWART vs R. L. CHAMPION Exo'r of JOHN L. CHAMPION. Debt. Judgment Confess'd for Note and Interest with Costs of Suit.

[Page 255]

The State vs DANIEL LANDEN. Assault.

1 ZACHARIAH CANTEY foreman, 2 MICHAEL GANTER 3 JAMES McCORKLE, 4 JACOB CHERY, 5 JOHN WHEAT, 6 JAMES NIPPER, 7 W'M WELLS, 8 ABRAM SHIVER, 9 JOHN LOCKHART, 10 LEWIS GRANT, 11 DAVID McMULLIN, 12 FRANCIS ADAMS.

[8 February 1797]

Guilty. ZACH'Y CANTEY, foreman.

ANDREW BASKINS Esquire & Capt. GEORGE EVANS having signified to the Court they they do not think themselves perfectly safe in continuing as Securities to WILLIAM MASSEY JUNIOR as Adminsitrator of the Estate of the Late Colonel JOHN MARSHEL any longer, and praying to the Court that the said WILLIAM MASSEY be Cited to appear & give such other security as may exonerate them from their said Securityship.

Ordered that a rule of this Court do issue to the said WILLIAM MASSEY to shew Cause why he should not give other security in order that they may be relieved or the Administration revoked on or before Friday next at Eleven OClock.

The Court then adjourned untill tomorrow ten O'Clock. JOHN KERSHAW, B. BOYKIN.

[Page 256] 9th Feby 1797

Agreeable to Adjournment the Court Met. Present JOHN KERSHAW, ISAAC DUBOSE, Esq'rs.

PATRICK McFADIAN vs ADAM McWILLIE. Debt. Abated by death of the Plaintiff.

JAMES GUNN vs THO'S SMYRL. Appeal. Dismiss'd at Plaintiffs Costs.

MOSES SARZEDAS vs SAMUEL TYNES. Debt. Plea With drawn. Judgment by Nihil Dicit.

Ordered that the Executor of JOHN L. CHAMPION Estate do Sell the Estate of the Deceased the first Saturday in March Next (after giving the legal Notice) for Cash.

Ordered that PRESTLY REEVES & JAMES REAVES Administrators of the Estate of MOSES REAVES do sell the property of the deceased the 4th March Giving Nine Months Credit (after giving legal notice)

Admi'x COUNTRYMAN vs JOSEPH McADAM & JOHN HOOD. Debt. We Confess Judgment for the Within Mentioned Debt & Costs 5 Months Stay of Ex'on.

WILLIAM AGLINTON vs JOSIAH SANDERS. SP. Judgment by Default.

HUGH YOUNG vs TURNER STARKE JUN'R S.P. Discontinued.

The State vs DANIEL LANDEN. Assault. Fined twenty Shillings With Costs of Suit.

[Page 257] 9 Feby 1797

JOHN TWADELL vs SAMUEL WEBB. Debt. We find for the Plaintiff $81. ZACH CANTEY, foreman.

DAVID BUSH vs BEN: EVANS, CH'S EVANS Guarnashee. Collateral. Issue.

HUGH YOUNG vs ISAAC ALEXANDER. Judgment Confes'd for the Amount of the two Notes and Interest With Costs of Suit.

MOSELEY COLLINS vs RICHARD WOOD. Att. Decree for L 5 s 16 d 8.

The Court then adjourned untill tomorrow Morning ten O'Clock, the Jury required to seal up their Verdict & delivered it in at that time in the Case. BUSH vs EVANS. JOHN KERSHAW, IS. DUBOSE.

[10 February 1797]

Agreeable to adjournment the Court met.   Present JOHN KERSHAW, BURWELL BOYKIN, ISAAC DUBOSE.

Ordered that a tax of One tenth the amount of the General Tax be levied for the Expences of the County & for the support of the poor thereof the present year & that the Collector of the General Tax be applied to collect the same.

[Page 258]

Ordered that the Sheriff be authorised to sell the Estray Cattle taken up by JOHN RUTLEDGE and JOHN ENGLISH at the plantation of the said JOHN ENGLISH on Saturday the 18th Instant giving due Notice of the same it being found too inconvenient & expensive to have them driven to the Court house.

Ordered that JOHN CHESNUT Esq'r & M'rs THOMAS BROOM be appointed Commissioners for the purpose of contracting for & building a bridge Over Pintree Creek on the Great Road to Charleston as laid out by THOMAS BROOM & JOHN KERSHAW appointed Commissioners for that purpose 11th February 1795.

CHARITY LOWRY vs JAMES WREN, MARY WREN.   Writ on the Case. Continued at the Defendants Costs.

Ordered that the Executors of JOHN DYE deceased Do sell the Property of the Estate on the first Saturday in March next on a Credit of twelve Months.

DAVID BUSH vs BEN: EVANS, CHA'S EVANS Garnashee.   on Att.   Verdict (Rendered in last Evening by Consent of the Parties) We find the Negro the Property of BEN EVANS.   ZACH'H CANTEY, foreman.

Ordered that the Administrator of MICHAEL CURRENT deceased do Sell the property of the deceased on the first of March next for Cash.

Ordered that the Administration of WILLIAM MASSEY JUNIOR on the Estate of Colo JOHN MARSHALL deceased be revoked and the same is hereby Revoked.

[Page 259]

DAVID BUSH vs ARCHELUS PAYNE, DANIEL PAYNE.   Case.   We find for the Defendant the Costs.   ZACH. CANTEY, foreman.

JAMES COWSAR In'd of W. SHROPSHIRE vs JOHN HOOD.   S.P. Decree for the Plaintiff according to Specialty the Ex'on to be lodged in the Shff's Office but Stay of Ex'on for three Months: With Costs of Suit.

The State vs STEPHEN DUKE.   Misdemeanor.   Dismiss'd at the Defendants Costs.

The State vs JOSEPH McCOY.   Stealing a Stear.   Guilty.   ZACHARIAH CANTEY, foreman.

Ordered that JOSEPH McCOY do stand Committed untill he pay the legal fine of ten pounds, or give Satisfactory Security to the Sheriff for the payment of it within one Month.   And that he pays the Costs of the Prosecution before his discharge.

The Court then adjourned untill tomorrow ten O'Clock.   JOHN KERSHAW, B. BOYKIN, IS. DUBOSE.

Agreeable to Adjournment the Court Met.   Present ISAAC DUBOSE & BURWELL BOYKIN Esqrs.

[Page 260] 11 Feby 1797

JOSEPH BREVARD vs EDWARD RUTLEDGE S.P. Decree for the Plaintiffs according to Specialty With Costs of Suit.

WILLIAM LANGLEY vs GEORGE PERRY. S.P. Decree for the Plaintiff for L 7 s 13 d 1 with costs of suit. Stay of Execution three Months in Shffs hands.

Ordered that the administratrix and administrator of the Estate of JAMES BROWN have permission to sell the Carpenters Tools belonging to the said Estate on a Credit of three months they first giving Bond and Making a return of appraisement to the Clerks Office.

CHARITY LOWRY vs JAMES WREN, MARY WREN. Case. We find for the Plaintiff L 15 d 8. ZACH. CANTEY, foreman.

1 ZACHARIAH CANTEY foreman, 2 JAMES McCORKLE, 3 JACOB CHERRY, 4 JN'O WHEAT, 5 JAMES NIPPER, 6 W'M WELLS, 7 ABRAM SHIVER, 8 JN'O LOCKHART, 9 LEWIS GRANT, 10 MICHAEL GANTER, 11 SAMUEL LEVY, 12 DAVID McMULLEN [FRANCIS ADAMS stricken].

SAMUEL LEVY vs JAMES BROWN. Debt. Judgment Confess'd for the amount of the note and In't With Stay of Execution three Months With Costs of Suit.

ROBERT McCREDIE Sur'vr vs JAMES BROWN. S.P. Decree. A nonsuit.

[Page 261]

Admor. & Admix of WILLIAM HOMES vs Admix of ROBERT LEE. Case. We find for the Plaintiff Six Pounds 13/7. ZACH CANTEY, foreman.

JOHN ADAMSON vs PHILIP BURFORD. S.P. Decree for the Plainitff for L 9 s 4 d 6 with costs of Suit.

MOSES SARZEDAS vs PETER RUSH. Debt. Judgment Nihill dicit. [entire entry stricken]

MOSES SARZEDAS vs REUBIN COLLINS. Debt. Judgment according to Specialty Subject to a Discount of L 3 and d 5 at the Date of the Note should the Calculation of the said Discount be found Just & True Which said L 3 d 5 is to be paid to DANIEL BROWN by DAVID BUSH.

REUBIN STARKE vs BENJAMIN McKENZIE. Att. Ordered that the Property attached in this Case be sold by the Sheriff for the best Price that can be got for the same and the Money arising therefrom to be paid to the Plaintiff on his giving good Security for the Return of the same; if by the Court required or Otherwise to Remain in the Shff hands Untill the Determination of this Cause and be Subject to the further Order of the Court. The Sheriff Giving Legal Notice.

[Page 262]

MOSELY COLLINS vs RICHARD WOOD. Att. Ordered that the Property Attached in this Case be Sold by the Shff.

BRICE MILLER vs ADAM TAMSON, FRANCIS ADAMS. Debt. Decree for L 6 s 10 d 6 from the 9th Decemr 1794 & Costs of a Summery Process to be taxed against the Defendants & the Plaintiff to refund to them the Extra Costs that he has put them to by Bringing an action instead of a Summary Process.

BENJAMIN CUDWORTH vs DAVID BUSH. Debt. Verdict for the Plaintiff.

[11 February 1797]

1 ZACHARIAH CANTEY foreman, 2 JAMES McCORKLE, 3 JACOB CHERRY, 4 JOHN WHEAT, 5 JAMES NIPPER, 6 WILLIAM WELLS, 7 ABRAM SHIVER, 8 JOHN LOCKHART, 9 LEWIS GRANT, 10 MICHAEL GANTER, 11 FRANCIS ADAMS, 12 DAVID McMULLEN.

TURNER STARKE vs RICHARD WOOD. Att. Ordered that the Property attached in this Case be Sold by the Sheriff for the best Price that can be got for the same and the Money arising therefrom to Remain in the Shffs. hands until this Case is Decided, if the Property is not Replevied.

BENJ. CUDWORTH vs DAVID BUSH. Debt. We find the the Plaintiff $277.13. ZACH. CANTEY, foreman.

ANDREW LEUTHOLD vs JOHN MARTIN. Debt. We find for the Plaintiff L 17 s 12 d 4. ZACH. CANTEY, foreman.

NATH'L RUSSELL vs WILLIAM TWADDELL. Debt. We find for the Plaintiff L 26 s 11. ZACH. CANTEY, foreman.

[Page 263]

SAMUEL McKEE vs LEWIS COOK. Debt. We find for the Plaintiff L 13 s 2 d 4. ZACH. CANTEY, foreman.

FRANCIS BOYKIN vs JOHN RUTLEDGE, WILLIAM NETTLES SEN. Case. Judgment Confes'd for L 14 s 12 d 1 With costs of Suit.

NATH'L RUSSELL vs WILLIAM DEASON. Debt. We find for the Plaintiff L 14 s 2 d 1. ZACH. CANTEY, foreman.

DAVID BUSH vs BENJAMIN EVANS. Att. We find for the Plaintiff L 20 s 3 d 10. ZACH. CANTEY, foreman.

JAMES WILLIAMS vs WILLIAM DOBY. Debt. We find the the Plaintiff.

SAMUEL KIRKLAND vs R. L. CHAMPION. Debt. Judgment Nihil Dicit.

EDWARD ROGERS vs THOMAS CREIGHTON. Debt. Judgment by Default.

JAMES WILLIAMS vs WILLIAM DOBY. We find for the Plaintiff $91.76. ZACH. CANTEY, foreman.

WILLIAM TWADDELL vs SAM'L WEBB. Debt. Judg't by Default.

DAVID R. EVANS vs Mess'rs McRA & CANTEY. On Motion of the Defendants Atty Ordered that the Depositions of JAMES CANTEY & THOMAS WHITAKER be taken De bene Esse in this Cause.

MOSES SARZEDAS vs PETER RUSH. We find for the Plaintiff L 12 s 11 d 11. ZACH. CANTEY, foreman.

[Page 264]

GEORGE PERRY vs REUBIN STARKE. S.P. Decree for the Plaintiff for L 5 with Costs.

THOMAS PACE being proposed by the Clerk as a Deputy Clerk he appeared in Court and Sworn in Accordingly.

SAM'L LEVY In'dse, BENJ. HUTCHINS & C'o vs GEORGE WADE JUN'R. Debt. Judgment by Default.

[11 February 1797]

BUMAN BROCKWAY vs GEO. & JANE BROWN. Sum Pro. on Note. Judgment Confessed according to Note with Int. and Defdts consents to the proceedings being filled up by the Clerk.

The Court adjourned till the 7th of May next. [names cut out]

[Page 265]

Agreeable to Adjournment the Court Met. Present ISAAC DUBOSE Esquire.

Ordered that Letters of Administration do Issue to WILLIAM BONDS on the estate of JOSHUA ENGLISH deceased the Security is DAN CARPENTER.

Ordered that the Property of JOSHUA ENGLISH be Sold by the Administrator after giving the Legal Notice on a Credit Untill the first of January next.

The Petition of MARY ENGLISH to have her Brother THOMAS ENGLISH appointed his [sic] Guardean. Ordered that THOMAS ENGLISH do Act as Guardean to MARY ENGLISH, daughter of THOMAS ENGLISH.

Ordered that the Administrator of JOHN ODANIEL Estate do Sell the Property after Giving the Legal Notice on a Credit of the

[cut out]

[Page 266] 9 May 1797

Agreeable to Adjournment the Court Met. Present ISAAC DUBOSE Esquire.

Ordered that the Following Persons are appointed Overseers of the Several Districts of Roads Within this County for the ensuing Year, each Overseer to appoint a Summoner for his District.

DANIEL PEAK, JACOB CHAMBERS, JOHN McCAA, WILLIAM COOK, SAM'L SMITH, GEORGE MILLER, ROBERT COLEMAN, THOMAS LANGFORD, ROBERT FORD, JOHN MARSHALL, FRANCIS BELL, WILLIAM ODANIEL, MICHAEL BARNET, LEWIS COLLINS, SAM'L JONES, W'M JONES, DANIEL MONAHAN, EVANS Overseer to J. ADAMSON, PETER CRIM, THO'S WATTS, WILLIAMS McRA's overseer, JACOB CHERRY, TOUSON GENOT, ELY FREEMAN, JAMES ENGLISH, JOHN BETHENY, ISAAC UNDERWOOD, THOMAS BROOM, WILLIAM COOK, JOHN ROBINSON, JAMES COWSAR, MATTHEW COLEMAN, JAMES WILLIAMS, ROBERT FORD, WILLIAM MALONE, JOHN KING, ARCH'D WATSON, JACOB CHAMPION, FRANCIS WREN, ROBERT MAHAFFEY, SAM'L TINES, JACOB FALKENBERRY, ROBERT WILLIAMS, JAMES CAIN, THO'S WATTS, ISAAC ROSS JUN'R, JOHN OQUIN, JOSEPH PAYNE, JACOB CHAMBERS, JAMES ENGLISH.

[Page 267] 9 May 1797

Ordered that all the Males liable to work on the high Road from the Plantation of FRANCIS BOYKIN to the County line between the Main Road and the River and the hands at CHAMBERS Mills be Summon'd in future to work on the Road from the County Line to ENGLISHES Ferry.

Ordered that W'M SOWDEN be permitted to Sell the Estate of WILLIAM PERKINS. The Wearing apparel for Cash, and a Mare for three Months Credit.

The Court Adjourned Untill the Seventh of August Next. IS. DUBOSE.

AUGUST TERM 1797

Grand Jury Drawn from Box N'o 1 to N'o 2.

1 ABRAM BELTON, 2 GEORGE EVANS, 3 GEORGE NOX, 4 ANDREW BASKINS, 5 SAMUEL HAMMONDS, 6 JOHN ADAMSON, 7 GEORGE SAUNDERS JUN'R, 8 ABNER ROSS, 9 WILLIAM BOND, 10 JAMES WREN, 11 DAN'L PEACH, 12 ISSAC ROSS JUN'R, 13 SION CATES, 14 JOHN DINKINS, 15 JOSEPH KERSHAW, 16 RAWLEY HAMMONDS, 17 ABRAHAM KELLY, 18 THOMAS WATTS, 19 THOMAS STRIPLAND, 20 REUBIN STARKE.

[Page 268]

Petit Jury Drawn from Box N'o 3 to N'o 4.

1 SOLOMON BRADLEY, 2 JOHN CATO, 3 JOHN COOK, 4 WILLIAM NORRIS, 5 WILLIAM KOY, 6 JAMES TRANTHAM, 7 JOSHUA TRANTHAM, 7 JOSHUA MARSH, 8 THOMAS BRADFORD, 9 ROBERT ROWEN, 10 BENJAMIN KING, 11 DAN'L McMULLIN, 12 MATTHEW SUMMERVILLE, 13 JAMES MILLER, 14 FRANCIS ADAMS, 15 HUGH BRANNEN, 16 THOMAS ADCOCK, 17 JOHN NIXON, JUN'R, 18 JOHN HALL, 19 WILLIAM RUSSELL, 20 TIDY LAYTON, 21 WILLIAM AGLINGTON, 22 JAMES FLEMING, 23 BURWELL CATO, 24 JOHN McCLUER, 25 JAMES HARP, 26 DANIEL TOUCHSTONE, 27 JOHN OQUIN L Creek, 28 JOHN ELDERS, 29 JOHN BURGESS, 30 BRYAN SPRADLEY.

Agreeable to Adjournment the Court Met.   JOHN KERSHAW, BURWELL BOYKIN.

HUGH YOUNG Vs RICH'D L. CHAMPION.   S.P. Judgment Confess'd for L 3 s 11 d 7 With Costs of Suit.

JOHN ADAMSON vs JOHN BOING.   Writ on Debt.   Judgment Confess'd for L 19 s 10 With Interest as P Specialty and Costs of Suit.

[Page 269]

Ordered that Letters of Administration do Issue to DICEY PAGE on the estate of THOMAS PAGE Deceased.   The Securities are GEORGE EVANS and WILLIAM McGEE.

JOHN BRADLEY as Petit Juror appeared in Open Court and Made his Excuse to the Court on Oath.

BENJAMIN HUTCHINSON & C'o vs LEWIS HUDSON.   S.P. on Note.   Judgment Confess'd according to Note One half to be paid in three Weeks the Remainder the first of December next with Cost of Suit.

WILLIAM LANG vs JOHN HAMILTON.   S.P. Abated by the Death of the Defendant.

The Court Adjourn'd Untill To Morrow ten OClock.   JOHN KERSHAW, B. BOYKIN.

Agreeable to Adjournment the Court Met.   Present BURWELL BOYKIN, JOHN KERSHAW.

JOHN KING vs JAMES WILLIAMS.   Assault.   Dismiss'd at Defendents Costs.

Ordered that letters of Administration do Issue to ANNY DAVIS on the Estate of MASON DAVIS Deceased, the Securities are JAMES MARSHALL SEN'R & JOHN EVANS.

[Page 270] 8th August 1797

WILLIAM STARKE vs GEORGE PERRY. Case. Refered to an Arbitration and the Award to be Made a Rule of Court.

Ordered that Letters of Administration do Issue to DANIEL OQUIN and REBECCAH OQUIN on the Estate of DANIEL OQUIN Deceased the Securities are

JONATHAN BARNS appeared in Open Court and took the Oath Prescribed by Law as Constable.

Ordered that the Administratrix of MASON DAVIS do Sell the Property of the Estate after giving the Legal Notice on a Credit of Six Months.

JESSE MINTON vs WILLIAM SKIPPER. Writ. Trespass. Nonsuit.

GEORGE SMITH vs JESSE MINTON. S.P. On note. Decree according to Specialty With Costs of Suit.

NATHANIEL RUSSELL vs WILLIAM LAYTON. Debt. We find for the Plaintiff the amount of the Note and Interest with One Cent Damage & Costs of Suit. FRANCIS BELL, foreman.

The Petit Jury Impannel'd & Sworn.

1 FRANCIS BELL foreman, 2 CHARLES RAYLEY, 3 JOHN TEAKLE, 4 LEWIS PEEBLES, 5 JONATHAN BUNKLY, 6 THOMAS CURRY, 7 JOHN PAYNE, 8 AARON ATKINS, 9 JOHN HOOD, 10 ARCHIBALD OWENS, 11 WILLIAM HOOD, 12 JACOB FAULKENBURY.

[Page 271]

The State vs WILLIAM DOBY. Ass't & Battery. True Bill. A. B. ROSS, foreman.

The Grand Jury Impannell'd & Sworn.

1 ARTHUR B. ROSS foreman, 2 ARTHUR CUNNINGHAM, 3 JACOB GREY ,4 JAMES ROCHELL, 5 WILLIAM NETTLES, 6 LEWIS COLLINS, 7 THOMAS ROACH, 8 SAM'L BROWN, 9 THOMAS BALLARD, 10 WILLIAM COLLINS, 11 WILLIAM PARKER, 12 ELY KERSHAW, 13 ALEX'R ARCHER.

The State vs WILLIAM FAIRFIELD. Assault & Battery. No Bill. A. B. ROSS, foreman.

JAMES BELL vs SAM'L THOMSON. S.P. Decree a Nonsuit.

JOHN BUNT vs WILLIAM DOBY. Case. Continued at the Defendants Costs.

GEORGE PERRY vs WILLIAM LANGLEY. Case. A Juror Drawn.

A negro woman named VIOLET HORN having been in Custody of the Faoler committed as a Runaway, came into Court & it appearing from the testimony adduced that she is free, was ordered to be discharged.

[Page 272]

JOHN BUNT vs WILLIAM DOBY. Case. Ordered that an Attachment Issue against ANDREW BASKINS Esquire to Bring him up to this Court to Answer for a Contempt for not appearing at this Court go give evidence in this Cause in Obedience to a Subpoena served on him by the Defendant.

WILLIAM BRACEY JUN'R vs HUGH FAIRFIELD. Case. Dismiss'd at the Defendants Costs.

Same vs Same. S.P. Dismissed at the Defendants Costs.

[8 August 1797]

THOMAS SMIRL vs BRYAN SPRADLEY. Judgment Confess'd for the Amount of Note & Interest Execution to be Lodged in Shff Office but not Executed for three Months.

The Court then adjourned untill tomorrow ten O'Clock. JOHN KERSHAW, B. BOYKIN.

Agreeable to Adjournment the Court Met. Present BURWELL BOYKIN, JOHN KERSHAW, Esq'rs.

The Court Sheriff apply'd to have REUBIN ARTHER appointed as a Deputy Sheriff for the County he appeared and took the Necessary Oaths.

[Page 273] 9th August 1797

JAMES PEIRSON vs Admor of ROB'T ROBINSON. Writ in Debt. Judgment Confes'd for L 14 17/5 Sterling and Interest thereon from 16th March 1796 With Costs of Suit.

JOHN ADAMSON vs WILLIAM BOWEN. S.P. on Note. Judgment Confes'd for L 6 Sterling & Interest thereon from the 19th July 1797 With Costs of Suit.

JONATHAN BELTON vs RICHARD McGILL. S.P. Decree for L 3 s 16 d 8 With Costs.

Ordered that Letters of Administration do Issue to RICHARD BERRY on the estate of PRETTYMAN BERRY deceased, the Securities are ELIJAH PAYNE & JOHN SHIVER.

GEORGE PERRY vs WILLIAM LANGLEY. Case.

Ordered that the Administrator of PRETTYMAN BERRY's Estate do Sell the Property of the Estate on three Months Credit after giving the Legal notice.

[Page 274]

ARTHUR B. ROSS vs Exo'r of the Exo'r of JOHN BELTON. S.P. ARTHUR B. ROSS attended with his Books and Proved his Original Entry in this Case. Decree for the Plaintiff for L 3 s 10 With Costs of Suit.

The State vs SUSANNAH MILLS, BURWELL MILLS, WILLIAM MILLS. Petit Larceny. Tru Bill. A. B. ROSS, foreman.

The State vs WILLIAM MOUNCE. Cattle Seatling. True Bill. A. B. ROSS, foreman.

The State vs W'M BOWEN. Stealing a Heifer. True Bill. A. B. ROSS, foreman.

The State vs JAMES DRAKE. Stealing a Hoe. No Bill. A. B. ROSS, foreman.

ELIAS JONES vs WILLIAM PAYNE. Trover. FREDERICK LAMB Enters himself as Security for the Costs of this Court payable When the suit is Ended in behalf of ELIAS JONES. FREDERICK LAMB.

Adjourn'd Until to Morrow ten OClock. B. BOYKIN, JOHN KERSHAW.

[Page 275] 10 August 1797

Agreeable to Adjournment the Court Met. JOHN KERSHAW, BURWELL BOYKIN, Esq'r.

JOHN ADAMSON vs WILLIAM BOWEN. S.P. on Account. Judgment Confess'd for L 6 s 17 d 2 & Interest from the 1st Jany Last With Costs of Suit.

GEORGE PERRY vs WILLIAM LANGLY. Case. We find for the Plaintiff L 17 s 10 Sterling with all the Costs of the Suit. FRANCIS BELL, foreman.

JESSE MINTON vs WILLIAM SKIPPER. Reinstated Case. We find for the Plaintiff L 5 sterling with Costs of Suit. FRANCIS BELL, foreman.

REID HUTT vs EDWARD CALVERT. Case. Dismiss'd at Defendants Costs.

JOHN BUNT vs WILLIAM DOBY. Case. We find for the Plaintiff $70 with the Costs of Suit. FRANCIS BELL, foreman.

MARY WILLIAMS vs ANNY DAVIS. S.P. Dismiss'd at Plaintiffs Costs.

Ordered that at the Request of POLLY TINSLEY, LEWIS COLLINS SEN'R is appointed as Guardian and that letters of Guardianship do Issue to him.

[Page 276] 10 August 1797

JOHN BUNT vs WILLIAM DOBY. Case. [stricken] Appeal Craven by Defendant and Granted.

The Court then adjourned till tomorrow Nine OClock. JOHN KERSHAW, B. BOYKIN.

Agreeable to Adjournment the Court Met. Present BURWELL BOYKIN, JOHN KERSHAW, Esq'rs.

HUGH YOUNG vs CHARLES EVANS. Case. Judgment Confess'd for L 18 s 18 d 3 sterling the same to bear Interest from this day until Pd. Execution not to be levied Untill the first of January next With Costs of Suit.

JOHN ADAMSON vs JAMES SHARPLIN. S.P. Decree for L 6 s 9 d 7 with Costs of Suit.

HUGH YOUNG Surv'r of WILLIAM YOUNG vs WILLIAM CASE Adm'x JN'O CASE. S.P. Dismiss'd at Defendants Costs.

WILLIAM STEPHEN vs JOHN ROBINSON Adm'x of ROBERT ROBERSON. S.P. Dismist at Defendants.

[Page 277] 11 August 1797

JOHN ADAMSON vs SAMUEL TYNES [stricken], WILLIAM DOBY. Debt. Judgment by Default against WILLIAM DOBY as P Specialty With Costs of Suit.

DAVID R. EVANS vs Mess. McRA & CANTEY. Writ. Ass't. We find for the Plaintiff $111 With Costs of Suit. FRANCIS BELL, foreman.

ROBERT HENRY vs JAMES BROWN. Sci: fa. The Defendant having Made Default, Ordered that the Judgment be Revived.

WILLIAM McDONALD vs W'M BRUMMET. Case. Judgment by Default.

JOHN McKINNEY vs Exor of the Exor of JN'O BELTON. Case. We find for the Plaintiff $72 with Interest from the Commencement of the last Suit With Costs of Suit.

[11 August 1797]

JAMES COWSAR vs WALTER SHROPSHIRE Indorsee of JOHN HOOD. S.P. on Note. Decree as P Specialty with costs of a Fuit. JA'S COWSAR Indsor of WAT. SHROPSHIRE against JOHN HOOD and the present costs.

The State vs SUSANNAH MILLS, BURWELL MILLS, WILLIAM MILLS. indictment. Petit Larceny. Not Guilty. FRANCIS BELL, foreman.

Ordered that the Defendents are hereby Discharged of the Indictment above.

[Page 278]

ALEXANDER McKEE vs ROBERT FORD. Writ on Sci: fa. The Defendant having made Default, Ordered that Judgment be Revived.

BENJAMIN HUTCHINSON vs JOHN GRAHAM. S.P. on NOte. Decree by Default as Pr Specialty With Costs.

SAMUEL THOMSON vs JOHN HOOD. On Motion of the Pltffs Atty Ordered that Special Bail be given in this Case.

HUGH YOUNG vs DOUGLAS STARK. Writ. Case. Non Suit: The Defendant Producing a Receipt in full on the Same Accounts that is in Suit.

The Court then adjourned untill tomorrow ten O'Clock. JOHN KERSHAW, B. BOYKIN.

Agreeable to Adjournment the Court met. Present JOHN KERSHAW.

The State vs WILLIAM DOBY. Ass't & Battery. Dismiss'd at the Defendants Costs.

[Page 279] 12 August 1797

Ordered that the Sheriff previous to the Next Court Do cause the present Jury Box to be so altered that there shall be not more than four divisions in the same & that those Names Which have heretofore been in the Special Jury list be placed One third in the Grand Jury list & the remaining two thirds in the Petit Jury List.

That the County Attorney be Requested immediately to take effectual Measures for recovering the Penalties Prescribed by Law from the Several Overseers of the Roads Who have been Presented by the Grand Jury.

SAMUEL THOMSON vs JOHN HOOD. Writ. Debt. Judgment Confess'd for the Amount of the Specialty with Interest and Costs of Suit. With a Stay of Execution untill the 1'st Jany 1798.

SAMUEL FRANCIS & Wife vs WILLIAM PARKER, JOANNA PARKER & MARIAH ANDERSON. Writ. Assault & Battery. Judgment by Default. Ordered that a Commission Do Issue to take the Deposition of M'rs SARAH MARTIN wife of Docter JAMES MARTIN.

DANIEL BROWN vs HUGH McDOWAL. Sci fa. Judgment Revived. Ordered that Execution do Issue.

- 114 -

[Page 280] 12 August 1797

The State vs WILLIAM MOUNCE. Ind't. Stealing Cattle. Not Guilty. FRANICS BELL, foreman.

And on Motion on the part of the Defendant, Ordered that the Defendent be furnished with a certify'd Copy of the indictment, the Warrent and affidavits fil'd in Court in this Case, the Jurors are FRANCIS BELL, CHARLES RAYLEY, JOHN TEAKLE, LEWIS PEEBLES, JONATHAN BUNKLEY, THO'S CURRY, JOHN PAYNE, AARON ATKINS, JAMES BROWN, ARCHIBALD OWENS, WILLIAM HOOD, JACOB FAULKENBERRY.

MINOR WINN vs SPENCER BRUMMETT. S.P. on NOte. Decree for a Nonsuit.

WILLIAM McDONALD vs WILLIAM BRUMMETT. Case Reinstated.

MATTHEW BOWEN vs ISAAC ROSS JUN'R. Case. Discontinued.

HUGH FAIRFIELD vs THOMAS ADAMS. S.P. Decree for the amount of Note & Interest JOHN MATTHEW LANGSTAFF is the Real Plaintiff & costs of Suit.

Admo'r of JOHN COUNTRYMAN vs PHILLIP BURFORD & RAWLEY HAMMOND. Debt. Judgment by Default according to Specialty with Costs of Suit.

DANIEL McDONALD vs JOSEPH PAYNE. S.P. on Note. Decree for the Defendant.

[Page 281] 12 August 1797

Admix of ROBRET LEE vs CHARITY LOWREY. By Consent of both Parties, Ordered that all Matters in Controversy in this Cause by Submitted to the Arbitriment final end and Determination of DUNCAN McRA & ZACHARIAH CANTEY Arbitrators indifferently and Mutually Chosen by the said Parties and that their Award Shall be a Judgment of this Court so that the same be Made in Writing and Return'd into this Court during the sitting of this Court or at any time before or at the Sitting of the Next Court to be held for this County.

Ordered that all the Estrays that have been Advertised the legal time be Sold Immediately after the adjournment of the Court on the last day of this term.

WILLIAM KIRKLAND vs EDWARD RUTLEDGE. S.P. on Case. At the reqeust of the Defendant this Cause Tryed by a Jury, We find for the Plaintiff $39.66. FRANCIS BELL, foreman.

On Application of the Sheriff Ordered that JAMES SPARKS is not hereafter to be Considered as a Deputy Sheriff of this County.

State vs JOHN BROWN. Ass't & Battery. IS. ALEXANDER. It appearing to this Court that JOHN BROWN has been detained in the Custory of JOHN FISHER Esq'r Sheriff of this County by Virtue of a Warran from FRANCIS BOYKIN Esq'r One of the Justices assign'd to keep the peace for Said County bearing Date the 9th August 1797 and it appearing unto the Court that there is no just cause for detaining the said JOHN BROWN in Custory. Ordered that the said JOHN BROWN be Discharged Out of the Custody of the Sheriff.

[Page 282] 12 August 1797

The Court then adjourned until Monday 10 O'Clock. JOHN KERSHAW.

14th August 1797. Agreeable to Adjournment the Court Met. Present JOHN KERSHAW, BURWELL BOYKIN, Esqr's.

WILLIAM KIRKLAND vs EDWARD RUTLEDGE. Case. On application of the Defendants Atty for an Appeal, Ordered that the same be granted. [entire entry stricken]

JOHN McKINNEY vs Exor of the Exor of JOHN BELTON. On application of the Defendants Atty for an appeal, Ordered that the same be Granted, Whereas it appeared to this Court that Mr. GEORGE BROWN a Constable for this County has levied Monies upon an Execution at the suit of WILLIAM BRACEY JUN'R against WIATT COLLINS, to the amount of Four pounds and two pence which the said GEORGE BROWN has neglected and refused to pay over Therefore Ordered, that the said GEORGE BROWN do immediately pay the sum of money into the hands of the Clerk of this Court, for the use of the parties entitled thereto, or otherwise than an Attachment issue against him.

[Page 283]

GEORGE PERRY vs WILLIAM LANGLEY. Case. On application by the Defendants Atty for a New Tryal, ordered that the same stand over for a New Tryal.

MARY LEE Adm'x vs CHARITY LOWRY. On Motion of Plaintiffs Atty, Ordered that the Award Return'd in this Case be Recorded to Wit, For the Plaintiff we award Eight Pounds Twelve Shillings & Six Pence Sterling With Costs of Suit in full of all Demands in this Suit. DUNCAN McRa, ZACH. CANTEY. Camden, 12th August 1797.

The State vs WILLIAM BOING. for Cattle Stealing. Ordered that a Warrant do Issue to apprehend MATHEW BOING the Prosecutor and the Witnesses to be bound in Recognizanes with Security to appear & give Evidence at the next Court.

The Court then adjourned untill the seventh day of November next. JOHN KERSHAW, B. BOYKIN.

[Page 284] 7th November 1797

The Court met according to adjournment. Present JOHN KERSHAW, BURWELL BOYKIN & ISAAC DUBOSE Esquires.

Ordered that the Clerk do make out Lists of the persons who have made default in working on the Roads in the same manner as is directed on the 9th May 1795 that the same proceedings be had thereon as is therein directed and that the said Order be considered as permanent & to be always observed in future.

Ordered that all the personal property belonging to the Estate of DANIEL OQUIN JUN'R deceased be sold at the Plantation of DANIEL OQUIN SEN'R on next Saturday three Weeks Conditions of the Sale to be one half to be paid on the first Feby next and the remainder on the first day of August following: The purchasers giving Obligations bearing Interest from the Day of Sale & Good Security for the payment thereof.

On Motion of DANIEL BROWN as Atty for GEORGE EVANS producing the Citation duly published, Ordered that Letters of Administration be granted to him s'd EVANS on the estate of RICHARD MARS, the said GEORGE EVANS attended and qualified as Administrator, JOHN EVANS & JAMES WILLIAMS are approved of as Securities therefor.

[7 November 1797]

JOHN EVANS, W'M McGEE & BENTLEY OUTLAW are appointed appraisers of the persons Est. of the said RICHARD MARS decased, Ordered that the said personal Estate be sold viz't at the Plantation of the deceased, on the 2'd Saturday in Decem'r next, conditions one third to be paid in Cash at the time of Sale and the remainder in twelve Months with interest from the Day of Sale, the Purchasers giving good Security to be approved by said GEORGE EVANS & He to give three weeks publick Notice thereof.

A Citation being returned duly published in behalf of DANIEL BROWN and JOHN FISHER Esq'rs, they applied for Letters of Administration on the estate of the Reverend THOMAS ADAMS. Ordered that the same be granted on their giving Security as usual; and DAN CARPENTER and JOHN BROWN were approved as Securities therefor. The said DANIEL BROWN & JOHN FISHER attended and were qualified as Administrators as aforesaid.

[Page 286] 7th November 1797

They named THOMAS BROOM, BENJ'N PERKINS, JOHN DINKINS and SAMUEL MATHIS as appraised & they were approved and appointed by the Court.

At the request of the said Administrators Ordered that they be allowed to sell the Personal Property of the said THOMAS ADAMS deceased viz't the Negroes at the Court House in Camden and the other Property at the House of the said deceased on the third Saturday in Decem'r next, on Six months Credit with Interest from the Day of Sale and the purchasers giving such Security as shall be approved by the said Administrators.

JOHN FISHER Esq'r produced to the Court a Citation duly published on the estate of NATHAN ELLIS deceased.... But the said JOHN FISHER not being able to shew to the Court that he was a Creditor of the said Deceased & it appearing that the said deceased died out of the County, the Court therefore refused to grant him Administration.

[Page 287]

The last Will and Testament of JOHN NIXSON was produced & proved by MILLEY GARDNER and TRAVIS NIXSON and THOMAS GARDNER the two Exors therein named appeared & qualified as Executors thereof; Ordered that Letters Testamentary be granted to them.

They named JOHN HORTON, ROBERT MEHAFFY, WILLIAM WILLIAMS & JOHN CRAIG as appraisers, they were approved & appointed as such.

Ordered that the personal Property of the said Deceased be sold viz't the Negroes at the Court House in Camden & The other part of the Property at the Plantation of the deceased on next Saturday three Weeks on twelve Months Credit with Interest from the Day of Sale & good Security.

DAN CARPENTER applied for Letters of Administration on the Est. of DEMPSEY ALSOBROOKS & produced the Citation duly published. Ordered that the same be granted on his giving the usual Security: He attended & was qualified; DANIEL BROWN & JOHN FISHER Esq'rs are approved as his Security & the sd D BROWN & J FISHER and also W'M LANG are appointed Appraisers of the said Est. Ordered that the said Est. be sold at the Court House in Camden.

[Page 288]

on the next Saturday three Weeks for Cash.

[7 November 1797]

The Letters of Administration that were heretofore granted on the Est. of Col'o JOHN MARSHALL deceased being revoked. GEORGE EVANS applied to the Court for Administration thereof at same time producing a Citation duly published, ordered that Letters of Administration be granted to him, & he attended & qualified, ZACH'Y CANTEY & JOHN EVANS were approved as his Security.

THOMAS WELSH, BENJ'N HAIL, SAMUEL TYNER, WILLIAM JONES & SAMUEL JONES were appointed Appraisers thereof.

Maj'r THOMAS BALLARD was appointed Guardian to ABEL & MAHALLY STAFFORD to take Charge of their Property, JOHN RUSSELL To be his Security together with GEORGE MILLER.

Ordered that the personal Estate of THOMAS PAGE be sold by the Administratrix on the 1st Monday in Decem'r next at the Plantation of the deceased on a Credit viz't one third to be paid in three months & the remainder in twelve months with Interest from the Day of Sale giving Bond with good Security.

The Court then adjourned until the 7th February next, the minutes being first read. JOHN KERSHAW, IS. DUBOSE, B. BOYKIN.

[Page 289] Feby 7th 1798

Grand Jury Drawn from Box N'o 1 to N'o 2.

1 MATTHEW COLEMAN, 2 JAMES CAIN, 3 ARCHIBALD ATSON, 4 DANIEL OQUIN, 5 JAMES CANTEY, 6 THOMAS ENGLISH, 7 MICHAEL BARNET, 8 JAMES PERRY S.C., 9 EDWARD RUTLEDGE, 10 SAM'L MARTIN, 11 GEORGE KERSHAW, 12 JOHN ENGLISH, 13 SAM'L JONES, 14 ISAAC KNOX, 15 LEWIS COOK, 16 JAMES KERSHAW, 17 THOMAS DINKINS, 18 RUSH HUDSON, 19 GEORGE GAYDEN, 20 FRANCIS WREN.

Petit Jury Drawn from Box N'o 3 to N'o 4.

1 JAMES CHESNUT, 2 JAMES MAXWELL, 3 MATHEW BOWEN, 4 ISRAEL MOORE, 5 JOHN GREYHAM, 6 HUGH HAMILTON, 7 JOHN GOODWIN, 8 DANIEL HALIDAY, 9 HOBS BRADLEY, 10 JAMES CUNNINGHAM, 11 AMBROSE BRYANT, 12 ANDREW SHEROR, 13 ANDREW GREYHAM, 14 THOMAS GRIFFIS, 15 JOHN MAUDIN, 16 DAVID SAUNDERS, 17 JAMES SMITH, 18 JOHN HIXON, 19 WILLIAM CLANTON, 20 JOHN COATS, 21 PATRICK McCAIN, 22 WALTER CARRUTH, 23 WILLIAM CAMPBELL, 24 NATHANIEL JONES, 25 WILLIAM EZAL, 26 WILLIAM ARCHER, 27 THOMAS HARDWICK, 28 JOHN GAYDEN, 29 WILLIAM DUNLAP, 30 LEWIS GRANT.

Agreeable to Adjournment the Court Met. Present ISAAC DUBOSE, BURWELL BOYKIN.

Ordered that Letters of Administration With the Will annexed do Issue to M'rs SARAH MARTIN on the Estate of Docter JAMES MARTIN her Securities are JOHN BOYKIN & JOSIAH CANTEY.

[Page 290] Feby 7th 1798

Ordered that Letters Testamentary do Issue to THOMAS ARCHER One of the Nominated Executors in the last will and Testamentary of JOHN McKEE deceased the Will being Produced in Open Corut and Proved.

Ordered that Letters of Administration do Issue to M'rs JANE SCOTT on the estate of JOSIAH SCOTT deceased, her Securities are REUBIN STARKE and DOUGLAS STARKE.

[7 February 1798]

Ordered that WILLIAM McCORKLE do Receive Letters of Administration on the state of WILLIAM McCORKLE deceased, his securities are FRANCIS ADAMS & PHILLIP BURFORD.

Ordered that Letters of Administration do Issue to ELIZABETH HOOD on the estate of JOHN HOOD deceased, her Security is PHILLIP BURFORD & JOHN LAKE.

Ordered that Letters Testamentary Do Issue to JAMES DICKEY One of the Executors Nominated in the Last Will & Testamentat of THOMAS LENORE deceased, the Will being Produced and Proven in Open Court and the Executor duly Qualified.

JOHN ADAMSON vs JAMES PERRY. Debt. Judgment Confess'd for the amount of the note & Interest With Costs of Suit.

JOHN ADAMSON vs MATTHEW BOWEN. Debt. Judgment Confess'd agreeable to Specialty With Costs of Suit.

[Page 291] 7th February 1798

JAMES HENRY vs JAMES ENGLISH Exor of the Exors's of JOHN BELTON. Judgment Confess'd for L 14 s 15 d 6 Subject to a Plea of Plene administravit with a stay of Execution Untill Next Court With Costs of Suit.

DAN CARPENTER vs GEORGE & JANE BROWN. S.P. Judgment Confess'd agreeable to Specialty With Costs of Suit. Wait Exo'n untill Orders from the Plaintiff.

Ordered that the Administratrix on the Estate of JOHN HOOD deceased Do sell the property of said Estate after giving Legal Notice the Negroe to be sold at the Court house in Camden the Remaining part to be Sold at the Plantation of the deceased on a Credit payable one half in Six Months from the day of Sale and the Remainder the first of January next.

SAMUEL BACOT vs ROBERT TUTLE. ROBERT TUTLE appeared in Open Court and took the Oath of an insolvent Debtor ordered that he be discharged from Confinement. The Court allowed him to retain the Articles Mentioned in the Schedule which is ordered to be filed in the Clerks office.

The Court then adjournd to tomorrow 10 Oclock. IS. DUBOSE, B. BOYKIN.

[Page 292] 8 Feby 1798

Agreeable to Adjournment the Court Met. Present JOHN KERSHAW, ISAAC DUBOSE.

DAVID BUSH appeared in Open Court and Proved the last Will & Testament of DINAH WYLY.

Ordered that JOHN McCAA do shew cause to the Court tomorrow morning at Eleven O'Clock why he should not be prosecuted for neglect of duty as overseer of the Road leading from Pinetree Bridge to Sanders Creek.

Ordered that ROBERT COLEMAN do shew Cause to the Court on the first day of the Holding Court next May term, why he should not be prosecuted for neglect of duty as overseer of the northern Fort Road from Camden Ferry to Pinetree Creek.

Ordered that letters of Administration do Issue to DINAH ADAMSON on the estate of THOMAS ADAMSON, her securities are JOSIAH CANTEY & JOSEPH BREVARD.

[8 February 1798]

Ordered that JOSEPH KERSHAW Esquire late Sheriff of Kershaw County do Shew Cause to the court to Morrow at twelve OClock Why Out of the proceeds of the Money levied by attachment & sale of a Studd horse in the case of JOHN LOCKART vs JAMES HARRIS he should not Pay Over to ARCHIBALD WATSON the sum of Seven Pounds Nineteen Shillings & Six Pence Pursuant to the direct of this Court Made in August 1794.

[Page 293]

The Petit Jury being Sworn and Impanne'd are as Follows

1 FRANCIS ADAMS foreman, 2 JAMES TRANTHAM, 3 THOMAS BRADFORD, 4 DANIEL McMULLIN, 5 JAMES MILLER, 6 THOMAS ADCOCK, 7 JOHN NIXON JUN'R, 8 WILLIAM RUSSELL, 9 JOHN McCLURE, 10 JAMES HARP, 11 BURWELL CATO, 12 BRYANT SPRADLEY SEN'R.

Admo'r of JOHN COUNTRYMAN vs JEREMIAH SIMMONS. Debt. We find for the Plaintiff With One Cent Damages and Costs of Suit. F'RS ADAMS, foreman.

The State vs WILLIAM BOWEN. Cattle Stealing. Not Guilty. FRANCIS ADAMS, foreman.

Ordered that THOMAS SCOTT do Receive Letters of Guardeanship for and on behalf of JOHN SCOT son of JOHN.

Ordered that the Money Arising from an Estray Bay Horse Bought by SAMUEL MATHIS after deducting the fees, be paid Over to M'rs ELIZABETH GRIFFITH.

The Court then Adjournd to tomorrow Morning 10 OClock. IS. DUBOSE, B. BOYKIN.

[Page 294] 9th Feby 1798

Agreeable to Adjournment the Court Met. Present JOHN KERSHAW, ISAAC DUBOSE, BURWELL BOYKIN.

LEWIS COOK In'ds of JOHN ADAMSON vs THOMAS SMYRL. Debt. Judg't Confes'd agreeable to Specialty with Costs of Suit. Stay of Exo'n Six Months.

SAM'L MATHIS vs WILLIAM WATSON exo'r of PETER CASITY. Judgment by Default.

ROBERT WILLSON Esq'r vs JOHN MARSHALL. S.P. Judgment by Default.

WILLIAM LUYTEN vs WILLIAM KENNEDY. Assumsit. Dismiss'd at Plaintiffs Costs.

JOHN CHESNUT vs JOHN HUDSON. Att. Judgment by Default against him Ordered that WILLIAM RANSOM DAVIS as Garnishee in this Case pay the debt & costs.

WILLIAM CAMPBLE vs OLIVER & JEREMIAH MEHAFFEY. Settled at the Plaintiffs Costs.

ROBERT DOW vs PAUL SMITH. S.P. Judgment by Default Stay 3 Months Stay of Exon.

THOMAS BALLARD vs BRICE MILLER. Att. Judgment by Default against the Defendant and Ordered that JOHN FISHER Garnishee in this Case do pay the Debt & Costs.

[Page 295] 9 Feby 1798

MATTHEW NUTT vs LITTLETON RAINS. Att. Judg't by Default, Ordered that the Property attached be Sold to pay the Debt & Costs.

John McCAA appeared agreeable to the order of this Court of Yesterday & made an excuse to the Court for the road of which he is overseer not being in the repair expected, which was deemed satisfactorey. He was then directed by the Court to give immediate Notice to the Inhabitants to assemble next week for the purpose of working on the Said Road. and JOHN NAUDIN was appointed to Warn the Inhabitants for the above purpose.

PETER TWITTY vs BARTLETT HILLARD. Att. PHILLEMON HILLIARD Garnishee appeared and Made Oath that he had No monies Goods or Chattels Debts of Effects of or Belonging to the Defendant in this case in his hands and that he is Not Indebted to him.

GEORGE PERRY vs WILLIAM LANGLEY. Case. We find for the Plaintiff $40 With Costs of Suit. FRANCIS ADAMS, foreman.

Defendants Atty moved for an appeal in this Case. Ordered that the same be Granted on Giving Bond in thirty Days or else an Execution do Issue.

[Page 296]

MATTHEW BOWEN vs WILLIAM BOWEN. Case. Settled at the Defendants Costs.

Ordered that the Administrator of WILLIAM BROWNs Est. Sell a Negroe Boy the property of the deceased after giving the legal Notice, for Cash.

Ordered that PETER TWITTY is appinted as Constable for this County; appeared in Open Court and took the Necessary Oaths.

WILLIAM STARKE vs GEORGE PERRY. Case. Abated by the death of the Plaintiff.

REUBEN STARKE vs BENJAMIN McKENZIE. Att. Settled at the Plaintiffs Costs.

JOHN KERSHAW vs JOHN HARDWICK Exo'r of RICHA'D EDGEWORTH decd. Debt. Judgment by Default.

Ordered that the Clerk of the County do refund the Money Received on Account of a Note Given by WILLIAM NARRIMORE, JOHN RUTLEDGE, WILLIAM NETTLES, WILLIAM MYERS & JAMES WILLIAMS Given to the Clerk for a fine against WILLIAM NARRIMORE for Hog Stealing amounting to Ten Pounds & the In't Which Note was Sued in this Court and Recovery had against JOHN RUTLEDGE in the name of FRANCIS BOYKIN the Same being Remitted by the Governors Pardon.

JOSEPH PAYNE vs JOHN SWETT. Att. Decree for the Plaintiff for L 8 s 18 d 9. Ordered that the Property attached in this Case belonging to the said SWEAT be Sold.

[Page 297] 9th February 1798

DAVID BUSH vs JOHN RUSSELL. S.P. Decree for the Plaintiff for L 9 s 3 d 10 With Costs of Suit. Stay Exon 3 Months.

The Court then adjourned untill tomorrow ten O'Clock. JOHN KERSHAW, B. BOYKIN.

10th Feby 1798. Agreeable to Adjournment the Court Met. Present JOHN KERSHAW, BURWELL BOYKIN, ISAAC DUBOSE, esq'r.

JOHN PALMER vs ISAAC DUBOSE. Debt. Note. Judgment Confess'd for the Amount of Note and Interest With Costs of Suit.

ELIAS JONES vs WILLIAM PAYNE. Trover. We find for the Plaintiff $13 With Costs of Suit. FRANCIS ADAMS, foreman.

SAMUEL THOMSON vs ZACHARIAH PETTY Bail of JOHN HOOD. Sci fa. Judgment against ZACHARIAH PETTY the Bail of JOHN HOOD & Costs of Suit.

BURWELL BOYKIN vs TURNER STARKE. Debt. Judgment Confes'd for the Amount of Note and Interest with Costs of Suit. Stay of Exo'n three Months.

[Page 298]

The Sheriff having Proposed to the Court FRANCIS WREN as a Deputy also JOHN McCAA & PETER TWITTY. The Court approved of them but as FRANCIS WREN Was too Unwell to attend to take the Oath of Office, The Court Consented that he should take the Oath of Qualification before the Clerk of the Court.

JOHN McCAA appeared in Open Court and took the Oath of Office.

THOMAS STARKE vs TURNER STARKE. Debt. Judgment Confess'd for the Amount of the Note & Interest With Costs of Suit With Stay of Exon three Months.

BENJAMIN CUDWORTH vs LOVICK ROCHELL. Debt. We find for the Plaintiff With One Cent Damages & Costs of Suit. FRANCIS ADAMS, foreman.

JOHN KERSHAW vs JOHN HARDWICK Exo'r of RICH'D EDGEWORTH dec'd. Debt. We find for the Plaintiff One Cent Damages & Costs of Suit. FRANCIS ADAMS, foreman.

Ordered that the Executor of THOMAS LENORE's Es't do sell the property of the deceased that is Not Mentioned in the Will as Legacys to the Heirs, and after giving the legal Time of Noitce on a Credit Untill the first of January Next.

GEORGE MONTGOMERY & JOHN CHAMBERS Exors of PATRICK McFADIN dec'd vs ADAM McWILLIE. Case. We find for the Plaintiff With One Cent & Cost of Suit. FRANCIS ADAMS, foreman. The Defendants atty Mov'd for an appeal in this Case. Granted on the Usual terms.

[Page 299] 10th February 1798

WILLIAM ANCRUM, EDWARD DARRELL & al vs LEWIS DINKIN & THOMAS DINKINS. Debt. L 90. Judgment Confess'd for the Specialty after deducting the Receipt from the District Sheriff for L 26 s 16 d 7 With Costs.

JOHN BOURSHETT vs JOHN DINKINS. Assault & Battery. We find for the Plaintiff $36 With Costs of Suit. FRANCIS ADAMS, foreman.

The Court then adjourned untill Monday Morning ten OClock, the Jury having Returned a Verdict in the last above Mentioned Case. JOHN KERSHAW, IS. DUBOSE, B. BOYKIN.

12 Feby. Agreeable to Adjournment the Court Met. Present JOHN KERSHAW, BURWELL BOYKIN.

JOHN MOTLEY vs DAN'L PAYNE. S.P. Dismis'd Each Party Pay their Own Costs JOHN ADAMSON the Real Plaintiff.

[12 February 1798]

BENJAMIN PARNELL vs ROBERT DUNLAP. N'o 47 a.d. Appeal. Judgment Reversed.

Ordered that Cap't BENJAMIN CARTER be authorized to Collect the arrears of the County Tax which were not collected & received by the late Collector of the General Tax. And that he also do collect one tenth the amount of the General Tax laid by the Legislature, for the use of the County & poor it being deemed necessary by the Judges of the County. The County Tax to be Payable at the same with the General Tax.

[Page 300]

Whereas JOHN CHENSUT Esquire & THO'S BROOM who were appointed Commissioners by this Court on the tenth day of February last for the purpose of Contracting for the building a Bridge over Pinetree Creek have not made any contract for the purpose nor caused a Bridge to be made, Ordered that their authority do cease & that SAMUEL MATHIS Esquire & JOHN KERSHAW be appointed Commissioners to Carry the said order of the tenth of February last into Effect.

Ordered that the Estrays which have been advertised the legal time be sold immediately after the adjournment of the Court.

The Sheriff produced his acc't against the County to the am't of L 12.10. The Clerk also produced his to the Court to the am't of L 6. They were both approved. Ordered that they be paid.

The Court then adjourned to the 7th May next. IS. DUBOSE, B. BOYKIN.

[Page 301] 7th May 1798

Agreeable to adjournment the Court met. Present BUR'L BOYKIN.

ELIZABETH HOOD Administratrix of JOHN HOOD made a return of the Appraisement of the personal Estate amounting to L 176.7.10. Ordered that the said Estate be sold at the plantation of the Dec'd on the first Saturday in June. The Conditions all sums under thirty shillings to be paid in Cash. All sums over ten PCent to be paid in Cash, the remainder on Credit till the first of January next, good security to be given for the payment and public Notice of this Sale to be advertised for three Weeks in three public places in the County.

Ordered that the motion for letters of administration on the Estate of SILAS CAMPBELL be postponed untill next Court and that the Parties interested then have Leave to come in and Contest the same.

[Page 302] 7 May 1798

Ordered that PETERS CRIM Admor in right of his Wife MARGARET CRIM Adm'x of DAVID JONES deceased sell all the remaining personal Estate unsold on the Second Saturday of next month giving due notice of the sale, on a Credit till the 1 of Jany next taking good Security for the payment and that he make return of the same & of the property heretofore sold on the 7 of August next.

JOHN CHAMBERS having applied to the Court for relief as Security for MARTHA CASE admx of JOHN CASE, It is ordered that MARTHA CASE do, on the Seventh day of August next give other security to exonerate said CHAMBERS from his Securityship, and on failure thereof that the Letters of Adm'n granted said MARGARET be then revoked and the administration of said Estate be committed to the said JOHN CHAMBERS.

Ordered that MARTHA CASE be served With a Copy of this order.

- 123 -

[Page 303] 7 May 1798

Ordered that JACOB CHAMBERS be appointed Guardian for a Mullatto Girl named PEG alias CHANA aged thirteen years in December last and that her guardianship do continue until she attains the age of eighteen years and that he do furnish her in the mean time with good wholesome meat & drink and good Cloathing.

The last will and testament of JOHN DIXON was this day duly proved in open Court by the oath of JAMES PERRY one of the subscribing witnesses to the same, which was ordered to be recorded.

Ordered that EDWARD RUTLEDGE, SION COATES, READ WILL and ISAAC KNOX or any three of them be appointed Appraisers, to appraise the personal estate of JOHN DIXON deceased late of Kershaw County as shall be shown them by SAMUEL DIXON. WILLIAM DIXON and JAMES PERRY executors of the last Will and testament of the said JOHN DIXON.

[Page 304]

And that they do make a true return on oath of the same at next August Court, and that WILLIAM KIRKLAND Esquire be appointed to administer the oath of appraisors to the said EDWARD RUTLEDGE, SION COATS, READ WILL and ISAAX KNOX.

WILLIAM DIXON appeared in open court and qualified as Executor of the last will and Testament of JOHN DIXON late of Kershaw County deceased.

[Page 305] 7th May 1798

The Court then adjourned to the 7th Aug't next. B. BOYKIN.

Jurors drawn to serve at the next Court.

Grand Jurors from Box N'o to Box N'o 2.

1 JAMES McCULLOUGH, 2 SAMUEL LEVY, 3 JAMES TATE, 4 ELY KERSHAW, 5 DAVID BUSH, 6 JAMES COOSART, 7 JOHN CREIGHTON, 8 CHARLES BARBER, 9 MICHAEL GANTER, 10 LEWIS COLLINS [WALTER SHROPSHIRE stricken], 11 JAMES MARSHAL SEN'R, 12 DOUGLAS STARK, 13 RICHARD DRAKEFORD, 14 PETER CRIM, 15 W'M ANDERSON, 16 SAM'L SMITH, 17 JAMES WILLIAMS, 18 JOHN RUTLEDGE S'R, 19 ANDREW NUTT, 20 REUBIN PATTERSON.

Petit Jurors for the Same Court from Box N'o 3 to Box N'o 4

1 GEORGE RICHARDSON, 2 JOHN ABBOTT, 3 SAM'L BRADLEY, 4 BENJ. COWHERD, 5 DAN'L GASKINS, 6 W'M PAYNE, 7 JOHN MOTLEY, 8 ALLEN PERRY, 9 JOHN MYERS, 10 JOHN RUSSEL, 11 CHARLES McCLELAN, 12 JOHN PEOPLES, 13 STERLING CLANTON, 14 DAVID COATES, 15 ZACH CANTEY 16 JESSE FLY, 17 BERRY ROBINSON, 18 BENJ. CARTER, 19 JAMES SHROPSHIRE, 20 BERRY KING, 21 W'M KING, 21 W'M McGILL, 22 JAMES LOGAN, 23 REED HUTT, 24 W'M PEACH, 25 ADAM TAMSON, 26 DAVID McMULLAN, 27 JOHN McARTHUR, 28 EDWARD RODGERS, 29 JAMES GUNN, 30 TRAVERS NIXON.

[Page 306]

At a Court held for the County of Kershaw on Tuesday the 7th day of February 1798. Present Judges ISAAC DUBOSE, BURWELL BOYKIN.

The following Persons were impanneled on the Grand Jury and Sworn.

1 JAMES CANTEY foreman, 2 DANIEL OQUIN, 3 SAMUEL JONES, 4 JAMES PERRY, 5 EDWARD RUTLEDGE, 6 THO. ENGLISH, 7 GEORGE KERSHAW, 8 ISAAC KNOX, 9 LEWIS COOK, 10 RUSH HUDSON, 11 MICH'L BARNET; 12 JN'O ENGLISH, 13 GEO. GAYDEN, Affs.

A Commission was presented to the Court under the hand and Seal of his Excellent CHARLES PINCKNEY constituting and appointing JAMES KERSHAW Esq. one of the Judges of this Court.

[Page 307] August 1798

[Commission copied in full, dated 19 May 1798.]

FRED'K SAML vs JOHN BOING. Debt. Judgment confessed for the Am't of the Note With Interest and Costs. Stay of Exon 2 M'o.

JAMES KERSHAW vs PETER DUNCAN. Debt. Confession D's 50 with In't' from 1 Jan. 1797 and Costs of Suit.

[Page 308] 7th August 1798

JOHN MARSHAL vs ROBERT McCAIN. Ordered that THO. BALLARD Esq. Do Certify to the Court on Thursday next the Proceed'gs had before him in this Case as a Justice of the peace. On Motion of M'r J. BROWN.

The following persons were impannelled on the Petit Jury & Sworn to execute Writs of Enq'y & Also for the trial of Issues.

1 MATHEW BROWN, 2 JOHN GRAHAM, 3 ISRAEL MOON, 4 AND'W SHERRAR, 5 HOBS BRADLEY, 6 [HUGH HAMILTON stricken] W'M CLANTON, 7 DAVID SAUNDERS, 8 JA'E MAXWELL, 9 W'M CAMPBELL, 10 AND'W GRAHAM, 11 [AMBROSE BRYANT stricken] JOHN NOWDEN, 12 W'M ARCHER Aff.

WALTER CAURTH in Sted of W'M CAMPBELL.

JOHN CHESNUT vs ELY FREEMAN. Pro. Decree for L5.15.8 & Costs. BREVARD.

SAM'L FRANCIS vs W'M PARKER, JOANNA PARKER & MARIA ANDERSON. Ass't & B'y. Ordered that the Case be dismissed. J. BROWN.

SAM'L MATHIS vs Admor & Admix JA'S BROWN. Debt. Judgm't for L44.1.3 with Int. from 21 Sept. 1798 & Cost of Suit.

[Page 309]

The State vs AARON STRIPLING. Ord'd that the Defend't be discharg'd from his Recognis'a he being bound over on a charge of bastardy.

Ordered that Letters of Administration be granted to LOUISA CAMPBELL on the estate of SILAS CAMPBELL deceased. RICHARD BERRY and JACOB SHIVER approved of by the Court as Security of the said LOUISA CAMPBELL.

Admor MYDDLETON vs JOSIAH CANTEY. Writ of Esq. BROWN. Find for plaintiff $58 In't 30 Cents & Costs of Suit. JOHN GRAHAM, foreman. D. BROWN, R. L. CHAMPION 4 vouchers.

ELIS'TH HOOD Admx of the Estate of JOHN HOOD made a return of the Sales of the said Estate amounting to ____ Dollars.

The following Bills of indictment were present by the County Atty, the Witnesses Sworn the Bills delivered to the Grand Jury.

[7 August 1798]

The State vs JAMES PEAKE. Larceny. STEPHEN BOYKIN. True Bill. JAMES CANTEY, foreman.

The State vs W'M LUYTEN. Assault & Batty. SAM'L LEVY, JN'O McCLOCKLIN. No Bill. JAMES CANTEY, foreman.

[Page 310] August 8th 1798.

The Court then adjournd to tomorrow Ten Oclock. IS. DUBOSE, B. BOYKIN.

The court met according to Adjournment August 8, 1798. JAMES KERSHAW.

WALTER CARRUTH inserted in the Petit Jury in the room of W'M CAMPBELL and was sworn to execute Writs of Enquity and also for the Trial of Issues.

Ordered that BENJAMIN CARTER Esq. Collector of the Public Tax of this County do pay to M'r JAMES WILLIAMS The Sum of Ten Pounds in pursuance of an order of Court passed at last February Court respecting the fine of W'M NARRIMORE which was remitted by the Governor.

The following Bills of Indictment were present by the County Atts. The witnesses sworn and the Bills delivered to the Grand Jury.

The state vs RICHARD BRYANT & SABER BRYANT. Hog Stg. JOSHUA LISSINBY, STEPHEN PEAK, JOHN WEBB.

The state vs SAM'L THOMPSON. Assault True. Bill. W'M HUDSON, MOSES STRIPLING, JAS CANTEY, foreman.

[Page 311] 8 August 1798

JOSEPH CASTON vs WILLIAM NUTT. Confessions L5.0.9. STay of Exon 2 Mo's.

BURWELL BOYKIN vs JOHN GREGG. Confession for the amount of the Note Interest and Costs.

Admx JA'S MARTIN vs DAN'L OQUIN SEN'R. Settled by the parties.

Bill of Indictment del'd to the Grand Jury.

The State vs SAM. LEVY. Assault. W'M LUYTEN, REUB. ARTHUR, JOHN McCAA. True Bill JAS. CANTY, foreman.

McDONALD vs McCOY. Confession for L7.7.7 as the Ball'ce of the Note in this Case after deducting the note in the Case of MARSHAL vs GASKINS.

JOHN RUSSIL vs FRANCIS ADAMS & ADAM TAMSON. Ord'd that W'M KIRKLAND Esq. do on or before Friday next Certify to this Court the Proceedings had before him in this Case as a Magistrate.

[Page 312]

The state vs JOHN PEAK. Larceny. The Grand Jury having found a Bill in this case against the Defendant and he not appearing. Ord'd that his Recognizance be estreated.

JAMES COOSART vs PHILEMON HILLARD. Pet'n & Pro. Judgment confessed for the am't of the Note Interest and Cost.

JOHN KIRKPATRICK vs WILL'M LANGLEY. [stricken] Postponed.

[8 August 1798]

JOHN CHAMBERS who is Security for the due Administration of the Estate of
JOHN CASE having appeared in Court and requested to be discharged from said
Securityship Ordered that he be accordingly discharged from the Same, and that
W'M ROPER be appointed Guardian to the Child of the decesaed JOHN CASE he
giving such Satisfactory Security for his Guardianship as shall be approved of by
the Court.

Ordered that the Estate of the said JOHN CASE be sold at Public Vandue on the
1 day of September next three weeks notice being previously given on a Credit
till the 1st February next the purchaser giving Bond with good Security for the
purchases made.

W'M COLLINS appointed, and sworn as a Constable for the ensuing year.

[Page 313] 8 August 1798

M'r ROPER having offered to the court ADWELL ATKINS and FREDERICK LAMB
[stricken] PETER HARKEY Security for the Due performance of his Guardianship
of the Child of JOHN CASE Deceased, the Court approves of them.

JOHN McDONALD vs JOSEPH PAYNE.   Pet'n & Pro.   Decree for the Pltf $33
with Int from April '95 & Costs.

GEO. PAYNE, JN'O PAYNE, JN'O McCAA, JO BREVARD.

Bill del'd to the Grand Jury.

State vs JOHN RUSSELL. Assault. True Bill.   JAMES CANTEY foreman.   W.
THOMPSON, THOMAS KELLEY, AND'R NUTT, P. TWITTY [stricken]

Bill del'd to the Grand Jury.

The State vs RICH. BRYANT, SABER BRYANT.   Receiv'g Stolen Goods.   JOSHUA
LISINBY, STEPHEN PEAK, JOHN WEBB.   No Bill.   JAS CANTY, foreman.

The State vs JN'O RUSSEL, THOMAS RUSSEL, JN'O KIRKPATRICK.   Assault.
JOHN HOOD, AND. NUTT.   Assault.   True Bill against JOHN RUSSELL.   JAS.
CANTEY, foreman.

[Page 314] 8 Aug 98

The State vs JOHN RUSSELL, THO. RUSSELL, JN'O KIRKPATRICK.   Assault
with Intent to Murder.   AND'W NUTT, JOHN HOOD.   True bill against JOHN
RUSSELL.   JAS. CANTEY, foreman.

The Court then adjournd to Tomorrow 10 OClk.   JAMES KERSHAW, IS. DUBOSE,
B. BOYKIN.

The Court met agreeable to adjournment 9 August 1798.

SOLOMON NEIGHBOURS & Wife vs SAM'L KELLEY and JOHN EVANS.   Debt.
Dismissed at the Defendants Costs.

SOLOMON NEIGHBOURS & Wife vs SAM'L KELLEY and PATRICK McCAINE.
Debt. Dismissed at the Defendants Costs.

[Page 315] 9 August 1798

On motion on the part of the Executors of CATHERINE SMITH deceased who was Executrix of JAMES SMITH deceased, Ordered that the Executors have leave to sell all the personal Estate of the said deceased, except the negroes, on 22d day of September next, at the Plantation of the said JAMES SMITH deceased on a Credit of twelve Months, taking good Security.

DENNIS BURNS vs THOMAS HANKS. SP. Judgment confest for L5 Cost to be equaly Devi'd.

The State vs JOHN PEAK. Larceny. The Same Jurors were sworn except WALTER CARUTH who was sworn in the place of W'M CAMPBELL and returned the following Verdict. Guilty. JOHN GRAHAM, foreman.

On which the Court ordered that Prisoner JOHN PEAK to receive five stripes on the bare back at the Public Whiping Post this evening and that he be committed to Gaol untill he pays the Costs of prosecution or swears off.

The State vs SAMUEL LEVY. Assault. The above Jury were Sworn and returned the following verdict, viz. Guilty. JOHN GRAHAM, foreman.

JOHN RUSSELL vs FRANCIS ADAMS & ADAM TAMSON. Aslt. Dismissed at JOHN RUSSELL cost.

[Page 316] 9 August 1798

Ordered that Letters of Administration on the Estate of JAMES REN be granted to MARY REN.

M'rs REN offered to the Court as her Security on the estate of JAMES REN, Mr. JOHN BOYKIN and WILLIAM KIRKLAND Esq'r which the Court approved of.

State vs SAM'L THOMPSON. Assault. Ordered that a Bench Warrant do Issue.

JAMES TRANTHAM vs MARY DIXON. Ordered that the Deposition of JAMES WILLIAMS be taken De Bene esse.

JOHN TRANTHAM vs MARY DIXON. The same Order and that the deposition of JAS. TRANTHAM also be taken De Bene esse.

JOHN PEAKE who was this day convicted of petty Larceny having re'd his punishment agreeable to the order of court not being able to pay the fees have Sworn off agreeable to Law and was discharged.

The Grand Jury having present the following Roads as being in a bad condition it was in consequence Ordered viz't

[Page 317] 9th August 1798

Ordered that PHILLIMON HILLIARD as overseer do call out as soon as convenient all the people liable by law to work on the Beaver Creek Road from the County line to said Beaver Creek, and that Capt'n ADAMS as Overseer do call out the people liable to work from Beaver Creek to White Oak, That THOMAS SMYRLE as Overseer do cause the road to be worked on from thence to Granny Quarter Creek by all the people liable to work thereon, and that the said roads be put in as good repair as can be within the time allowed by law for working on public roads, and that the Clerk do issue warrants accordingly, also

Ordered that RUSH HUDSON as Overseer do immediately call out all the inhabitants liable to work on the Rocky mount Road from the County Line to Beaver Creek and put the same in good order.

[9 August 1798]

Ordered also, that JESSE LEE as Overseer do work with those who was liable to work from thence to the forks of the Road.

[Page 318]

That FRANCIS BELL as Overseer do work from Granny's Quarter Creek to BRYANT SPRADLEY's, and that the Clerk do issue Warrants accordingly.

MATTHEW COLEMAN vs BRYANT SPRADLEY, JOHN KERSHAW. Debt. Find for the Plaintiff L 14 with Interest and Cost of Suit, Interest according to Note. JOHN GRAHAM, foreman.

J. MARSHALL, D. RUSSELL adv ROBERT McCAIN. Witness JOHN'N DINKINS, MICHAEL GANTER, ISAAC ALEXANDER, DUNCAN McRA. Ape'l Magistrate. Judgment affirmd.

The Court then adjourned to nine O'Clock in the Morning. JAMES KERSHAW, IS. DUBOSE, B. BOYKIN.

[Page 319] 10 August 1798

The Court met agreeable to Adjournment. Present BURWELL BOYKIN, ISAAC DUBOSE, JAMES KERSHAW, Judges.

Mr. FRANCIS GENOE was appointed a Deputy Sheriff of this County with the approbation of the Court and Sworn in according to Law as a Deputy Sheriff for the County.

JOEL CHERY vs BRYANT SPRADLEY. S.P. Judgement confessd for the amount of Note and Interest.

MATTHEW NUTT vs LITTLETON RAINS. Att. Settled at the defendants cost.

JAMES MARSHALL vs JOSIAH CANTEY. Case. Settled at the defendants costs.

State vs JOHN RUSSELL. Assault. The Same Jurour was sowrn who returned the following viz't. Guilty. JOHN GRAHAM, foreman. Witness WILLIAM TOMSON, PETER TWITTY, THO'S BALLARD.

State vs W'M DOBY. Assault. Dismistd at the Defendants Costs be compromised by the parties after Bill found.

W'M BRACEY vs JAS. SHARPLIN. S.P. lay over by mutual consent.

[Page 320]

JOHN L. DEBUSSY vs LEWIS HUDSON. S.P. J. BREVARD. Decree for L 8 s 9 d 3 with cost of Suit. L. 8.9.3.

MATTHEW COLEMAN, BRYANT SPRADLEY, JOHN KERSHAW. Writ. Order for a new Trial.

TURNER STARKE vs RICHARD WOOD. Att. Find for the Plaintiff $43.62. JOHN GRAHAM, foreman. SAD'K PERRY, GEORGE PERRY.

The State vs JOHN RUSSELL. Indictment for an assault &c with an intent to Murder. On Motion of the County Attorney, Ordered that the Defendant be taken into Custody until he shall give Security for his Appearance at the next Court of General Sessions for Camden District; and that the two Bills of Indictment against him be put up to the said district to be then tried And that the Prosecutors & the Witnesses be bound in Recognizance for their appearance at the said District Court to give Evidence in behalf of the State upon the said two Indictments.

[Page 321] 10 August 1798

W'M McDONALD vs W'M BRUMMIT. Writ in Case. Find for the Plainitff L 19 s 14 d 8. JOHN GRAHAM foreman. ZACH CANTEY. L19.14.8.

Ordered that a Stray Steer told some time ago by BURWELL BOYKIN Esq'r be Sold on Saturday the 25 August 1798 at his plantation the Steer being difficult to drive and the great warmth and that the Clerk do advertize the Same.

The Court was adjourned to Ten O'Clock in the morning. JAMES KERSHAW, B. BOYKIN.

[Page 322] 11 August 1798

The Court met agreeable to adjournment. Present ISAAC DUBOSE, JAMES KERSHAW, Esq'rs.

Whereas it was ordered at the last Court that letters of administration should issue to DANAH ADAMS on the State of THOMAS ADAMS deceased, but no appraisors were appointed therefore the following Freeholders now appointed to appraise the sd. estate on oath viz. DAN CARPENTER, ROBERT DOW and MICHAEL GANTER.

MATHEW BOWIN vs ISAAC ROSS JUN. Writ. We find for the Plaintiff $27.56 with Interest thereon from the 23 February 1797. JOHN GRAHAM, foreman. Witness JOEL CHERRY, F. LAMB, M'r LAMB.

FURMAN STARKE vs RICHARD WOOD. At. Ordered that the Sheriff of this County pay to the Plaintiff the ballance remaining in his hands of the Sales or the property attached in this Case According to the Shffs filed in Court.

JOHN McDONALD vs JOSEPH PAYNE. Ordered that this Case lay over till next Court.

[Page 323] 11 August 1798

JOHN KIRKPATRICK vs WILLIAM LANGLEY. SP Decree for the Plaintiff L 3 s 3. Execution not to be levied untill the 10 of December next. M'r MITCHELL.

JAMES SPRUNT vs GEORGE PERRY & SAMUEL THOMSON. SP Decree L 7 s 10 & Int. from 15 Dec'r 1797.

BRYANT SPRADLEY vs W'M KENNEDY. Decree for Plaintiff twelve shillings 8 1/2 d and cost. M. GANTER, B. SPRADLEY, Witness sworn.

MICHAEL FITZGERALD vs SAMUEL BRILEY. SP BREVARD. Decree according to specialty.

DAVID BUSH Ind'see of W'M BRACEY JUR vs JAMES TATE. SP Decree according to Specialty.

ANN BOWLES vs JOHN GREGG. SP of BROWN on Note. Decree on Default accord'g to Specialty.

[Page 324]

DANIEL BROWN vs MATTHEW COLEMAN. W'M MATHIS. We find for the Plaintiff $88.49. JOHN GRAHAM, foreman.

[11 August 1798]

JOSEPH ARTIST vs BRYANT SPRADLEY. SP Decree for Plaintiff for L 3 s 13 d 9. Witness's sworn JO PAYNE, A. SHIVER, A. BELTON, F. GENOE, J. McLAUGHLIN.

DANIEL BROWN Esq against MATTHEW COLEMAN. Case. [stricken]

MOSES SARZEDAS vs ELI FREEMAN. D. BROWN. Debt on two Notes Plea withdrawn. Judgment according to Specialties for Principal and Interest & Costs of Suit.

The State vs JOHN RUSSELL. Ind't for assault & c'a. NUTT Prosecutor. The Defendant to be discharged on Payment of the Costs of Prosecution.

The State vs JOHN RUSSELL. Indictment for Assault & Ca. JNO HOOD Prosecutor. Same order as above.

[Page 325]

BENJ. PERKINS vs BRYANT SPRADLEY SEN. S.P. J. BROWN. Decree for the Plaintiff $15 with Cost of Suit. Witness's sworn JOHN CANTEY, JOHN MARTIN, JO. KERSHAW.

Admo'r of RICHARD MIDDLETON vs JOSIAH CANTEY. Case. The plaintiff appeared in open Court prayed an appeal to the Circuit Court from the Decision of this Court which reversed the Verdict of the Jury on a Writ of Inquiry which was executed during the setting of this Court, Ordered that the same be granted.

WILLIAM HIDE vs WILLIAM PAYNE. Case. Witnesses ALLEN PERRY, Mr. PULLAM, JOHN KERSHAW. [entire entry stricken]

A. B. ROSS vs DANIEL CARTER. Judgment by Default.

N. RUSSELL vs Ex'ors R. GIBSON. Decree for Plaintiff.

[Page 326]

HUGH YOUNG vs Admo'r of W'M MAXWELL. Judgment by Default.

JAMES PEIRSON vs JAMES GUNN. [stricken]

ROBERT HENRY vs JOSHUA DINKINS. Judgment revived.

BRYANT SPRADLEY vs ROBERT McCAIN. Judgment by Default. Ordered that on Motion the Plffs' atty that Defend't be held to Special Bail.

DAVID BUSH vs JOSHUA GRAHAM. On Mot'n Plffs Atty Ord'd that Defend't be held to Special Bail.

W'M HYDE vs W'M PAYNE. Case. J. BROWN. We find for the Deft. with Costs of Suit. JOHN GRAHAM, FOREMAN. The Same Jury. Witness's sworn ALLEN PERRY, BEN PULLUM, JOHN KERSHAW.

GEO. EVANS vs JOSIAH CANTY. Writ of Enq. We find for the Plf D's 18 with Costs of Suit. JOHN GRAHAM, foreman.

[Page 327]

JOHN RUTLEDGE J'R vs RICHARD WOOD. We find for the plaintiff $128.57 with Cost of Suit.l JOHN GRAHAM, foreman.

Issue ED RUTLEDGE.

The Court then adjourned to Monday morning at ten O'Clock. IS. DUBOSE, JAMES KERSHAW.

[Page 328] 13 Augt 1798

The Court met agreeable to adjournment ISAAC DUBOSE, JAMES KERSHAW, Esq'rs.

JAMES PEIRSON vs JAMES GUNN. S.P. Decree according to note.

State vs SAM LEVY. A & B. Guilty. The Court Sentenced him to pay a fine of $20 and give Security for good behavior 6 months and pay cost.

State vs JOHN RUSSELL. The Court sentenced him to pay a fine of $10 and give Security for his good behaviour 12 months and pay cost.

Ordered that the Estrays be sold this afternoon by the Sheriff that has been tolld the legal time.

The Court then Adjournd to Nov'r 7th next. IS. DUBOSE, JAMES KERSHAW.

[Page 329] 7th November 1798

Agreeable to Adjournment the Court Met. Present ISAAC DUBOSE, BURWELL BOYKIN, JAMES KERSHAW, Esquires.

Ordered that letters of administration do Issue to MARY McCOY administratrix on the Estate of JOSEPH McCOY deceased, her securities are WILLIAM MALONE and JOHN MARSHALL.

Ordered that letters of Administration do Issue to FRANCIS ROBINSON and CHARLES ROBINSON on the Estate of NICHOLAS ROBINSON deceased their Securities are JOHN NAUDIN & JOHN KIRKPATRICK and the Appraisers are THOMAS FLAKE, REUBIN COLLINS, JONATHAN DUREN, PAUL SMITH and DAN CARPENTER. And Ordered that the Property Belonging to the Estate be sold as follows viz't The Negroes to be sold on twelve Months Credit, and the remaining Property, Cash for all sums not exceeding Forty Shillings & two Months Credit for all sums over forty shillings; The sales to be at Camden on the 1st Saturday in January next, at the Mill of the Deceased on the second Saturday in January & at the Plantation where ROBERT FORD lives on Lynches Creek the third Saturday in the same month; But it is considered that the said Adminsitrator & Administratrix do give Bond & Security before they make the said Sales.

[Page 330]

GEORGE PAYNE having returned a Citation duly published, appeared & qualified as Adminsitrator of the Estate of his Father GEORGE PAYNE SEN'R deceased & Ordered that Letters of Administration be granted to him upon his giving Bond & Security.

The Rev'd ISAAC SMITH & JACOB SHIVER are approved of Securities for the said GEORGE PAYNE. DAVID PEOPLES, JOHN JONES, CASON SCOT, ABRAHAM SHIVER and RICHARD BERRY are appointed Appraisers of the said Est. and ordered that the said Estate by sold at the Plantation of the said deceased on the last Monday in the present Month & the Day following and that twelve Months Credit be given from the 1 Jany next for all Sums over forty Shillings & all sums not exceeding forty Shillings to be paid down in Cash at the time of Sale.

Ordered that the personal estate of JOSEPH McCOY be sold on a Credit of twelve Months, the purchaser giving Bond and Security for all Sums above forty shillings, and all Sums under forty Shillings to be paid in Cash at the time of sale.

Ordered that JOHN FISHER be admitted as a Security with JOSEPH BREVARD in the Room of JOSIAH CANTEY on the Estate of THOMAS ADAMS deceased.

[Page 331] 7th November 1798

Ordered that the goods and Chattels of the Est. THOMAS ADAMS Deceased be sold on the 28th Instnat on a Credit till the 1st of May next for all sums over 40/. taking Bond and security for the payment with Interest from the sale. The beds & Bed furniture returned in the Inventory are excepted from this order of sale.

Ordered that Letters Testamentary do Issue to ROBERT DOW on the Estate of ALEXANDER GOODALL Deceased, the Will being Produced in Open Court & Proved.

Ordered that the Personal Estate of JAMES WREN deceased be sold on the Plantation of the decesaed and for all Sums above Forty Shillings on a Twelve Months Credit all Sums under to be Sold for Ready Cash after giving the legal Notice for the Sail.

Ordered that a Road from Camden ferry in a direct line leading to Compties Bridge be laid Out as soon as possible and that SAMUEL DOHERTY, CORDAL HOGAN and WILLIAM HOGAN be Commissioners of Said Road and that CORDAL HOGAN is appointed Overseer of Said Road.

On application to the Inspector of the revenue for Stampt Paper he inform'd the Court that DANIEL STEPHENS Esq'r Supervisor for the District of South Carolina Wrote him Word that the Stamp Act of Congress did not extend to Bonds of administration.

[Page 332]

Whereas WILLIAM ROPER appointed last Court Guardian to the daughter of JOHN CASE has not complied with the Order of Corut in not giving the security required, therefore Ordered that JACOB CHAMBERS be and is hereby appointed guardian to the child of the said JOHN CASE, and the said WILLIAM ROPER is no longer to be considered as such, and that ADWELL ADKINSON be liberated from the security of the Guardianship of the said WILLIAM ROPER.

The Court then adjourned till tomorrow morning at 10 o'Clock. B. BOYKIN, IS. DUBOSE, JAMES KERSHAW.

[Page 333] 8 November 1798

Agreeable to Adjournment the Court met. Present BURWELL BOYKIN, JAMES KERSHAW, Esq'rs.

Ordered that the following persons be appointed overseers of the Road leading from the ford of Sanders Creek to Lynches Creek by the Plantation of JOHN LOCKERT (that is to say) BENJAMIN MARR from Sanders Creek to JOHN LOCKERT; WILLIAM JONES from LOCKERT to Col. MARSHAL's old Saw Mill; and BURWELL CATO From MARSHAL's mill to Lynches Creek.

MARGARET JONES returned & Accot. of the administration of the Est. of DAVID JONES deceased from the 7th Novr 1793 to the 1 Augt 1797 which was examined & approved, & ordered to be filed.

PETER CRIM & Wife returned & Accot of Sales of the remaining part of DAVID JONES's Est which was ordered to be filed.

Ordered that Letters Testamentory do Issue to ROBERT DOW on the last Will and Testament of JAMES BERKLEY deceased the Will being produced and proved in Open Court.

[8th November 1798]

Ordered that a Road be laid Out from the Rocky Mount to take Out Near TOLLISONS old Field and crop twenty five Mile Creek near WELLS ford & from there in the nearest directly to the Winnsborough Road and that ARTHUR BROWN ROSS Esq'r, JOHN BURNS and WILLIAM NETTLES appointed Overseers.

[Page 334]

Ordered that the Letters of Administration on the Estate of JOHN CASE heretofore granted to MARTHA CASE be Revoked. The Court having Considered the same as done When the Security was discharged.

Ordered that ROBERT DOW Executor of the late ALEXANDER GOODALL do sell all the live Stock of Cattle, Geesee and One horse; also all the personal Estate of the said ALEXANDER GOODALL, giving the legal notice of Advertising three weeks previous to the day of sale. Conditions Six months Credit for all sums over forty shillings.

Ordered that ROBERT DOW Executor of the late JAMES BRACLAY do sell all the personal effects, giving the legal notice of advertising three weeks previous to the day of sale of the said JAMES BARCLAY. Conditions Cash.

Adjourned till to morrow morning at 10 o'Clock. B. BOYKIN, JAMES KERSHAW.

[Page 335] 9th November 1798

Agreeable to Adjournment the Court Met. Present BURWELL BOYKIN, ISAAC DUBOSE, JAMES KERSHAW, Esq'rs.

Ordered that the Administrator of GEORGE PAYNE's Est be allowed to sell the personal Property belonging to the said Est at the time before mentioned or on the last Wednesday in December next & the Day following at the same place & upon the same Conditions that are mentioned in the former Order in this Case.

The Clerk of the Court having Produced to the Court his Acc'ts With Vouchers up to this day and after they were examined they were approved of and Passd. The balance of L7.12.4 to be Paid into the hands of his Successor.

M'r BOYKIN having given in his Resignation as Clerk of the Court w'ch was accepted. The Court then Proceeded to an Election when STEPHEN BOYKIN was duly elected Clerk. It is therefore Ordered that the books & papers belonging to the Court be deposited in his hands.

[Page 336]

The Court then adjourned to the 7th day of February next. B. BOYKIN, IS. DUBOSE, JAMES KERSHAW.

[Page 337]

COMMENCEMENT OF FEBRUARY TERM 1799

The Court met on Thursday the Seventh day of February agreeable to adjournment and proceeded to draw the Jurys to serve in August Term next, which are as follows Viz.

[Page 338] 7th Feb 1799

Grand Jury drawn from N'o 1 to N'o 2.

1 EDWARD COLLINS, 2 DANIEL KIRKLAND, 3 JOHN NIXON, 4 DAN CARPENTER, 5 THOMAS BROOM, 6 ROBERT COLEMAN, 7 WILLIAM DARKER, 8 SAMUEL BREED, 9 JOHN CRAVEN, 10 JAMES DUNLAP, 11 THOMAS WHITAKER, 12 ADAM McWILLIE, 13 JOHN DEACH, 14 WILLIS WHITAKER, 15 GEORGE MILLER, 16 DANL SMITH, 17 PETER TURLEY, 18 JAMES PERRY Singl'n C, 19 JAMES ENGLISH, 20 RUSH HUTSON.

Petit Jury for the same Court from N'o 2 to N'o 4.

1 EPHRAM CLANTON, 2 JOHN CLANTON, 3 WILLIAM MALONE, 4 JOHN BELTON [stricken], 4 MARK STEPHENS, 5 JOHN BROWN B.C., 6 WILLIAM McGEE, 7 THOMAS ROWLAND, 8 JOHN CHAMBERS S.C., 9 JOHN CHERRY, 10 JESSEE GILES B.C., 11 WILLIAM WALLEN, 12 WILLIAM WILLIAMS, 13 REUBIN WINDHAM, 14 ROBERT BARCLAY, 15 NICHOLAS BARROT, 16 WILLIAM REYNOLDS, 17 WILLIAM HUX, 18 SHAW BROWN, 19 TOUTRAINT GENOE, 20 JOHN EVANS, 21 JOHN NELSON, 22 RABIN COLLINS, 23 JAMES BROWN Esq'r, 24 WILLIAM NUTT, 25 JAMES STEPHENS, 26 JAMES McCULLUM, 27 MAM FURGESON [stricken] THOMAS DUREN, 28 ANTHONY PRESTLEY, 29 WILLIAM CATO, 30 GEORGE SAUNDERS JUN'R.

[Page 339]

JAMES KERSHAW having been previously appointed Clerk of the County Court of Kershaw County appeared in open Court and produced his Commission and took the Oaths of office.

Ordered that he give Bond & Security agreeable to Law by tomorrow at twelve o'Clock.

M'rs PHERIBA GOODALL appeared in Court and qualified as Exet'r of ALEXANDER GOODALL deceased. Ordered that letters Testamentary be granted.

[Page 340]

Ordered that Mr's SARAH MARTIN Administratrix to the Esta. of Doct'r JAMES MARTIN be permitted to sell all the personal Esta. of said deceased giving three weeks notice upon a Credit, One half payable on the first day of May next and the remainder payable on the first day of January next, giving Bond and Security for all Sums above Two Pounds.

No. 11. JOHN ADAMSON vs WILLIAM WATTS. Confession of Judgements for L 16 2/5.

PETER CRIM rendered an Account of the Receipts and Expenditures of DAVID JONES's Esta. from 1st of Augsut 1797 to 1st January 1799 which was examined and approved and Ordered to be deposited amongst the papers of said Esta.

JOHN RUTLEDGE JUN'R vs RICHARD WOOD. Fi fa in case. Ordered the Sheriff do return the Execution in this Case on Saturday next & Shew cause why the Money is not collected and paid over to the Plaintiff.

The Court then Adjourd to Tomorrow 10 Oclock. IS. DUBOSE, B. BOYKIN.

[Page 341] 8th February 1799

Mr. JAMES CLERK applied for letters of administration on the Esta. of WALTER SCOTT [stricken]

Ordered that the Clerk do issue a Citation to the said JAMES CLERK. [stricken]

Mr. RICHARD RANSOM GWYN appeared and qualified as Executor of the last will and testament of THOMAS LENORE deceased. Ordered that Letters Testamentary be granted to him.

N'o 7a. BEN CARTER vs M. POTTER. Trover. Ordered that the Defendant do plead within two days after the service of this rule or judgment will be entered against him by default.

ISAAC ALEXANDER and WILLIAM LANG Esquires being appointed by the Legislature as Justices of the Quorom appeared in open Court and qualified according to law.

SAMUEL MATHIS Esquire being appointed by the Legislature a Justice of Peace for the County of Kershaw appeared in open Court and qualified accordingly.

[Page 342] 8th February 1799

Mr WILLIAM WHITAKER appeared in Court and qualified as Executor of the last will and testament of THOMAS LENOIR deceased.

M'rs MARGARET LOVE as Administratrix of the Esta. of JAMES LOVE has satisfied debts of said Esta. to the Amot of One hundred and thirty two pounds nine shillings and five pence; and she maketh Oath that she knows of no other debts due by the said Esta.

No. 9a. S. S. ROSS vs THOMAS BROOM. S.P. Dismissed at defendants costs.

WILLIAM KIRKLAND Esquire being appointed by the legislature a Justice of Peace for the County of Kershaw appeared in open Court and qualified according to law.

23. JOHN ADAMSON vs FREDERICK LAMB. App'tn. Judgement Confessed for L 24 14/1 Sterling and Interest from the first Instant.

DANIEL BROWN vs MATHEW COLEMAN. Fi fa is Case. Ordered that the Sheriff do return this Execution tomorrow with a due return thereon, or else shew Cause why an attachment should not issue against him.

[Page 343] 8th February 1799

JACOB CHAMBERS Esquire being appointed by the legislature a Justice of Peace for the County of Kershaw appeared in open Court and qualified accordingly.

No. 25. ADAM McWILLIE vs JAMES RUSSELL & JESSE GILES. Debt. Judgment Confessed for $199.10 with Interest thereon from the 29th day of December 1797.

State vs SAMUEL THOMPSON. Indict. Assault. Bill found. Compromised with the prosecutor WILLIAM HUDSON who pays costs.

The Court then Adjourned to Tomorrow 9 oClock. IS. DUBOSE, B. BOYKIN.

KERSHAW COUNTY COURT MINUTES 1791-1799

[Page 344] 9th February 1799

The Court met agreeable to adjournment.

No. 16 GEORGE PERRY vs ISAAC REYNOLDS. Debt. Settled at REYNOLDS costs.

No. 3. A. F. BRISBANE JUN'R vs JOHN KIRKPATRICK. S.P. Settled at defendants Costs.

No. 9. McRA CANTEY and C'o vs Exor & Exix of ZACHARIA DUNSDUM. Case. Dismissed at Plaintiffs Costs.

Ordered that all recognizances in state business and all Persons bound in any Manner to appear in Criminal Cases at this Court be continued over to next Court & that all such persons then attend.

No. 10 BURWELL BOYKIN vs JOHN CASTON, JOSEPH CASTON. Debt settled at defendant Costs.

No. 13. SAM'L MATHIS vs JOHN CASTON. S.P. Judgement by default for Amot. of Account as appear on the back of the process.

[Page 345] 9th Feby 1799

No. 22. JAMES PEIRSON vs ISAAC ALEXANDER. S.P. Judgement by default for note and Interest.

39. THOMAS BROWN & C'o vs JAMES ROPER. Debt. Ordered that a Commission do issue to take the deposition of Witness's out of the State.

No. 17. PETER TWITTY vs BARTLETT HILLIARD. Att. The Garnishee being sworn and having no property in his hands and non being actually attached dismissed at plaintiffs Costs.

No. 20. JAMES CLARK vs S. S. ROSS. App'l from a Magistrate the following Witness sworn for appellant JOHN McCAA, WILLIAM LUYTON. for applee JOHN HOUSE. Judgment of the Magistrate Confirmed and the Appellant left open to his Action against the Plaintiff.

The Clerk of the Court Produced the Bond with legal Securities given by him for Performance of the duties of his Office W'ch was accepted by the Court & Ordered to be Recorded.

[Page 346] 9th Feby 1799

JOSEPH BREVARD Esq'r appeared in Court and was Qualifyed as a Magistrate.

The Court then Adjournd to Monday 10 OClk. IS. DUBOSE, B. BOYKIN.

11th February 1799.

No. 28 FRANCIS ROGERS vs NICHOLAS JOHNSON. Debt. Discontinued.

JAMES KERSHAW being appointed and qualified as Clerk of this Court, having given bond for the performance of his duty as such, He is therefore to have the Custody and care of the books and papers belonging to said Office. Ordered that the same be delivered up to him.

The Court then adjourned to the Seventh of May next. B. BOYKIN.

[Page 347] 7th May 1799

At an intermediate Court held the 7th of May 1799. Present ISAAC DUBOSE, Esquire.

Ordered that letters of Testamentary do Issue to THOMAS BROOM on the Esta. of ELIZA BROOM deceased. IS. ALEXANDER and ZEBULON RUDOLPH his securities. ISAAC ALEXANDER, JOHN ADAMS, JONATHAN BELTON, appraisers.

Mr. JAMES SHAW having produced a Citation for Letters of Administration on the Esta. of WILLIAM SHAW deceased. Ordered that the same be granted on the usual terms Mr. FISHER and Mr. JOHN BROWN on his securities. Mess'rs FITZPATRICK, SIMON TAYLOR, SAMUEL GREEN appointed appraisers to said Esta.

Mr. WILLIAM LUYTON present a Citation for letters of Administration on the Esta. of MARY LUYTEN deceased. Ordered the same be granted, he offering as his securities JOHN McCAA & JAMES CLARK, JOHN BROWN, JOHN FISHER and JOHN McCAA as appraisers.

Ordered that Letters of administration be Granted to JAMES CLARK on the Esta. of WALTER SCOTT deceased, he having offered DAN CARPENTER and JOHN McCAA as his securities. and JOHN FISHER, JOHN McCAA and JOHN BROWN as appraisers.

[Page 348] 7th May 1799

The Court then adjourned till the seventh of August next. IS. DUBOSE.

COMMENCEMENT of AUGUST TERM. WEDNESDAY 7th AUGUST 1799

The Court met agreeable to adjournment.

Application being made by Colonel CANTEY for letters of Administration on the Estate of HUGH FAIRFIELD. Ordered the same be granted on the usual terms. Doct'r ALEXANDER, JOHN ADAMSON & WILLIAM LANGLEY as appraisers and BEN CARTER & DUNCAN McRA as Securities.

The will of WILLIAM BECKHAM was deliver in Court and proved therein by JEAN GARDINER. SIMON BECKHAM qualified as executor to the said Will.

The Will of SAMUEL LEVY was present and proved in open Court by DAN CARPENTER. Ordered that SARAH LEVY be qualified as executrix to the due execution of said Will.

[Page 349]

WILLIAM LANG Esquire presented a Commission as a Judge of the Court from his excellency EDWARD RUTLEDGE Esq'r, Governor in and over the State of South Carolina, and took the oaths of office. [Commission copied into minutes, dated 12 July 1799]

[Page 350]

DANIEL PAYNE vs MATHEW COLEMAN. Tres. Judgement Confess'd for Three dollars & three quarters.

JOHN HALL vs TURNER STARK. SP Judgment confessed stay of execution for three months.

The Grand Jury empanelld and Sworn. WILLIS WHITAKER, foreman.

EDWARD COLLINS, DANIEL KIRKLAND, JOHN NIXON, DAN CARPENTER, THOMAS BROOM, ROBERT COLEMAN, WILLIAM PARKER, SAMUEL BREED, JOHN CRAVEN, ADAM McWILLIE, PAUL SMITH, PETER TURLEY, JAMES ENGLISH, GEORGE MILLER.

[7 August 1799]

The Petit Jury impaneled and Sworn.

JAMES BROWN foreman. WILLIAM WILLIAMS, EPHRAM CLANTON, WILLIAM MALONE, JOHN BROWN, THOMAS ROWLAND, JOHN CHAMBERS[stricken], RABIN COLLINS, ROBERT BARCLAY, JESSE GILES, TOMAINE GENOE, JOHN EVANS, ANTHONY PRESLEY.

[Page 351]

JOHN KERSHAWS Vs JOSEPH PAYNE. ELIJAH PAYNE Bail. ELIJAH PAYNE appeared and entered himself special bail to the action and surrender up his principal in discharge of his bond.

Ordered that the Sheriff keep the said defendant in safe custody till delivered by due course of law and that the said ELIJAY PAYNE be discharged from his said bail bond.

Ordered that MICHAEL GANTOR, ABRAM CHILDERS, HARTWELL MEKINS, PAUL SMITH and WILLIAM BRUNSON be and are hereby appointed Appraisers of the personal property of WILLIAM BRUMMIT deceased lying within the County.

DAVID BUSH vs JOSHUA GRAYHAM. RUSH HUDSON Bail. RUSH HUDSON the bail of the defendant in this case having surrendered the body of his principal to the Sheriff in Court, and prayed to be discharged from his bail bond.

Ordered that the Sheriff do keep the Defendant in safe Custody till delivered by due Course of Law and that the said RUSH HUDSON be discharged from his said bail bond.

[Page 352]

JOHN KERSHAW vs JOSEPH PAYNE. On motion in behalf of the plaintiff, Ordered that the defendant be ruled to special Bail.

State vs JOHN DILMORE. Hog Stealing. No Bill. WILLIS WHITAKER, foreman.

JOHN CRAWFORD vs JOHN DINKINS. Settled between the parties at Defendants Costs.

Application being made by HUGH McDOWELL for letters of Administration on the Esta. of DANIEL McNEAL deceased, Ordered the same be granted on the usual terms, he offers ADAM McWILLIE, THOMAS BERRY securities. MICH GANTER, CHRISTOPHER ATTLER & AARON appraisers.

Application being made by HUGH McDOWELL for letters of Administration on the Esta. of MATHEW MORRISON. ADAM McWILLIE, THOMAS BERRY securities. M. GANTER, C. ATTLER & M'r AASON. Ordered the same be granted on the usual terms.

[Page 353]

The Court then adjourned to half past nine O'Clock in the Morning. B. BOYKIN, IS. DUBOSE, WILLIAM LANG.

The Court met agreeable to adjournment

Application being made by GEORGE MILLER for Licence to retail Spirituous Liquors. Ordered the same be granted.

Application being also made by THOMAS BROWN and Company for Licence to retail Spirituous liquors. Ordered the same be granted.

[8 August 1799]

Application was made by Major THOMAS BALLARD, JOHN GRAHAM, and ANDREW GRAYHAM for letters of Administration on the Esta. of FRANCIS GRAYHAM.

[Page 354]

Ordered the same be granted. ADAM McWILLIE & GEORGE GAYDEN, securities. Appraisers THOMAS BRADFORD, PHIL BUFORD, and THOMAS CREIGHTON.

JONATHAN BELTON vs EDWARD RUTLEDGE. Debt on Note. Judgement Confessed for Thirty eight pounds two shillings and four pences with Interest from the 21st day December 1797, Execution not to be levied before 1st day of January next.

JOHN McDOWELL vs JOSEPH PAYNE. Refered to the Abritrament and award of DUNCAN McRA, Colonel CANTEY, WILLIAM NETTLES and JACOB CHAMBERS and their Umpire. their Award to be a judgment of Court.

Mrs. SARAH LEVY offered as appraisers to the Esta of SAMUEL LEVY: DAN CARPENTER, STEPHEN BOYKIN and JOHN McLAUGHLIN which were approved.

Mrs SARAH ENGLISH and JOSEPH ENGLISH appeared in open Court and qualified as Executrix and Executor to the last Will and testament of JOSHUA ENGLISH deceased.

WILLIAM KIRKLAND vs REID HUTT. Discontinued.

State vs WILLIAM FAIRFIELD. As't. True Bill. WILLIS WHITAKER, foreman.

[Page 354]

MATHEW COLEMAN vs BRYANT SPRADLEY, JOHN KERSHAW. Debt. Petit Jury. JAMES BROWN foreman, EPRAM CLANTON, WILLIAM MALONE, JOHN BROWN, THOMAS ROWLAND, REUBIN COLLINS, WILLIAM WILLIAMS, ROBERT BRACY, JESSE GILES, TOUSAINE GENOE, JOHN EVANS, ANTHONY PRESLEY.

Sworn REUBEN ARTHER, MICH GANTER, Mrs CAT GANTER.

We find for Plaintiff Seven Pounds, sixteen shillings & two pence. JAMES BROWN foreman. MATHIS paid the Jury.

JOHN ADAMSON vs ALEXANDER DOUGLAS. Debt. Judgment Confessed for Amo't of Note and Interest with Costs of the action.

The State vs MARY ADAMS. Assault. True Bill. Grand Jury WILLIS WHITAKER foreman, EDWARD COLLINS, DANIEL KIRKLAND, DAN CARPENTER, THOMAS BROWN, ROBERT COLEMAN, WILLIAM PARKER, SAM'L BREED, JOHN CRAVEN, ADAM McWILLIE, PAUL SMITH, PETER TURLEY & GEORGE MILLER.

WILLIAM BRACEY vs JAMES SHARPLIN. S.P. Judgement for Amot of Note With Interest.

The Grand Jury Discharged.

[Page 356] 8 August 1798

JACOB SHIVER vs JOHN McDOWELL. Refered to the arbitrament and award of DUNCAN McRA, ZACHARIAH CANTEY, WILLIAM NETTLES and JACOB CHAMBERS and their Umpire. Their Award to be made a Judgment of Court.

[8 August 1799]

The State vs WILLIAM FAIRFIELD. Ordered the defendant to appear or forfeit his Recognizance.

JOHN REID vs ROBERT FORD. Same Jury. Debt. We find for the plaintiff L14.2.9 1/2 having deducted 40/ off one of the notes on amount of subscription in Raffle of a Pheaton.

The Petit Jury were dismissed till tomorrow half past nine oClock.

Adjourned to half past nine O'Clock tomorrow morning. IS. DUBOSE, B. BOYKIN, WILLIAM LANG.

[Page 356] 9th August 1799

The Court met agreeable to adjournment.

JAMES SPRUNG vs THOMAS BALLARD, THOMAS CREIGHTON. Debt. Judgement confessed for L 10 8/ sterling with interest thereon from the 1st of January 1797 and costs of suit. execution not to issue until the 15th of November next.

VERNON MORTIMER & C'o vs WILLIAM CARTER. Debt. Judgement confessed in this case for L 37 4/7 with interest thereon from the 28th March 1796 execution to be stayed until the 1st of Jany 1800.

JUDITH DAUGHERTY vs STARK HUNTER, TURNER STARK. Debt on Note. Judgement confessed by STARK HUNTER for L 38 sterling with interest thereon from the first day of 1797.

JOHN KERSHAW vs JOSEPH PAYNE. On motion and by consent of parties it is ordered that all matters and difference between the parties in this cause be refered to the Arbitrament final end and determination of THOMAS BROOM and ABNER ROSS with power to chuse an umpire and that their award when returned, be the judgment of this Court.

[Page 357] 9 August 1799

The Grand Jury Drawn from N'o 1 to N'o 2

1 LEWIS COLLINS, 2 WILLIAM COLLINS, 3 CHARLES BARBER, 4 THOMAS ROACH, 5 WILLIAM BOND, 6 PETER CRIM, 7 SAMUEL JONES, 8 GEORGE GAYDEN, 9 SAMUEL HAMMONS, 10 SAM'L BROWN, 11 ISAAC ROSS JUN'R, 12 THOMAS BALLARD, 13 LEWIS COLLINS Rev'd, 14 JOHN RUTLEDGE SEN'R, 15 MICHAEL GANTER, 16 JAMES MARSHALL SEN'R, 17 JOHN ENGLISH, 18 DANIEL PAYNE, 19 SCION COATS, 20 ELY KERSHAW, 21 MICHAEL BARNET, 22 RUBIN STARK, 23 DANIEL GARDNER, 24 ALEXANDER ARCHER, 25 GEORGE EVANS, 26 ISAAC KNOX, 27 JOHN CREIGHTON, 28 LEWIS COOK, 29 GEORGE SAUNDERS J'R, 30 JOHN CHESNUT Esq'r.

The Petit Jury drawn for same Court from N'o 3 to N'o 4.

1 JOHN BOEN, 2 THOMAS FLAKE, 3 WILLIAM JONES J'R L.C., 4 JOHN SHIELDS, 5 HARMON HORTON, 6 JACOB CHAMPION, 7 HENRY EDEY, 8 EDWARD WATSON, 9 JOHN DRAKEFORD, 10 WILLIAM RUSSELL, 11 THOMAS SMYRL, 12 WILLIAM HUTSON, 13 GEORGE SAUNDERS, 14 DANIEL MARTIN, 15 ALEXANDER McKEE, 16 JOSEPH ROBERTS, 17 SOLOMON BELTON, 18 WILLIAM DANIEL, 19 JACOB SHIVER, 20 JOHN WEB, 21 BARWELL EVANS, 22 JOHN PILTON, 23 ISAAC WILLIAMS, 24 ARCHIBALD McFEE, 25 DILLARD SPRADLEY, 26 CORNELIUS MALONE, 27 JESSE WINDOM, 28 WILLIAM MACKEY, 29 EDWARD PARISH, 30 JOSEPH PAINE J'R.

[Page 358] 9 August 1799

ISAAC REYNOLDS vs GEORGE PERRY, ZADOCK PERRY. Debt. Judgement confessed for eleven Pounds sterling with Interest from 12th May 1795.

THOMAS WHITAKER Esquire appeared in open Court and qualified as a Justice of Peace for the County and took the oaths of Office accordingly.

GEORGE WAYNE vs THOMAS HAWFIELD. Debt. Settled between the parties and dismissed at defendants Costs.

GEORGE KERSHAW vs BRYANT SPRADLEY. Appeal from a Magistrate. Judgment Confirmed.

WILLIAM BRACEY vs JAMES SHARPLIN. S.P. Decree for five pounds.

[Page 359]

GEORGE PERRY & DAVID RUSSELL ads CHARLES BARBER. On motion of M'r BREVARD in behalf of the nominal plaintiff in this case, and it appearing to the Court that the real plaintiff was not CHARLES BARBER but DAVID BUSH, who was nonsuited in this action for his own default and the default of CHARLES BARBER, and it having also appeared that the defend't will know the real Plaintiff, and that CHARLES BARBER was only the nominal Plaintiff. Ordered that the Execution issue in this Case against the said CHARLES BARBER for the Costs of nonsuit be set aside.

The Court then adjourned to half past nine o'Clock tomorrow morning. IS. DUBOSE, WILLIAM LANG, B. BOYKIN.

[Page 360] 10 August 1799

The Court met at half past nine o'Clock agreeable to adjournment. Present WILLIAM LANG Esquire.

Admor & Admx N. ROBINSON vs REUBIN HARRISON. S.P. Petit Jury. JAMES BROWN fom, EPHRAM CLANTON, WILLIAM MALONE, JOHN BROWN, THOMAS ROBINSON[stricken], THOMAS ROWLAND, REUBIN COLLINS, WILLIAM WILLIAMS, ROBERT BARCLAY, JESSE GILES, THOUSANE GENOE, JOHN EVANS, ANTHONY PRESLEY. We find for the defendant. JAMES BROWN, foreman. Witnesses ROBINSON, R. HARRISON, Cap. CARTER.

BRYANT SPRADLEY vs JOSEPH PAYNE. Case. Refered to the arbitrament and award of JOHN ADAMSON and JAMES WILLIAMS and their umpire.

Note JOHN CHAMBERS was sworn on the petit Jury in the place of JAMES BROWN and appointed foreman.

WILLIAM JAMES vs WILLIAM BRUNSON. Debt. Judgement confess for Amo't of Note stay execution Six months.

[Page 361]

A paper was produced in Court purposely to be the last Will of FRANCIS GRAHAM deceased, it appearing to the Court that two of the Subscribing Witnesses are interested & by the Testimony of the other that the making the Will was occasioned by urgency & undue influence on the mind of the deceased in his extreme moments and no Evidence to publication thereof after signing And the WIll not being Sealed adjudged that the same is void & be set aside & the administration granted this Court confirmed.

THOMAS BROOM & C'o vs THOMAS MINTON. Judgement by default.

[10 August 1799]

JOHN MOTLEY vs FREDERICK ROBINSON. Ass. dismissed at defendants Costs.

[Page 362]

WILLIAM ANCRUM vs Exr & Exix ALEXANDER GOODALE. S.P. decree for the plaintiff L 9 14/6 subject to the judgement that may hereafter be had upon the plea of plene administravit to be filed in this case.

M'r ARTHUR sworn.

WILLIAM ANCRUM vs Admix T. ADAMS. S.P. decree for the plaintiff L 4 10/7 subject to the judgement that may hereafter be had upon the plea of plene administratvit to be filed in this case.

M'r ARTHUR sworn.

HINSON DAVIS vs WILLIAM SNEED. S.P. Decree for the defendant. Witness R. McCAIN, JNO TRANTHAM, W'M YOUNG, JAMES TRANTHAM.

Adjourned to Monday morning at nine O'Clock. WILLIAM LANG.

AUGUST TERM Monday the 12th 1799

The Court met agreeable to adjournment. Present BURWELL BOYKIN, WILLIAM LANG, ISAAC DUBOSE, Esquires.

Same Jury Sworn.

BRYANT SPRADLEY vs ROBERT McCAIN. Case. Settled between the parties each to pay their own Cost.

BRYANT SPRADLEY vs JOSEPH PAYNE. Case. This case being referred to arbitration, the Arbitrators returned their award thereby they award to the plaintiff nine shillings and 8d the defendant having by discounts lessened his demand to that sum.

JOHN McDOWELL vs JOSEPH PAYNE. S.P. This case having been referred to arbitration, the arbitrators returned the following award "We are of opinion from evidence brought before us that the note on which this suit was commenced has been settled" ZACH CANTEY, JACOB CHAMBERS, W'M NETTLES (W his mark), JOHN ADAMSON.

[Page 364]

PETER TWITTY vs JAMES SPRADLEY. Case refered to the Arbitrament & award of JAMES WILLIAMS and JOHN KIRKPATRICK and their umpire their award to be a judgement of Court.

ISAAC ROSS JUN'R vs FREDERICK LAMB. Case. We find for the Plaintiff L 30. JAMES BROWN, foreman. Jury proved by FR ROSS. Witnesses DAVID JAMISON, Col. CANTEY.

Application being made by WILLIAM BRACEY and ELIZABETH BRACEY for letters of administration Esta of GAYETON AIGUIRE, Ordered the same be granted. JOHN NAUDIN & THOMAS BROOM securities. THOMAS BROOM, JOHN NAUDIN & WILLIAM LANGLEY the appraisers.

JOHN TRANTHAM vs MARY DIXON. Case. Refered to the Arbitrament and award of Colonel CANTEY and RICHARD DRAKEFORD and their umpier and their award to be a judgement of Court.

[12 August 1799]

THOMAS DUSON vs BRYANT SPRADLEY. Debt. Judgement confessed pertecting [sic] persons for the amot of note. Stay execution till the 19th day of November next.

[Page 365]

WILLIAM LUYTON vs WILLIAM KENNEDAY. Debt. The defendant appeared in Court and surrended himself in exhoneration of his bail. Wit: JAMES BROWN, SAM'L BROWN. Ordered that the bail be discharged. We find for the Plaintiff L22.4.7. JAMES BROWN foreman. HUGHES note deducted.

JAMES KERSHAW came into Court and offered himself as Special bail in this Case, which was approved of and entered as Such.

JOHN McDOWELL vs ELY FREEMAN. Debt. We find for the plaintiff L16.6.6. JAMES BROWN, foreman. Wit: CHA'S COOK, F. GENOE.

SAMUEL BROWN vs WILLIAM LUYTON. S.P. Decree Dol's 19 87 1/2 Cents. Wit: SAM BROWN, JOHN McCAA, JOHN O'CAIN.

PETER TWITTY vs JAMES SPRADLEY. Case. We the arbitrators met to settle between PETER TWITTY & JAMES SPRADLEY as award that the said JAMES SPRADLEY do pay the said PETER TWITTY $14 within 20 days from the date hereof & each man pay his own cost of the within named suit. Certified by us the 12th day August. JOHN KIRKPATRICK, JAMES WILLIAMS, ISAAC ROSS JUN'r.

[Page 367]

JOHN McDONALD vs JOSEPH PAYNE. S.P. We are of opinion from Evidence brought before us that the note on which this suit was commenced has been settled. ZACH CANTEY. [entire entry stricken]

GEORGE EVANS vs CHARLES EVANS. Debt. We find for the plaintiff L 94.6.5 or $404.34. JAMES BROWN, foreman.

Note Mr. LANG left the bench.

WILLIAM LANG vs Exor & Ex'x HENRY RUGELEY. Debt. We find for the plaintiff one Cent Damage & Costs of suit. JAMES BROWN, foreman.

ADAM TAMSON vs WILLIAM RAY Esta. Att. Judgement by default against CHARLES BARBER Garnishee.

The Extrs JOSEPH KERSHAW vs JAMES BROWN. Sci fa. Defendant came into Court proper persons and confessed Judgment for L=18.12.1 with int't thereon from 21 Jan 1797, but it is agreed that an Order in for L12.14.6 for JAMES BETTY's amount against RICHARD WADSON with interest thereon from the 15th day of September 1787 be admitted in discount thereof provided the same be agreed to by the Trustees of Colonl JOSEPH KERSHAWs Estate. Stay execution till 1st Jany next. [entire entry stricken]

RICHARD KING vs ISAAC ROSS JUN'R. Debt. Judgment confessed according to Bond with stay of Execution till 1st Decr 1799.

[Page 367; no page numbered 368] 12 August 1799

ROBERT DUNLAP vs WILLIAM JONES. Case. Motion made that the defendant be allowed to pay into Court the sum of Money that he looks upon to be due in this Case. Ordered that the same be granted, whereupon the defendant paid into the hands of the Clerk the sum of Ten dollars.

[12 August 1799]

Ex'rs PATRICK McFADDEN vs ADAM MCWILLIE. Debt. Wit: SAM'L THOMPSON deft, MICH BRANNON deft. JOHN BROWN, PETER TURLEY, W'M ANDERSON, EPHRAM CLANTON, plaintiff.

The Jury were devised to deliver their verdict in the morning sealed up.

The Court then adjourned to half past nine o'Clock tomorrow morning. WILLIAM LANG, IS. DUBOSE.

[Page 369] 13 August 1799

The court met agreeable to adjournment. Present BURWELL BOYKIN, Esq., WILLIAM LANG Esq'r, ISAAC DUBOSE, Esq're.

McRA & CANTEY vs WILLIAM KENNEDAY, WILLIAM LUYTON. On Motion on behalf of the Plaintiffs, Ordered that the defendants be ruled to Special Bail.

GEORGE MONTGOMERY & JOHN CHAMBERS Ex's PATRICK McFADEN vs ADAM MCWILLIE. Debt. Same Jury sworn yesterday to try this cae deliver'd their Verdict sealed up. We find for the Defendant. JAMES BROWN, foreman. MATHIS paid the Jury.

ROBERT DUNLAP vs WILLIAM JONES. Aspn. Same Jury. We find for the Plaintiff L2.3.1. JAMES BROWN, foreman. Witness's COOK. BREVARD paid Jury.

NATHANIEL RUSSELL vs CHARLES EVANS. Debt. Same Jury. We find for the Plaintiff One Cent Damages & Cost of Suit. JAMES BROWN, foreman.

[Page 370]

BRYANT SPRADLEY JUN'R vs DAVID BIRD. On motion and affidavit of defendant of the absence of a metrial Ordered that this cause stand over till next Court.

JOHN LISONBE vs CHARLES EVANS, JAMES WILLIAMS. Debt. Same Jury We find for the Plaintiff one Cent damages and Cost of Suit. JAMES BROWN, foreman.

Wit: JNO FISHER. MATHIS paid the Jury.

Ex'rs of Col JO KERSHAW vs BREED and BROWN. Colonel KERSHAW appeared in Court being the Attory for the Trustees of the Esta. and not agreeing to the Judgement entered up yesterday, Ordered the same be revoked and expunged from the minutes.

THOMAS DINKINS vs THOMAS FLAKE, WILLIAM McCORKLE. Trespass. We find for the Defendants. JAMES BROWN, foreman. Witnesses JOSHUA DINKINS, JOHN DINKINS, JOHN POLLOCK.

THOMAS BROOM & C'o vs JAMES ROPER. On motion on behalf of the Plaintiffs, Ordered that the defendant be ruled to Special Bail. Mr. DAN CARPENTER comes into Cort and enters himself as Special Bail in this Case and the court uapproved of the same.

[Page 371]

THOMAS BROOM & C'o vs JAMES ROPER. Debt. Same Jury. We find for the Plaintiff $131.59. JAMES BROWN, foreman. ALEX MATHESON, JAMES WHITE.

DAVID BUSH vs JOSHUA GRAYHAM. Debt. The defendant came into Court in proper person and confessd Judgement for Amot of Note and Cost of Suit.

[13 August 1799]

WILLIAM LUYTON vs MATHEW COLEMAN. Case. On Motion of the plaintiff in this Case for the defendant to be held to special Bail, Ordered that the defendant be ruled to special Bail.

Adjourned to 9 O'Clock tomorrow Morning. IS. DUBOSE, WILLIAM LANG.

[Page 372] 14 August 1799

The Court met agreeable to adjournment. Present BURWELL BOYKIN, ISAAC DUBOSE, WILLIAM LANG Esquires.

DAVID BUSH vs ARCH WATSON. Debt. Lays over till next Court.

BEN CARTER vs MILES POTTER. Trover. Same Jury as yesterday. We find for the Plaintiff $40. JAMES BROWN, foreman. HUGH YOUNG. Jury paid P plaintiff.

JOSIAH WOOD vs BENJAMIN CARTER. Debt on Note. Defendant came into Court and confessed Judgment for the amount of the Note & Interest Deducting therefrom Seven shillings and 6d for a P Shores delivered to Plaintiff the 21st Novr 1798 as P Discount filed.

FRANCIS BELL vs DINAH ADAMS Ex'x desontort of THOMAS ADAMS deceased. Judgement confessed according to note subject to note the plea of plene administravit ad so as not to offset the private Esta of the Executrix but to come in with Creditor's.

The plea to be filed the next intermediate court with an account of the Administration[stricken]. in equal decree of the Estate of the Deceased for a Distribution of the Assets.

[Page 373] 14 August 1797

JOHN FISHER Sheriff of this County having produced his Account against the County to the 7th inst., amounting to L18.15. which was approved of. Ordered that he receive payment for the same.

ROBERT DUNLAP vs WILLIAM JONES. Case. On motion to tax magistrates Cost on a Verdict given in this case ordered the motion be discharged & that the plaintiff have full Cost.

Ordered that Letters of Administration on the Estate of JOHN BROWN Esq deceased be granted to REBECA BROWN the Widow of the Deceased and that the Clerk issue a Dedimus to qualify her on Security to the satisfaction of two of the Judges.

DAVID BUSH vs JOSHUA GRAYHAM. The defendant in this Case having rendered in a Schedule of all his estate in discharge of himself in this action and the same consisting of one tract of Land and a Rifle Gun, it is Ordered that the same be assigned except the Gun unto JOSEPH BREVARD real plaintiff in this suit in part satisfaction of the debt and cost, and that the said JOSHUA GRAYHAM be discharged from confinement.

[Page 374]

The Court then adjourned to the Seventh day of November being the next ensuing intermediate court. B. BOYKIN, WILLIAM LANG, IS. DUBOSE.

INTERMEDIATE COURT Nov'r 7th 1799

The Court met agreeable to adjournment. Present ISAAC DUBOSE Esq'r.

Application being made by DAN CARPENTER for letters of Administration on the Esta. of JOHN BURCHET deceased, Ordered the same be granted on the usual terms. Col. CANTEY & JAMES CLARK, Securities.

[Page 375] 7th November 1799

Mrs SARAH LEVY applied for leave to sell all the personal property of SAMUEL LEVY deceased. Ordered that the personal Esta. be sold on the first Tuesday in December next in Camden. Conditions Cash. Ordered the appraisement of the Esta. of SAMUEL LEVY be recorded.

The Court then adjourned to 12 o'Clock to morrow. IS. DUBOSE.

The Court met at 12 o'Clock agreeable to adjournment.

ISAAC DUBOSE & WILLIAM LANG Esq'rs.

The will of JONATHAN BUNCKLEY was proved in Court by WILLIAM THOMPSON one of the subscribing witnesses. LEWIS COLLINS and CHAMBERS qualified as executors to the last will & testament of JONATHAN BUNKLEY deceased.

[Page 376] 8th November 1799

The Court having examined and approved Mrs SARAH MARTINs Accounts of Administration of the Esta. & JAMES MARTIN for the years 1797 & 1798. Ordered that they be deposited with the inventory and appraisment of the said Estate in the Clerks office of this Court.

Ordered that the Estate of FRANCIS GRAYHAM deceaed be sold the second Saturday in December next on the following terms. "All sums under twenty shillings Cash, All sums of 20/ 12 Months Credit."

The Court having examined and approved the papers returned by the Extrix of the Esta. of JOHN BROWN, Ordered that they be deposited with the inventory and appraisement in the Clerks Office of this Court.

M'r DAN CARPENTER qualified as Administration of the Esta. of JOHN BURCHET.

Col. CANTEY, JAMES CLARK, JOHN FISHER and Rev. Mr. SMITH & MATHEW COLEMAN, appraisers.

Ordered that the Esta. of JOHN BURCHET be sold the first Saturday in December next in the Town of Camden. Conditions Cash.

[Page 377] 8th November 1799

Adjourned to 12 O'Clock tomorrow. IS. DUBOSE, WILLIAM LANG.

The Court met at 12 o'Clock agreeable to adjournment. Present ISAAC DUBOSE Esq. & WILLIAM LANG Esq.

Ordered the Esta. of HUGH FAIRFIELD be sold on the first Tuesday in Camden. Conditions

Adjourned to the next Court in Course. IS. DUBOSE, WILLIAM LANG.

KERSHAW COUNTY COURT MINUTES 1791-1799

Gardner cont.
Milley 117
Richard 102
Robt. 55
Susannah 96
Thomas 36,57,63,73,96,
117
Thos. 16,55
Garnder, Daniel 102
Garner, Richard 95
Richd. 7
Garns, George 56
Gaskins, _____ 126
Danl. 124
Gaston, Joseph 97
Gather, Thomas 4,13
Gaton, George 2
John 3
Gaunt, Samuel 37
Gaunter, Michael 14,24,29,
45,84
Gayden, Geo. 125
George 41,81,97,118,140,
141
John 8,66,81,82,118
Richard 35
George 7
John 8
Geno, Francis 80
Touson 95
Genoe, F. 131,144
Francis 129
Thousane 142
Tomaine 139
Tousaine 140
Toutraint 135
Genot, Touson 109
Gibson, Luke 7,16,17,18
R. 131
Roger 1,8,13,14,16,17,
23,25,26,28,29,30,31,
34,45,57,76,77,78
Gidbon, Luke 48
Giles, Jesse 80,136,139,
140,142
Jessee 135
Gillaspie, Nacey 51
Glandall, Stephen 35
Glanden, Stephen 23
Glaze, Mary 86
Goodall, Alexander 1,43,
133,134,135,143
Alexr. 28,29,45
Mrs. Pheriba 135
Goodwin, John 118
Goyen, Drury 66
Wm. 44
Gragg, Henry 37
Graham, Andrew 3
Andw. 125
Francis 80,142
John 2,80,82,91,114,125,
128,129,130,131,140
Joshua 131
Grant, Lewis 3,95,103,104,
107,108,118
Graves, John 55
Gray, Jacob 53
Sherod 53
Grayham, Andrew 53,140
Francis 140,147
Joshua 139,145,146
Green, Samuel 138
Greg, John 81
Gregg, John 98,126,130
Henry 58,59
Greham, John 16
Grey, Charles 3
Jacob 2,7,16,85,97,102,
111
Sherod 53
Greyham, Arthur 55
Andrew 8,118
John 27,53,118

Greyham cont.
Jonathan 7
Wm. 7,55
Griffin, William 3,74
Griffis, Thomas 118
Griffith, Elizabeth 120
Grig, Henry 78
John 78
Gueery, John 7
Guignard, John G. 89
Gun, James 13,36
Gunn, Gabriel 57
James 19,24,27,37,42,
53,57,59,62,70,76,78,
79,97,105,124,131,132
Robt. 24
Gwyn, Richard Ransom 136

Hail, Benjn. 118
Haliday, Daniel 118
Hall, John 110,138
Hamilton, Hugh 118,125
James 81
John 110
Hammond, Rawley 81,115
Rowley 35
Rawliegh 104
Hammonds, Rawley 110
Samuel 110
Hammons, Samuel 141
Hampton, Wade 68
Hanks, Thomas 128
Hannah, James 64
Hardwick, John 121,122
Thomas 118
Harkey, Peter 127
Harkins, Daniel 3,69,73
Harold, Cader 37
Harp, James 110,120
Harris, James 42,44,45,
61,120
Harrison, Reuben 68
Reubin 38,61,70,92,142
Samuel 93
Hart, Phillip 76
Harvell, John 26,46,57
Harwell, John 32
Havis, Andrew 79
Hawfield, Thomas 31,67,
100,142
Hays, George 2,48
Jesse 29,53
Heath, Frederick 9
Helton, Samuel 95
Henry, James 119
Robert 13,19,37,44,49,
57,104,113,131
Hester, James 88,95,96,97
Zach 86
Zachariah 62,80,97
Hickman, Wm. 2,11,12
Hickson, John 7,16,17,18
Hide, William 131
Wm. 62
Hill, Andrew A. 55,73
Hillard, Bartlett 121
Philemon 53,70,103,126
Phillimon 90
Hilliard, Bartlett 137
Philemon 5,95
Philimon 27
Phillemon 88,104,121
Phillimon 128
Hinson, William 25
Hixon, John 118
Hogan, Cordal 133
William 133
Holley, James 95
Holliday, Daniel 95
Hollis, Moses 70,90,92
Holly, James 9,13
Richd. 55
Holmes, Finely 32
William 32,33,34,39,80

Holzendorf, John 41,45,62
Homes, William 107
Hood, Elis'th. 125
Elizabeth 119,123
Jno. 131
John 16,60,82,86,87,88,
97,98,102,105,106,111,
114,119,122,123,125,
127
Robert 20,24,29,31,74,
88,90,104
Robert A. 86
Robt. 12
William 102,111,115
Hooper, Thomas 4,100
Horn, Violet 111
Horten, Daniel 56,75,96
Henry 16
Mary 67,71
Wm. 35
Horton, Daniel 67,72
Harmon 141
Henry 7,24,65
John 2,7,26,102,117
House, Averet 56,67
Everet 71
John 137
Houston, William 25,26
Howard, Ferraby 15
Heli 58
Lydia 15,32
Martha 15
William 15
Howze, Saml. 63
Hudson, _____ 85
Henry 7,10,16,18,23,25,
30,32,33,34,43,49,55,
62,67,78,80,86,89
Jeffry 59,72,74,80,86,
88,90
Jefry 17
John 120
Lewis 13,42,100,104,110,
129
Rush 13,35,62,80,82,118,
125,128,139
William 58,136
Wm. 70,126
Hughes, _____ 144
Henry 29,93
Hughs, Church 48
Wm. 48
Huland, Cullin 26
Edward 26
Hulin, Edward 90
Hunter, David 10,18,29,34,
39,40,42,44,46,52,55,
58,78
Henry 3,41,87,92
James 10,11,27,40,42,62
Stark 141
Starke 16,73,104
Hutchens, John R. 24
Hutchins, Benj. 108
John R. 18,24,44
Sarah 51,63
Hutchinson, Benjamin 110,
114
Hutson, Jefry 16,18
Rush 135
William 141
Hutt, Read 66
Reed 90,124
Reid 113,140
Susannah 90
Hux, William 135
Hyde, Wm. 131
Hye, Joseph 35

Ingram, Arthur 91
James 16,85
Jas. 2
John 2
Wm. 52

153

McAfeee, Archibald 29
McArthur, John 124
McCaa, Jno. 127
  John 57,64,98,103,109,
    119,121,122,126,137,
    138,144
McCain, Patrick 6,16,34,
    55,77,85,96,98,99,100,
    118
  R. 143
  Robert 4,17,27,28,74,78,
    79,125,129,131,143
  Robt. 66
McCaine, Patrick 127
McCambridge, John 16,20
McCaw, Jno. 10
  John 1,43
McCay, Chs. 59
McClelan, Charles 124
McClester, Hugh 25,28
McClocklin, Jno. 126
McCluer, John 110
McClure, John 7,120
McCorkel, James 95
McCorkle, James 103,104,
    107,108
  William 119,145
McCoy, _____ 126
  Benjamin 39
  Jo. 14,24,25,34,36,38
  Jos. 14
  Joseph 6,7,12,16,17,24,
    30,35,36,41,48,51,57,
    59,77,96,101,106,132
  Joseph P. 42
  Mary 132
  Wm. P. 42
McCredick, _____ 74
McCredie, Robert 99,107
  & Young 79,81,89
McCullough, James 124
McCullum, James 135
McDonald, _____ 126
  Archd. 96
  Archibald 22,46,47,50,98
  Daniel 115
  Jeremiah 36
  John 127,130,144
  Margaret 47,50
  Middleton 76
  William 91,113,115
  Wm. 130
McDowal, Hugh 114
McDowel, Hugh 36,45,53
McDowell, Hugh 82,139,140,
    143,144
McDowl, Hugh 6,12,23,38,
    59,61,68
McFadden, Patrick 145
McFaddin, Patrick 85
McFaden, Patrick 145
McFadian, Patrick 105
McFadin, Patrick 122
McFee, Archd. 26
  Archibald 66,141
McGee, Hugh 11,21,29,30,
    46,49,58,71,76,81
  William 110,135
  Wm. 117
McGill, Richard 112
  William 16,17
  Willm. 80
  Wm. 18,55,124
McGinney, Charles 16,28,
    32,62,66,76,88
  Charless 30
  Chas. 45
McHenry, Joshua 5,11
McKain, Robert 96
McKay, C. 31
  Chas. 30
  John 36
  Saml. 3

McKee, _____ 80
  Alexander 83,114,141
  Alexr. 7,55
  John 7,55,118
  Saml. 55
  Samuel 41,108
  Wm. 60
McKenzie, Benjamin 107,
    121
McKerkey, John 30
McKernan, Peter 60
McKey, William 80
  Wm. 94
McKinney, Benjamin 4
  John 63,76,113,116
McKinnie, John 62,68
McKinnon, Peter 41,42
McLaughlin, J. 131
McLaughlin, John 140
McLeland, Charles 66,76
  Chas. 7
McLeod, _____ 40,58
McLester, Hugh 16,26,28,
    29,55,66,76
McManus, James 13,17
McMaster, John 48
McMillan, Daniel 59
McMillian, Danl. 7
McMullan, David 124
McMullen, David 95,107,
    108
McMullin, Daniel 95,120
  Danl. 110
  David 103,104
McNeal, Daniel 139
  John 12,13
McNeil, Archd. 14
  John 80
McRa, _____ 15,49,58,68
  Duncan 12,13,22,23,44,
    45,51,64,80,100,102,
    104,115,116,129,138,
    140
  Williams 109
McRa & Cantey 75,87,97,
    100,108,113,137,145
McWillie, Adam 72,74,79,
    105,122,135,136,138,
    139,140,145
  John 71
MacKay, Robt. 7
Mackey, John 30
  William 72,89,141
MacMullin, Daniel 103
Magoune, Joseph 43
Mahaffey, Robert 109
  Robt. 94
Mahaffy, Robert 55
Major, Benjamin 66
  Danl. 48
Malone, Corenlius 2
  Cornelius 74,141
  William 73,109,132,135,
    139,140
  Wm. 55,94
Man, James 75,90
  Richard 102
Marks, James 27
Marr, Benjamin 133
  Richard 95
Mars, Richard 116,117
Marsh, Joshua 110
Marshal, _____ 126
  Col. 133
  John 72,125
Marshall, J. 129
  James 7,16,57,71,129
  James Jr. 55
  James Sr. 48,56,95,103,
    110,124,141
  John 2,4,7,17,29,42,55,
    94,106,109,118,120,
    132
  Robert 8,9,11,12,75

Marshall cont.
  Robt. 3,7,48
Marshel, John 105
Martin & Trent 96
Martin, Daniel 141
  David 3,23,36,37,38,47,
    66
  James 78,79,80,91,96,
    114,118,135,147
  Jas. 68,126
  John 2,14,86,108,131
  Joseph 51,79
  S. 3
  Saml. 7,18,118
  Samuel 16,17,75
  Sarah 21,114,118,135,147
  Zachariah 11,38,40
Massay, Arthur 64
Massey, William 105
  William Jr. 55,100,104,
    105,106
Massy, _____ 51
  Arthur 24,51,55
  William 99
Matheson, Alex 145
Mathis, _____ 4,9,10,11,
    12,13,17,18,19,21,53,
    140,145
  Israel 91
  Mr. 4,27
  Robert 90
  S. 11,60
  Sam 83
  Saml. 38,43,49,96,125,
    137
  Sam'l. Sr. 19
  Samuel 25,26,33,44,51,
    86,87,93,101,103,117,
    120,123,136
  Wm. 130
Mattocks, James 36
Maudin, John 118
Maxwell, Jae. 125
  James 118
  John 69,72,90,92,96
  Sarah 80,88
  William 69,72,92
  Wm. 7,96,131
Mehaffey, Jeremiah 120
  Oliver 120
  Robert 73,74
Mehaffy, Robert 117
Mekin, Hartwell 62,79
Menkins, Hartwell 139
Melone, Wm. 85
Meyer, David 9
Mickle, Elizabeth 50
  John 1,2,50,81,92,96
  Thomas 74
Middleton, Jo. 78
  John 7,23,74
  Rd. 2
  Richard 16,74,75,131
  Richd. 7,50
  Wm. 85
Milhous, John 92
  Sam 92
  Saml. 96
  Samuel 92
Milhouse, John 51
Miller, Brice 107,120
  Geo. 34,94
  George 7,14,16,17,39,40,
    58,71,72,81,85,97,101,
    109,118,135,138,139,
    140
  James 16,17,18,19,110,
    120
  Joseph 29
Millhouse, John 15,32,49
Millin, Hugh 57
Mills, Burwell 97,98,112,
    114
  Susannah 80,112,114

155

Other Heritage Books by Brent H. Holcomb:

Bute County, North Carolina Land Grant Plats and Land Entries

*CD: Early Records of Fishing Creek Presbyterian Church,
Chester County, South Carolina, 1799-1859*

CD: Kershaw County, South Carolina Minutes of the County Court, 1791-1799

CD: Marriage and Death Notices from The Charleston [SC] Observer, *1827-1845*

CD: South Carolina, Volume 1

*CD: Winton (Barnwell) County, South Carolina Minutes of
County Court and Will Book 1, 1785-1791*

*Early Records of Fishing Creek Presbyterian Church, Chester County,
South Carolina, 1799-1859, with Appendices of the Visitation List of
Rev. John Simpson, 1774-1776 and the Cemetery Roster, 1762-1979*
Brent H. Holcomb and Elmer O. Parker

Kershaw County, South Carolina Minutes of the County Court, 1791-1799

Marriage and Death Notices from The Charleston Observer, *1827-1845*

*Winton (Barnwell) County, South Carolina Minutes of
County Court and Will Book 1, 1785-1791*

CPSIA information can be obtained at www.ICGtesting.com
Printed in the USA
LVOW10s1243160816

500523LV00064B/831/P